States, Markets and Wars in Global History

Giulio Sapelli

States, Markets and Wars in Global History

Economic and Political Developments Between the Advent of Globalization and the COVID-19 Pandemic

palgrave
macmillan

Giulio Sapelli
University of Milan
Milan, Italy

ISBN 978-3-031-26715-4 ISBN 978-3-031-26716-1 (eBook)
https://doi.org/10.1007/978-3-031-26716-1

The translation was done with the help of an artificial intelligence machine translation tool. A subsequent human revision was done primarily in terms of content.
Translation from the Italian language edition: "Nella Storia mondiale: Stati Mercati Guerre" by Giulio Sapelli, © Edizioni Angelo Guerini e Associati 2021. Published by Edizioni Angelo Guerini e Associati. All Rights Reserved.

This Palgrave Macmillan imprint is published by the registered company Springer Nature Switzerland AG
The registered company address is: Gewerbestrasse 11, 6330 Cham, Switzerland

Man has always lived in history but all human cultures, except for the Western one, have spent treasures of creative energy to mask the historicity of existence.
Ernesto De Martino, The end of the world.

Contribution to the analysis of cultural apocalypses

All things converge into each other: good into evil, generosity into justice, religion into politics, years into epochs, the world into the universe. To those who take this into account, the evolution of the species will appear as a tiny and banal process within that same movement.
Thomas Hardy

To Claudia, my love.

Acknowledgements

This book is the fruit of a long brooding. A brooding of years. The traces are evident in every line.

A brooding that I shared not only with the beloved Claudia Sonino, who always corrects with her inflexible accuracy as a scholar my disordered rides, but also with a group of friends who have been putting up with my intemperance for some... decade: Lodovico Festa, Pasquale Alferj, Augusto Carena, Veronica Ronchi, Giuseppe De Lucia Lumeno and Antonio Pilati have always been and are for me an intellectual reference point without which I would lose the compass more often than it always happens to me in research and curiosity.

In more recent times two friends have not only encouraged me. A young scholar like Edoardo Toffoletto who always opens new borders for me. A Master like Alessandro Mangia, from whom I never stop learning and who again convinced me - as happened for a long period of my life thanks to the unforgettable Alberto Predieri - that the philosophy of law opens those infinite worlds without which the theory of no longer segmented societies cannot exist.

All these scientific and relational experiences have been able to settle, especially after my university retirement, in that extraordinary community that has been and is, not only for me, the Eni Enrico Mattei Foundation, of which I have been a Board Member and Associate Researcher for more than twenty years. The dear friends Alberto Meomartini and Domenico

Siniscalco, already unsurpassed Director and now President of the Scientific Committee of the Foundation, have accompanied me on this journey for many years and for this I am deeply grateful to them. As I am grateful to the younger managers and researchers of this institution, of this very special business foundation, perhaps unique in the world, for all that they have given me in these long years.

Angelo Guerini, finally, is remembered not only among long-time friends, because his role has always been dual, in our long journey of life. As an old Turin resident, for more than thirty years in him I see not only the friend, but also the ideal publisher that the works of Piero Gobetti had taught me to love when I was very young.

His collaborators breathe that mysterious aura of the Gobettian publisher: I have always drawn great comfort from it and my gratitude must also reach them.

In Mario Mancini, also an unmatched publisher not only digital, I have always found—starting from the antipodal common love for New Zealand and the Olivettian world that shaped us in a regretted youth - the thread of a political and civil passion that never leaves us.

The same love for the Olivettian world I have shared for a lifetime with Mario Citelli: a job that was more than a passion... it was a destiny.

Giulio Sapelli

Contents

List of Figures

CHAPTER 1

Introduction

The content of this book is a research *Des choses cachées depuis la fondation du monde*, to resume the inspiration of René Girard's masterpiece [1], that is a research on the deep origins of what happened to the world during the years of the so-called "globalization" up to the global pandemic crisis of 2020.

My research is based, like all my previous works, on the basis of the "sacred texts" of the theory common to the "global humanistic thought", a thought rejected with hysterical and ideological disdain by the "published imbeciles" globally: annoyance, disdain, and hysteria incomprehensible unless resorting to Jungian or Freudian psychoanalysis.

My deep conviction is that the prevailing cause, the independent variable, in short, of everything that has happened lies in culture and not only in the *landscapes* symbolic [2].

It is primarily about the hegemonic victory [3] of ordo-liberalism theorized in the Thirties in the USA and in the Forties of the twentieth century in Germany.

If we do not remember clearly, once again, those theories and those socio-economic conditions that they—in more than sixty years—have helped to create in the world, we cannot understand what will happen in the post-pandemic.

Indeed, if we do not pay attention to what were the conditions of the economy and world societies before the coronavirus, we understand

G. Sapelli, *States, Markets and Wars in Global History*,
https://doi.org/10.1007/978-3-031-26716-1_1

nothing of what awaits us in the future, if "the Resurrection" does not come.

The global "pre-pandemic" foundations of property systems and the deep roots of socio-economic formations have remained structurally the same until today.

Political transformations, on the other hand, have been profound and have effectively culminated worldwide in the weakening of Weberian state structures, gradually replaced by extended forms of patrimonialism ranging from African states, where it has post-colonial, territorial, and clan roots, to the South American model that has exacerbated the neo-caudillismo described by Joaquín Costa in his masterpiece on Spanish political life [4], published in 1901 but increasingly current. It goes from the fragmentation of political parties into clans dominated by political and economic entrepreneurs grouped in small groups, to the model of the States with *common law* where the plutocratic caucuses of business have mixed with the "quasi groups" [5]. Afro-American multiethnic places of interest, *wasp*, black and Latin in a formidable mosaic for variety and freedom of expression, up to the European polyarchy dominated by States weakened by the subtraction of sovereignty from above for the ordo-liberal technostructures of the treaties that have followed from Maastricht and beyond.

With all the "regulations" that bind us, it is well understood how parties have crumbled in Europe with the sole exception of Germany, along with a handful of Scandinavian states also with surviving parties "inside" and "around" strong Weberian ordo-liberal states by the book. The same phenomenon of crumbling of historical political parties occurred in South America, with the dissolution of Apra in Peru, with the literal political-institutional disappearance of *desarollismo* radical in Argentina, with the rapid decomposition of the historical "liberal" Colombian parties (while the civil war and the clandestine armed struggle—which enjoys immense support among the rural populations—continue instead).

Not to forget what happened in Mexico, where the fragmentation of institutionalism—which had guided the liberalization and destruction of welfare—has been affirmed without giving that historical nation a stability that allows to defeat drug trafficking and mass murders caused by *narcos* to govern such vast territories and threaten the State with terror [6].

The USA are naked in front of everyone's eyes, with the profound transformation of their political classes: the party system, however, has remained intact, but in recent years the military-industrial complex—which is the fundamental engine of North American power—has forced the arrogant destructive prevalence of unregulated finance, with the consequent dysfunctions in the circulation of Pareto elites.

In conclusion, the great transformation that has taken place in the world since Bretton Woods seemed similar to the one that occurred between the Congress of Vienna and the First World War; but in substance, it was exactly the opposite.

Then the modern world was founded and the market was generated not by the State, but by the *haute finance* and the *big corporations*, with the corrections to the same market constituted by political parties: they, while organizing democracy, as Ostrogorski first understood [7], which Gaetano Quagliariello made known in Italy many years ago [8], built a relationship between State and citizens based on welfare systems. A role always underestimated and not recognized by the same theory on the party machine. They did that miracle, the mass parties *rank and file*, giving life to the foundations of the "welfare society", between the two wars and during the European civil war against the USSR, phase of world history that follows that well described by Karl Polanyi in his immense book that is *The Great Transformation* [9].

What happened after the Second World War was complex and in many ways unpredictable. For a brief span of years, it seemed to continue intact the world that I have evoked, while instead laying the foundations for its profound transformation.

From Bretton Woods to today, what has happened, as I have tried to describe in some of my works and as two French scholars [10] have meticulously and wonderfully reconstructed with the tools of intellectual historiography, is a transformation perhaps even deeper than that described by Polanyi. Unfortunately for humanity, this transformation is still ongoing. The years that have passed from the end of the Second World War to the eighties of the twentieth century, which seemed to be—for many—the foundation of a new social democratic order that elevated the European system of mixed economy and welfare as a model, were essentially, instead, only the decaying fruit of global economic growth in the post-Korean war conjuncture.

In the eighties of the twentieth century, in fact, everything would have changed.

I am referring to the "revelation", which after the years of growth—from the fifties to the seventies of the twentieth century—occurred of that new economic liberalism that had built, in the world's indifference, the European and global institutional construct based on a series of treaties and on the dominance, in Europe, of the ideas of Teutonic ordo-liberalism and the French school of regulation. It was the European response to North American neoliberalism, which was no longer based on the rejection of state action, to leave free rein to a phantasmagoric market inhabited by Robinsonian actors that was supposed to exist in nature, as it existed in the physiocratic imaginary and in that of the Austrian school in economics. Not existing in nature, the State had to make it real.

After the Second World War, thanks to the intellectual work of groups of scholars often not even linked to each other, both in the USA, and especially in Germany, the foundations of today's world were laid.

Cultural foundations, not economic ones, which today dramatically slow down and will slow down the global exit from the pandemic on the economic, social, and above all, cultural level: the most important of all the others.

That neoliberal world prevents the "Resurrection" after the pandemic tragedy, as the "letter" of Saint Paul to the Romans always urges us to do eschatologically. What we are prisoners of today is written in the works not of great thinkers, of immense intellectuals, but of severe academics of great honesty and sober lifestyle who do not reach the heights of science or philosophical glory: officials of "regulated capitalism", supported by the State and the law and by de facto orders when both laws and Constitutions are silent.

Illegitimate elites govern the world.

And here we understand the tragedy we have incurred, between Hollywood and the illiberal twist of democracy.

I am referring to the thinkers who founded the world that prepared societies for crumbling under the blows of the pandemic: Walter Lippmann (his *The New Imperatif* is fundamental) [11] and above all, equally and perhaps even more fundamental, Walter Eucken [12].

To be clear, these modest thinkers would never have been portrayed in a "School of Athens" by the divine Raphael. But their ideas, adopted by the situational powers of finance and even before the great *corporations*, have dominated and dominate the world between "TV series" and the illiberal regimes that we have been building for many years as humanity endowed with vital worlds devoid of humanistic culture.

Opposing this transformation, in the bourgeois world and not in the Marxist and Soviet one, was until the sixties of the twentieth century the

French critical thought that had in Charles de Gaulle and Jacques Léon Rueff [13] its illustrious champions, but which was defeated when it came to rebuilding the world economy starting from a Europe in danger due to Soviet pressure. It was then decided, after 1957, to give a new face to Europe: an ordo-liberal face.

Those who advocated and advocate, yesterday as today, the role of the State not only to impose the market economy, but also to impose a detailed regulation of it, through the creation of international institutions all inspired, even in their technocratic dress, by the utopia of universal peace characteristic of the UN and even earlier to the Briand-Kellogg Pact, of 1928 [14]. Only that IMF, OECD, World Bank, World Health Organization, and, finally, the European Treaties, successively followed, are not the advocates of universal peace. What happened in Paris, in 1928, in the Salon de l'Horologe of the Quai d'Orsay, where the Briand-Kellogg Pact was signed, and where the first meeting of the League of Nations had already been held in 1920, was nothing more than the anticipation of the increasingly compulsive transformation of world governance that occurred with increasing intensity from the end of the seventies of the twentieth century, with the advent of deregulated finance and the North American families nourished and brought to power by it. A power that will no longer be based on the principle of realism dictated by Vegetius: "Igitur qui desiderat pacem, praeparet bellum", but, as I will discuss in this book, on the contrary, on the principles of neocon humanitarianism, following the ideological footsteps of Leo Strauss [15]. The unipolarist war, as defined in his fundamental works by David Calleo [16], veiled by an increasingly oppressive ideology and based on the falsehood of the *landscapes* of *political correctness*, will become the new universal creed of the "Internationalists" [17]. They are, moreover and consequently, the perennially active proponents of unelected technocratic government, delegated [18].

Europe, a tragic and clear example of the fulfillment of this adventure of the spirit, Europe subjected to the control of the Treaties does not have a Constitution [19], but only national power relations shielded by regulations, unknown to most and primarily to those who should make them act through national democracies. They, the national democracies, still stand, but without any vital force.

The conflict of power is, in fact, at the base of a set of States not united by a constitutional or federal or confederal design, with a jurisprudential profile of the order sought from time to time with increasing difficulty through the dominance of the market paradigm.

Paradigm continuously imposed by a host of unelected in the guise of ideologically shielded technocracy, thus creating a veil that obscures the truth and scenographically feeds an illusory stage.

On the world political stage, a handful of mercenary companies perform. The issue has worsened when the other great transformation appeared on the scene: the transformation of neoliberal capitalism into capitalism with deployed finance.

The exogenous crisis of simultaneous demand and supply blockage caused in 2020 by the pandemic did not stop finance and its technological virulence. On the contrary, thanks to the same innovation that allowed us to rebuild relationships among the living in virtual conditions of interactive communication through magnetic waves (it is always Marconi who has given us everything that concerns the technohuman domain of the ether) the world has moved forward between *webinars* and constructs of artificial intelligence [20]. The latter has left the field of military research to flow into the creation of "Kondratiev waves" that spread in the regulated civil economy.

The global economy arrived at the appointment with COVID-19 in the worst possible situation, with high debt vulnerability and high speculative financial leverage: the pandemic had a catalytic effect amplifying a whole series of social dramas that had been evident for some time and that had to be brought, by the pandemic crisis, to an unprecedented explosion.

The speculative bubbles on credit and *equity* that circulated before the coronavirus were waiting for the fuse of the exogenous crisis to explode: the financial crisis, after all, would have come anyway, even just for a simple recession. And this is because the global model of capitalism with deployed finance is based on excess leverage, on lowering incomes, on huge speculative debt and weak investments in the real economy for the secular deflation in which we are immersed, central banks and non-central banks.

Here is a socio-economic system, not only European but global, that depends on how much debt one is able to make without taking into account the quality of the debt and its use. Quality of debt that is instead essential to avoid or not avoid cyclical crises: they are avoided, albeit for a short time, if the rate of debt growth is lower than the rate of economic growth, thanks to investments in capital stock, in organic capital [21].

All this in a constant decay of the real incomes of 99% of the world's living humans. Public and private debt, on the other hand, has been growing for thirty years more than income and attempts are made to support it with financial leverage causing continuous systemic crises. They started with the Asian crises at the end of the second millennium (Thailand) and continue cyclically until today.

Debt becomes, together, on the one hand, a theoretical European and global prohibition and, on the other, the condition of the artificial life of the same European and global capitalism.

It is a new version of the capitalist contradictions understood in a Marxian sense between social relations of production and development of productive forces: it is undeniable, even if today's bourgeois economy does everything not to see and to hide [22].

It is because of this contradiction, for example, that Europe is dividing: between states that slowly fold towards greater non-ordo-liberal self-regulation but of "mixed economy", effectively raising the issue of an increasing return to national economic policies (the states that with France at the head refuse, in 2020, to resort to the aid of the so-called ESM that is subject to rules based on the ordo-liberal rejection of debt *tout court*) and states that are, instead, determined to make—thanks to their situational power in fact, the result of social and ideological cohesion—the ESM a tool to move towards stronger control (national, note) of the technocratic levers of Europe. However, the decisive factor is always the national and asymmetric control—together with the quality of the people appointed—of the appointments of European bureaucrats, so as to have possession, by regulatory means, of the economic and social life of all other states [23].

Germany—due to the effects of the historically endemic conflict with France and within itself between the de facto situational powers of its polyarchy—could diverge between supporters of absolute ordo-liberalism, as described, and another Germany, which is slowly dragged towards change by virtue of its own Bourbon and Bavarian history, that is, from the historical, ideal, and economic bond with Italy [24], Spain, and the South of Europe, all the way down to Turkey: Turkey, which, after all, is already in the very heart of German social life with worker migrations and is destined for a new international role in the power conflict between the weak Eurasian Russian giant and the dominion of that Atlantic lake, which is the Mediterranean, is now contestable. In this way, Turkey challenges US dominance and downgrades Italian and French presences in the area. It can do this strong with the support of the polygamous Sunni states and Egypt. Egypt stands out in history as the new Germany of the Greater Middle East, after Syria, due to the Iranian wars of Shiite fundamentalism against the Wahhabi-origin Sunni one—and therefore Saudi—destroyed that ingenious agreement which was the Franco-English Sykes-Picot Treaty [25]. Today it has been devastated by the emergence—here is a new very dangerous form of state disintegration—of proxy war in Iraq, in Yemen, and in Syria and throughout the Greater Middle East. Hence the emergence of that asymmetric state, which is Islamic fundamentalism [26], which is nothing more than a terrible chapter of what I want to discuss in this book: the de-statization of the world.

Europe is inert in the face of these tragic processes. The French Empire cannot dominate them and Russia must rebuild its Eurasian power. Only the democratic awakening and therefore the confederal or federal rearmament (whatever it is as long as it is the result of what is tragically lacking today: a European Constitution), only the rearmament of Germany can change the course of events. If this does not happen, the spirit of the German scorpion will rise again and kill the frog that carries it to the shore, making everyone drown, not just Europe.

And on this I will say in conclusion of this complex of reasoning.

The temptation to suicide is always present in German history.

A great change is underway and binds and connects, without unifying, all the jagged faults, the uncertain fractals of the world that emerges from the pandemic crisis, revealing everything.

Moreover, as I try to discuss and propose in a central part of this book, the fundamental link to grasp among all the ongoing transformations is that of the changing structure of world polyarchies.

I speak of the growing role of technocratic situational powers gradually conquered by unelected structures endowed with non-legitimized compulsive power, but imposed, instead, by the transformation undergone by national legal systems due to the growing role assumed by de facto transnational systems, of a technocratic nature. De facto systems that once, before the Second World War—if we make the exception of the UN, an institution born from the Wilsonian brain of the dreamers of perpetual Kantian peace—did not exist.

It is this global institutional transformation that makes us say that the deepest legacy that a national culture has given to today's world, the world that most believe to be that of so-called globalization, is, instead, the return of Prussian cameralism. It is the “magical” legacy of a very powerful national culture in terms of formative power to the *Zeitgeist* of today. It was unsurpassably interpreted—and not by chance—on the North American shores at the beginning of the twentieth century by Albion Small [27], who wrote the best book on such cameralism in the heart of the emerging most powerful state monopoly capitalism in the world. This reference to Small is fundamental for me to interpret how current it—cameralism—is, more than it was yesterday, to understand today. A topicality, moreover, already wonderfully evoked by Schiera [28] and Miglio [29] in the fervent years of my youth.

In cameralism, as is known, elements of administrative science, economics, finance science, politics, and agricultural and industrial technique aimed to establish—as it was—a “possible” unitary science of the State. The State was understood as a “machine” that could achieve social balance by avoiding conflict, thanks to the continuous recourse to an “order” composite and multidisciplinary, imposed legally or with “de facto” regulations. All this without addressing the perennial problem of political science: that is, that always open and always dangerous problem for both order and economic growth which is the Constitution and what follows from it: parliamentary democracy.

Hence the relevance today of cameralism when the State built “around” and “for” parliamentary democracy is unraveling all over the world. Hence the role of neo-cameralism in what, more and more, is defined as “globalization”. It is nothing else, instead, than “the search for an economic interdependence” at least superior to that prevailing in the world before the First World War.

In this book, an attempt is made to give a non-transient explanation of this very complex phenomenon, which is presented in veiled forms by the ideologies of Kantian peace or by the equally unrealistic revanchist wills of neo-anti-Semitic and neo-fascist, Weberianly aimed at understanding. The State and the welfare of the State are the center of social order: the public finance system is the possible solution and at the same time the perennial problem of national order. In this sense, the “cameralists” were not economists, but “unelected theorists of politics”, politics that they were called to exercise without popular mandate.

Hence the “silent” overcoming of any theory of sovereignty: it was replaced by the theory of the State [30].

But there is a problem that should make it clear to the whole world what global neo-cameralism cannot solve and much less what global ordo-liberalism can deploy. I am talking about the immense problem of migrations, the destruction of stable human settlements that are shattered and dissolved with immense clouds of pain, suffering, death, and obfuscation of any humanitarian thought (where have the theorists of perpetual Kantian peace gone?). Mass emigrations are the most devastating and painful phenomenon of the present time. Only politics as a "virtue of the best" [31] can solve problems of this kind.

In the past, the time of the creation of the expanded accumulation of capitalism (on which, it must be admitted, Marxism or not Marxism, Rosa Luxemburg [32] wrote the essential and unmatched pages), the State, the States, set themselves the task of coordinating and regulating, with the collaboration of intermediate bodies (religious organizations *in primis*), human trafficking that was supposed to guarantee capitalist accumulation and often the creation of new global capitalist nations with overseas migrations. Today, however, the market and therefore the deregulation administered by the underworld fulfills this task that is not "accompanied" by the action of the immense "regulatory" superstructures. They, while spreading the humanitarian thought of the cowards in the face of war, mass death with new genocides, rampant neo-slavery, withdraw from the role they should instead fulfill. A role that the numerous NGOs certainly cannot replace. All this is shaping up as a vile lie that hides the power struggle behind the veil of the lost lives of millions of suffering people, in a world upset by local wars and national conflicts.

A tragic human comedy is based on a deployed liberalism that allows crime and human trafficking to spread, while that dominant neoliberalism fails to find an "order" that can not only resolve, but at least contain the problem.

The mask of the world is a satanic grin: the grin of a weak thought that cannot hide the infamy. Or rather: it succeeds very well. And this is a real tragedy: spiritual.

In this global context of institutional dissolution that the professionals of magic and the neoliberal and ordo-liberal exorcists call globalization, the "Old Mole" of history returns: it digs. But in which direction? The "political planet" is immobile and dragged into the dust by the *soft powers* external, which are no longer just those of the European powers or the North American one, but Chinese.

And the USA is hit by an internal conflict never seen before, with a polyarchy that is quickly moving towards increasing losses of international power.

And China is collapsing [33]. It is the power struggle that is veiled, also in this case, as I try to explain in this book: veiled by the unrealistic ideology of the heirs of Leo Strauss [34] who have forgotten the realism of Kissinger to actually hide the power struggle.

Only recently has there been a forced return to realism, as happened in the run-up to the two world wars of the twentieth century due to the emergence of a revisionist power. Then it was Germany: today it is China. It too, like Germany, has benefited from the "new Munich Treaties". Today the spirit of Munich is represented in its resurgence from China's entry into the WTO in 2001. And today as yesterday, the divisions between nations permanently established in the global power game are essential to understand what is happening: then it was France against Germany, while the USA was enticed by possible isolationism until Pearl Harbor. Today it is Germany divided from the USA on the attitude to take towards a China now decidedly aggressive all over the world, starting from the Pacific and Eurasia. Evidence of this is both the always latent Sino-Indian conflict and the continuous violations of maritime law in the South China Seas and the Indian Ocean, which also signal the Chinese maritime military effort (also here with impressive similarities with the pre-war situations of the twentieth century).

It is astonishing (as astonishing were the cowardice and blindness of the ruling classes before the two world wars) the blindness of the peaks of European capitalism incapable of centralization and that of global finance despite numerous real and proper manifestations of this aggression.

And it would be enough to read, as an example of such guilty blindness or interested cowardice, the texts of a refined intellectual like Yan Xuetong [35], who presents us with a refined exemplification, but no less threatening, of the designs of the current Chinese leadership group.

It is necessary that we realize, in the present history, the danger that civilization is running, and it is necessary that everything does not resolve into a historiographic problem: once again.

This time the reproduction of civilization would be seriously endangered. As it was, moreover, in the face of Hitlerian and Stalinist threats.

But as I try to demonstrate in this book, China is collapsing under the weight of the inherent contradictions in its structure of monopolistic state capitalism and terrorist dictatorship. So what will happen?

Will it drag the whole world with it?

These questions well express the drama of this time.

It is certain, however, that the great global game is only, again, once again, at the beginning. And this time, again and again and again, it will be the conflict between sea powers and land powers that will decide the future of the world.

The USA seems to be waking up from a long sleep and no one predicted it. The USA made manifest, at the end of July 2020, a transformation of their geopolitical orientation that could not have been clearer. The meaning of the naval exercises that took place simultaneously in the Indian Ocean in cooperation with the Indian Navy and in the Pacific in close cooperation with the Japanese Navy was evident to all. They were directed against China.

A new course of world foreign policy began that sees the USA laying the foundations, at the same time, both for the abandonment of the ruinous unilateralism on which David Calleo [36] wrote prescient pages, and at the same time inaugurating a new cold war. This, while targeting China, will inevitably lead to an unstoppable strengthening of the USA's approach to Putin's Russia. The Indo-Pacific Command, based in Hawaii, controls 52% of the planet's waters and more than any other example makes manifest the thalassocratic power of the USA. At the same time, further east, in the Philippine Sea, the US Navy was engaged, as I said, in a maneuver that saw the Royal Australian Navy and the Japanese Self-Defense Naval Force united. Everything took place on that eastern passage of the quadrant of the South China Sea, which the Pentagon—and now, it seems, also the State Department—has identified as a containment bulwark against Beijing. The bipartisan agreement in the USA was ratified in 2020 between the parties and the situational powers of fact—always unstable—of the North American polyarchy, which sets in motion its global servomechanisms, despite the very tough electoral confrontation, proving the historical importance of the decisions taken.

The USA once again demonstrated their unsurpassed global centrality.

But the weakness of the powers that base their dominance on the sea, as history well explains from the Peloponnesian Wars to the Napoleonic Wars and the Second World War and as Alfred Thayer Mahan, still unsurpassed theorist of maritime power struggle, is however based on the need to defend heterogeneous and distant territories. Thalassocracy is a form of exercise of power, therefore, extremely expensive and to understand it just think how much a well-armed fleet in the growing global technological confrontation requires huge investments, not only in materials, but also in troop training, more specialized than ever.

The shift of resources from ground troops to those of sea and air (with the consequences in the distribution of the military-industrial-bureaucratic power that derive from it) will have to be, if the confrontation with China is definitively accepted, enormous. As US Secretary of State Mike Pompeo significantly stated in that fateful 2020, and as the diplomatic incidents that followed in 2020 in the US against the spy network of Chinese parallel diplomacies demonstrate, the path chosen by the US was then traced and the consequences in every field of associated life will be enormous. Even Xi Jinping had to face the problem of controlling the armed forces, greatly reducing the power of the Army—prince of war when the enemy was the USSR and then Russia—to shift the weight of weapons and therefore of the centralized military-industrial complex of the CCP on the navy and aviation, which are the tools par excellence of maritime power. After all, the US faces this problem with NATO: but the fall of the USSR was not followed by the possibility of reducing the price to be paid to land defense to shift, instead, all the axis of resources towards the weapons of the sea and sky to which the future of the threat of war and therefore of world peace belongs.

Europe, as the events of 2020 demonstrated in relation to anti-pandemic economic intervention plans, is sinking in the quicksand of land power. Only Atlantic France and Mediterranean Italy, with the Southern States, Greece, Spain, and Portugal together with French imperial power, could face the new battles that await European states in the Mediterranean when the neo-Ottoman and neo-pharaonic pushes of Turkey and Egypt will threaten the power of European states in Libya, in Cyprus, even in Israel itself, squeezed between a declining Lebanon and a very fragile Syria with dangerous tendencies to dismemberment throughout the Greater Middle East. The only trend that can oppose such dismemberment is the evolution of the economic, political, diplomatic relationship, therefore, between Israel and the Arab states of the Gulf, despite their schismatic divisions, as seems to be confirmed after the agreement between Israel and the United Arab Emirates of 2020. Certainly in anti-Iran function and against the neo-imperial expansion of Turkish power in neo-Ottoman version, but certainly decisive, and this trend is destined to change the fate of the Mediterranean and the Greater Middle East, thus changing the fate of the world.

Italy returns, with the states of Southern Europe [37] and with France, to have a fundamental role in ordering the irreversibly contestable Mediterranean—whether it wants to, understands it or not—while the solely terrestrial German power cannot absolutely succeed in representing and unifying its economic destinies with all of Europe. Without an army, German geopolitical weight can only strengthen in the void of military power and therefore only by always allying itself with the enemies of the USA and other European states that threaten its dominance, as has always been the case in German history, since Prussia found its alliances against the Austro-Hungarian Empire and with the United Kingdom against France, as fully revealed in the nineteenth and twentieth centuries and as it now awaits to reveal itself again. History cannot be escaped. China is now this "resulting" power, which serves Germany to assume that geopolitical role that it cannot assume without an army, if not by fighting against those medium or large powers that should be, instead, its allies. Now and always the same story repeats itself. China is much weaker than it appears. But, as the history of the last thirty years of Europe shows, that is, after the fall of the USSR and the German reunification that none of those historical powers desired, the alliance between all European states and the USA is essential for world order. A power without an army like Germany can lose its head and do more damage than one might think, precisely because it is a disarmed power, but economically powerful. The void that it causes in the system of thalassocratic alliances must be filled by vassal powers of the imperial maritime power. For this reason, Italy becomes, with its own geographical positioning, potentially strategic in the new balance of world power, whatever its government. Indeed, for the powers with imperial impulse, the more technically unprepared the better: they, geopolitically more prudent, could—as already happens "fractally"—use its geopolitical potential, and it is to be hoped that they are not destructive powers. The power of China must be contained, in fact, also in the Mediterranean, which is the door of Africa and the Greater Middle East.

It is this danger of dispossession that European governments run when they are prevalent constructs of internationally multi-affiliated mercenary companies to the powers that compete for what can be conquered in the international power system, while the new cold war is outlined. But the pivot of the thalassocratic powers has always been the need to have loyal allies with whom to face the costs and strategic challenges of world domination through the seas and skies. Let's remember recent European political history. Even the Balkan wars of the nineties of the twentieth century constituted an unexpected and, for most, an unpredictable turning point. Action had to be taken and the dominance of the skies and seas was again essential, as was the unfolding of the US thalassocratic dominance.

The stakes have been masterfully summarized by Alessandro Mangia:

> It is an area, the Franco-German one, all of land that is today under pressure from the sea both from the west and from the south, that is, from the Mediterranean, through Italy. The ongoing occurrences are not casual, for the simple fact that geopolitics has its own logic and that, as Schmitt understood very well seventy years ago, the mythological monster of land, the Behemoth, is destined to always be strangled by the mythological monster of the sea, the Leviathan. Once the American power balances have finally stabilized, it will only be a matter of time before the Anglosphere regains control of the small giant of Earth, and reduces to reason a tool - actually an experiment - of regional government that has slipped out of the hands of its creators and that has been sold to the populations of this part of Eurasia as a "European dream", stuffing it with references to Kant, to "perpetual peace", to the ideology of rights in impossible, perennial expansion, to the "balanced" economy of ordo-liberalism, and to other amenities of the kind. [38]

For this reason, the European land swamp must be cyclically reclaimed from obstacles that oppose this dominance. But will the means to do this still be found?

The answer risks not being affirmative if we look at the cultural changes taking place in the so-called Western world, that is, in that cradle of universal civilization that were Europe and Mesopotamia and the other civilizations that sprouted from the "European miracle" and the Greater Middle East: the USA and Latin America.

This is what Giambattista Vico reminded us of:

> ... Now with such a Recourse of Civil Human things ... let's reflect on the comparisons, which throughout this Work in a large number of subjects have been made about the first and last times of the Ancient and Modern Nations; and the whole History will be explained, not just particular, and in time of Laws, and of the deeds of the Romans or the Greeks; but on the identity in substance of understanding, and diversity of their ways of explaining themselves: we will have the Ideal History of eternal Laws, on which run the facts of all nations, in their risings, progress, states, declines, and end, even if it were, which is certainly false, that from Eternity were born, from time to time, Infinite Worlds. [39]

The finiteness of the present time is made evident by the destruction of the historical statuary on which the image of the becoming of nations is based, with that overwhelming and different thing that always accompanies their history. It now denies itself with the rites of the scapegoat that, as Girard taught us, emanate from the foundational mimicry of human beings. Nowadays mimicry is rampant, with a worldwide regularity and based on the national tragedies of the nations that have been the cradle of the world in the time of modernity. Yes, mimicry is rampant, whether it is triggered by sexual difference in births no longer recognized as foundational of being or whether it is triggered by agnatic roots overflowed from the times of the formation of the modern world of emerging extractive and once slaveholding capitalism. Well, these differences do not become a reason for spiritual enrichment, as they should and as Vico always teaches us.

They are the result, instead, of mimetic laceration, foundational of the scapegoat, which Girard masterfully discusses in chapter XII of his masterpiece, dedicated to "The Demons of Gerasa". Here is what it reads:

> What can motivate an entire herd to self-destruct without being forced by anyone? The answer is obvious. It's called herd spirit, the one that makes a herd a herd; in other words, the irresistible tendency to mimicry. It is enough that a first pig falls into the sea, by chance or for any reason, due to sudden fear or the convulsions caused by demonic invasion, for all its congeners to do the same. The frenzy of following along goes perfectly well with the proverbial docility of the species. Beyond a certain mimetic threshold, the one that defines possession, the entire herd instantly reproduces any behavior that seems out of the norm. It's a bit like the phenomenon of fashion in so-called advanced societies, in the sense in which we say advanced that of Gerasa. [40]

These are the unforeseen but recurring phenomena that will mark the fate of future societies.

CHAPTER 2

Extraordinary Changes

Recent human history shows substantial changes in the international correlation of economic and political forces on a global scale, imposing a reflection on the reconfiguration and rearticulation of the world political system.

The heart of the global crisis is in Europe.

How long will that thread that holds together the European nations without its tearing plunge history back? Will it throw it back to the Treaty of Verdun that marked the end of the Holy Roman Empire and paved the way for the painstaking construction of a concert of nations that lasted in European history only a moment, after the industrialization of the continent?

That is, in that span of time that the already mentioned Karl Polanyi [41] defined as "the peace of a hundred years": from 1815 to 1846 peace was, in fact, guaranteed by the armies of the "Holy Alliance" after Napoleon's defeat.

A peace that bends the social storm of industrialization thanks to the role that was also played, unlike today, by that social force that Maurice Lévy-Leboyer [42], in his unforgettable 1964 book, first defined as *l'haute finance*. That is, the redistributive force, private and public, which on the one hand determined the balance of power of nations—since none of them trusted each other and there was a need for a clearing room of power—and on the other provided the financial means to build a

G. Sapelli, *States, Markets and Wars in Global History*,
https://doi.org/10.1007/978-3-031-26716-1_2

relative social peace on which the first experiment of Bismarckian welfare and the first social insurances (of which the Italian Ina was a clear example in the Giolittian age) would rise: here is the "European Concert", which from the Franco-Prussian War onwards determines a balance of power that no one challenges until the First World War. From 1815 to 1914, the great European powers suffered and provoked only eighteen cumulative months of war (the main one is the terrible one between Prussia and France that lasted only one year), while in all the previous centuries more than half was spent in war. This kind of miracle was made possible for Polanyi [43] by the simultaneous affirmation of four "institutions": the balance of power system between France, unified Germany, and the United Kingdom; the international gold standard (governed by powerful social forces and dedicated institutions); the emerging capitalist market; the liberal state. In this context, international finance, completely self-regulating without any kind of supranational infrastructures as are today the technocracies of the International Monetary Fund or the OECD or the EU, structured itself as an organic link between the political and economic organization of the world. It provided the tools for public debt, disciplined the states, worked in concert with them, and, when they arose, linked itself to the national central banks without however depending on them.

High finance was a sort of "sovereign agent" that enjoyed the trust of national states and international investors: in this way, in case of crisis, a regulation mechanism between economy and politics could always be regenerated, because homeostasis was a social product, not artificially generated: the national power forces constituted, with their *entente cordiale*, the balance of these international "natural" and "functional" institutions and prevented the entropy of the system.

This entropy is instead what is creeping in Europe today, where the fixed exchange rate system through a single currency operates without political unity, without integrated fiscal systems, without agreed welfare systems, with financial deregulation that plays against the states with speculation on debt instead of working as it once did to its integration with the states and their political classes. Hence the European disintegration that we are witnessing every day in a condition of impotence because the technocratic European institutions are not homeostatic and work against each other armed. Hence the resurgence of the spirit of power crudely called sovereigntism, neonationalism, and so on, proving the ignorance and lack of culture in which the world of the published and the publishable has sunk.

The great finance described by Polanyi worked, instead, for peace among the great powers because its long-term investments were based on stability, monetary, and political, in a way completely different from what happens today.

Hence the disintegration and the impossibility of reconstructing a *entente cordiale* European, subjected as they are to the role of finance that operates in a very short time in a steel cage that is much more rigid than the golden base, because it predetermines politics and the circulation of the same political classes, preventing their formation on the basis of consensus on economic policies. These, instead, are imposed from above with an autopilot. Naturally, the most abstract and invisible to the people was chosen, such as ordo-liberalism, which is based, precisely, on the inverse principle of Polanyian peace: the automatic and algorithmic processing of debt with the growing liberalist disintegration of social forces and political forms that had historically formed on the basis of the national needs of the people. These have been replaced, instead, by rules that only work in German, Dutch, and Scandinavian cases, and which are historically inapplicable in the French and Italic part of continental Europe and the South. Hence the crisis of almost all European political systems: there is not one that functions in classic forms, that is, as described by traditional political science: the circulation of elites in democratic polyarchy has jammed and only power elites are formed against each other. The inability to form parliamentary political majorities in almost every European state is the consequence of the process briefly described here and not its cause, as is commonly said.

Italy is no exception, indeed it is the case immediately understandable according to this model, if the disintegration of the international system is superimposed on this reasoning, which sees the USA unable to escape from the trap of unipolarity in which they fell thanks to the advent of a deregulating finance that has formed a speculative alliance with the Chinese power elites against the military and industrial forces of the North American establishment. The struggle that has been going on for years in the establishment in the USA is nothing but the reflection of this process.

Only a new *entente cordiale* between the USA and Russia can overcome unipolarity and the disproportionate force of deregulating finance. But to do this, the void of European politics must be filled by giving the system a non-entropic operation as the current one: reactivating an organic alliance with the USA, dismantling the autopilot of economic policy not regulated by national forces that gradually find consensus on individual specific points instead of, as today, being dominated by impersonal algorithmic forces. A return of "good" politics, in short. Something that seems impossible today.

The values of the West such as democracy, freedom, and human rights must be discussed today in a new scenario.

A cultural and value autonomy is affirmed by the countries of the so-called—once—third and fourth world that complete the decolonization process: the political subjects emerged after the end of European colonialism today claim their own state *governance*.

But it is precisely the State that is in disintegration or in the inability to form all over the world.

The de-statization or non-statization currently taking place all over the world is a complex phenomenon that has few points of continuity with the historical forms of polyarchic construction. Where the modernly understood State has been realized, it is subject to a drift that resides in the absence of compulsiveness of the concept of sovereignty.

My thesis is that this drift, on the one hand, and the constructive inability, on the other hand, are determined by the ever-increasing interdependence in international relations of those forces that gradually shatter the States by subtracting sovereignty and the possibility of reproducing and building communities of destiny, without which States cannot exist.

Technocracies and international organizations do not make up for these absences: they also realize them.

The key concept for understanding the process of de-statization is Eisenstadt's neopatrimonialism [44], which in 1973 warned us that institutional modernization is not a linear process, but rather it is multiple: it feeds hybridizations and selective absorptions of changes.

The elements of traditional (patrimonial) authority merge and confuse with elements of legal-rational authority, as well as with desacralized charismatic power. The point is that the reality of modern administrative organizations shows mixed profiles: survivals and unexpected combinations of traditional and modern administrative traits. The recourse to the concept of neopatrimonialism implies, therefore, the rejection of a unilinear vision of Western modernization and the attempt to find new categories capable of accounting for the complexity of the functioning of large public and private organizations in contemporary society.

The risk of distortions is high, as the constant reference to deteriorating phenomena such as nepotism, clientelism, corruption, conflicts of interest, use of the law to obtain privileges, and so on, recalls.

In comparative studies, neopatrimonialism has been seen as a variant of non-democratic regimes and recently has been referred to in the analysis of democratic transitions and hybrid regimes: it has been referred to Latin America, Southern Europe, Asia, and Africa.

To deeply understand what is happening today, for example in Africa, a wide-ranging comparative analysis is essential. Let's examine some topical phenomena.

The new forms of conflict in wars for raw materials that destabilize resource-rich states through their progressive socio-economic impoverishment have as victims the losers of globalization. Consider the case of the numerous "asymmetric wars" in sub-Saharan Africa, the basis of the so-called "African patrimonialism". This type of regime involves the head of government (usually a president) retaining authority through a system of *patronage* clientelism.

The reward for public officials is the opportunity to appropriate the opportunities offered by public institutions and control of society ("prebendal regime").

Starting from this symptomatic framework, some variants of African neopatrimonialism have been identified: "personal dictatorships" (Zaire, Somalia, Malawi); "military oligarchies" (Nigeria, Uganda, Sudan, Ethiopia); "plebiscitary single-party systems" (Togo, Congo, Cameroon, Madagascar); finally, the "competitive single-party systems" (Tanzania, Kenya, Zambia, Cape Verde).

It is clear today that the protagonists of de-Westernizing revisionism are not only the marginal countries from a global point of view, but also those better integrated because they are looking for their own attractiveness.

In Asia, an emblematic case in this sense is the Chinese one built on "market socialism", led by an authoritarian political system, capable, however, of adapting its political institutions in the new global course.

Gradually, China has imposed itself, going through strong conflicts much more powerful than what happened in the case of post-Soviet Russia, as one of the main actors on the global economic scene, beyond external imbalances, environmental and human costs, and corruption.

In fact, the Chinese model is oriented towards authoritarian corporatism and not towards an effective liberal democracy, as many stolid interpreters of the relationship between "quasi-market" and liberalism think.

Another noteworthy case is India, which had to suffer the consequences of a profound anthropological and social mutation dictated by globalization.

The result is the birth of a numerically small upper-middle class that has enormous wealth and a more extensive and desperate *underclass*. The design was supported and financed by multinationals that do great business in India and have a huge reservoir of low-cost labor to which they turn for jobs that in the West would weigh more heavily on their budgets [45]. The trans-caste establishment has chosen to indicate an internal enemy (the Muslims) to vent the anger of millions of Hindus.

A strategy that is at the origin of the massacres that occur periodically and claim victims in the religious minority, then fueling that silent conflict between India and Pakistan, which began in 1947 immediately after independence, and constitutes a constant threat to the stability of all of Asia, culminating twice in open war for the possession of the Kashmir region, the borderland that, in the opinion of many independent political analysts, could trigger a nuclear conflict in a short time in the absence of an agreement [46].

Here too: State (that is, what remains of British colonization) in disintegration and in constant incomplete reaggregation.

In Latin America, on the other hand, neopatrimonialism has ended up indicating the evolution or the manifestation of new paradoxes of liberal-democratic regimes that were created after the dictatorships ended in the eighties, with intense processes of "privatization of the public" and "economization of politics" [47]. This is the case of the neoliberalist wave, not neoliberal, that swept the subcontinent during the nineties, a wave colluding with clientelistic systems of selling public assets and the deconstruction of entire socio-economic constructs in a privatistic key [48].

From the ashes of this process arose the *socialism of the 21st century* of Chavezian memory that imposed *by military force* a system of redistribution through the logics of neo-indigenism and the exploitation of mineral resources based on the periodic high cost of oil and that can therefore be questioned by a lowering of the prices of *oil and gas*.

The process, as is known, has touched all the Andean countries and marked the "turn to the left" of Argentina of the Kirchner couple. Starting from the presidency of the Republic, the western and colonial institution par excellence, the *socialism of the 21st century* has reconfigured various state apparatuses in a pre-Columbian key, see the Bolivian case of Evo Morales.

The recent turn to the right of the entire subcontinent and the economic collapse of militarized Venezuela have expanded the strength of the attempt at neo-judicial re-vertebration promoted by the USA with anti-corruption campaigns (the well-executed export but with political protagonists—right-wing—different from the Italian ones—left-wing).

This attempt at re-vertebration was not a re-statization, but a technocratic polyarchic superimposition of a media-democratic nature, which delivered and delivers a "quasi State" to a military technocracy and hetero-directed (by China, Russia, and Iran) together.

This process, which is imposing itself in all South American republics with a model always similar to the Italian one of the nineties of the twentieth century, raises the question of how the State will reconfigure itself in the face of new economic challenges, first of all the collapse of the highly de-statized Brazilian economic system that is facing an international recession of unheard-of violence.

Analytically, it is important, in this light, to value those studies that—deepening the theme of political-institutional transformation—explain the complex dynamics that determine a voluntary choice of political elites to reform the system, which make possible a spontaneous "de-statization by exhaustion" of the previous polyarchic forms and that lead to the creation of social, economic or cultural spaces capable of escaping the control of the State, following the studies of Juan Linz [49] on the transformation of democracies.

Certainly this passage from the preface by Friedrich Engels to the brilliant work of Karl Marx *The 18th Brumaire of Louis Bonaparte* is too drastic and harsh, underestimating the (Crocean) role of the Spirit in history, but it serves well, however, to sociologically and anthropologically frame the political period that the whole world is going through:

> It was Marx himself – Engels wrote – who first discovered the great law of historical evolution, the law according to which all struggles in history, whether they take place on political, religious, philosophical, or other ideological grounds, are in reality nothing more than the more or less clear expression of struggles between social classes; according to which the existence, and therefore also the collisions, of these classes are in turn conditioned by the degree of development of their economic situation, by

> their mode of production and by the mode of exchange that results from it. This law, which has the same importance for history as the law of energy transformation has for the natural sciences, also provided him with the key to understanding the history of the second French republic.

And this is exactly what is happening today not in France, but all over the world: disintegration of the middle classes [50] frightened by the reform of pension schemes to which it is difficult to provide shelter; submission of large layers of *state clerks* to privatistic regimes that subject them to the law of the market and the continuous search for a job having completely lost the *status* of lifelong servants of a State articulated in bodies as well as in public apparatuses; devaluation of the principle of *status* for most of the teachers subjected to income regimes insufficient to reproduce general educational and cultural knowledge and subjected to the pressure of families and school directors lacking in the culture of educational relations. In the manufacturing industry, the crisis subjects managers of every low and medium level to the nightmare of unemployment in which they are barbarically thrown in not young age but in mature age, when it is not possible to find another occupation. Discrepancy of *status* between multimillionaire top managers and the intermediate managerial class and non-manual workers subjected to job insecurity. Growing fear creeping among the alveolar manufacturing bourgeoisie; small and artisanal businesses for the continuous risk of failure they run, subjected as they are to suffocating bureaucratic and fiscal pressures. The working class is paralyzed by the fear of unemployment and by the neo-slavery regime to which it is subjected in the majority of companies with intermittent contracts and short term, under an unheard-of ideological and moral pressure that has made it sink into anomie.

Youth that does not work and does not study, also sunk into the deepest anomie. Secularization has produced a classist neo-paganism of the "high ecological classes" that has spread in the symbolic worlds of all human settlements.

The masterpiece by Franz Neumann on "Fear and Politics" [51] that I have often mentioned is the most important text—along with the one cited by Marx—to understand the modern planetary drama.

The crisis due to anomie prevails because the Mortatian [52] "material constitution" has been destroyed—which are not the "strong powers", as I hear from fools everywhere, dominant in the published and visualized, but instead the large mass parties that in fragile States replaced and replace the State itself with processes of benevolent integration and that promoted and replaced together (again, the replacement...) the communities of destiny typical of mass political parties.

The reaction of the nineties of the twentieth century with the destruction of mass parties opposed to privatizations by subordinate globalization, which moved from Europe to Latin America and then to Asia and Africa, is the result of the universal emergence of the non-democratic and repressive polyarchy "via judiciary and via negative anthropology" of the human.

The North American exception should be noted here, so well explained by Theodore Lowi and Mauro Calise [53]: it continues to see the reproduction, in the mixed variant of *caciquismo* proliferating over vast areas *rank and file*, of mass parties.

This has given rise to a formidable divergence of social orientations and especially of the symbolic universes of the masses around the world.

CHAPTER 3

The Invertebrate World

"Indeed: the absence of the 'best' has created in the mass, in the 'people', a secular blindness to distinguish the better man from the worse man, so that when privileged individuals appear in our land, the 'mass' does not know how to take advantage of them, and often annihilates them": Ortega y Gasset, especially in *Invertebrate Spain. Second part. The absence of the best* [54], had well described, prophetically, the current political situation of the planet.

We must go beyond the classic dichotomy of rulers-ruled at the base of every social organization.

The theory of Gaetano Mosca [55] of the elites that bring order and progress precisely because they institutionalize elitism as a form of political government has been realized in reverse.

Electronic democracy (which was recently tried to be implemented in Congo with terrible outcomes in the electoral contest that marked the apparent end of the Kabila family's rule) hides the reality of the fact that certainly only a minority can guide the mass.

But does this mass—in a Canettian sense—exist only to be directed, influenced, represented, organized from above passively? It is not inevitable. Today in the world the *select minority* that according to Ortega [56] is able to subdue an undifferentiated agglomerate of hetero-directed individuals and thus promote the stability of the political order, instead presents itself as the servant of the people, its benevolent midwife in the

G. Sapelli, *States, Markets and Wars in Global History*,
https://doi.org/10.1007/978-3-031-26716-1_3

world of rights and creates a formidable world of mirrors once it has taken over, as it has, part of the national governments around the world.

The dominant Rosicrucian rhetoric today of those who have realized the political surplus value of representing the "people of the abyss" destroys day by day with the cries: "honesty! honesty!", or: "all thieves!" "prohibition of prescription!", and "all guilty!", that *realistic democracy* that accentuates the directive functions of a ruling minority. But every day it emerges that this minority has not been selected based on merit rather than power and dominance, wealth or strength, or the threat of the use of force [57].

This is what is not fully realized in every part of the planet, this minority. And this is due to the violent transformation through the anguished way of the *mass-man* Ortega-Gassetian by the small group of those who draw strength and will to power from the depressive solitude of the masses, generating with their appearance one of the most clamorous triumphs of media conformism, with a decline of civilization comparable only to the period of the Late Empire. Hence the barbarization and impoverishment of customs, with national languages reduced to a simplified caricature by the universal adoption of a "monkey language" para-Anglistic, so called for the possibility of learning its rudiments even by immense sectors of cognitively invertebrate human beings.

And this generates a mass hysteria that pervades both the "people of the abyss" and the financial bourgeoisie and its mass substitutes: the people *radical chic* of the ex-liberal professions, fanatical ecologists, and nutritionists who polemicize together with those who are against vaccines and fossil hydrocarbons with the same hysteria and conduct a political polemic also anguished, confusing politics with charity and mercy; just as others confuse political initiative on the issues of global mass migrations with racism.

But neither charity nor racism can replace political initiative, especially government.

For Ortega, the once elitist minorities succumbed under the dominion of an irresponsible, spoiled humanity, not spiritually tied to any social class, *deraciné par excellence*. Ortega y Gasset saw in the future a Europe and a world of despotisms, of homogeneity that nullify differences, with rampant conformism and vulgarity: a Europe and a world of barbarism dominated by an irresponsible humanity without historical memory, which enjoyed the wonders of technique without moral brakes.

Today Europe is the world.

The only hope, following one of the thinkers who, with Gaetano Mosca and Emmanuel Mounier [58], has most influenced my spiritual formation, is to revive the historical mass parties.

Of course, it would only be the beginning of a long and necessary refoundation of civic virtues that must lead to gather—before it withers forever—what is indispensable for the refoundation of politics: the legacy of the great liberal reformist, Catholic-social and socialist world traditions. But let's read Marco:

> At that time, Jesus said to the crowd: "Is the lamp brought to be put under the bushel or under the bed? Or is it not rather to be put on the lampstand? For there is nothing hidden that shall not be manifested; neither was anything kept secret, but that it should come abroad. If any man have ears to hear, let him hear!".

Appropriate words to define those who dominate the whole world in the times in which we survive.

We must live and not just survive.

CHAPTER 4

Theory for the New World

What struggles to emerge is a new "theoretical order", before a new historical-concrete order of world power structures.

The fundamental work of a great Master, Henry Kissinger, is indispensable to reconstruct that order.

And the main way is that of "geopolitical realism". Thinking of "realism" we can only think of Hans J. Morgenthau [59] and the "neorealism" of Kenneth Waltz [60], who transform the anthropological pessimism of the first into a more sociological consideration of the relations between powers, not only state ones. Power, after all, as a potent factor in the organization and reorganization of international power space—both for "realism" and "neorealism"—remains the only horizon through which one can have awareness and therefore interpret what the international connections between States are. Robert Gilpin [61] has given an important development to neorealist theories with a creative intertwining between the historiography of international relations and political thought, against the background of the theoretical hypotheses of reflection on *common goods*.

Geography has powerfully returned, in recent times, to the methodological scene of scientific reflection on international relations [62]. It tends to replace, with a sort of transposition in the field of studies just mentioned, neoclassical economics, with its algorithmic games and prisoner's dilemmas [63]. Gilpin, although strongly inspired by a neoclassical macroeconomic theory approach in his studies, escapes the simplicity

G. Sapelli, *States, Markets and Wars in Global History*,
https://doi.org/10.1007/978-3-031-26716-1_4

of hypostatizations to resume a long-term historiographic approach that allows him to develop a theory that exercises on a multidisciplinarity that becomes, precisely, "neorealist". We read that he states this in his main work just mentioned:

> ... presumes that the creation, maintenance, and successful functioning of a liberal international economy require the exercise of political leadership. Some mechanism of governance must supply such collective goods as a stable currency and promote open markets. In international economic relations there are frequently powerful incentives to cheat at the expense of other actors, and political leadership is needed to perform a managerial or policing role.

Paradoxically, the modern welfare state ... have increased rather than minimized the need for a leader [64].

Gilpin, with accents that are already present in the historiographic narration *événementielle* of Kissinger, argues the need for the presence of a "hegemonic" nation [65] that guarantees international stability, "stability" that is nothing but the absence of a destructive war. As is known, the first scholar who developed such a theory was the great Charles Kindleberger in *The World in Depression: 1929–1939* [66].

Reconsidering this theoretical work makes us understand why *the devil is in the detail.*

The trap of hegemonic theories that are based, as Gilpin does, on a too imperfect translation of neoclassical economic theories, is the trap of a model far from reality and therefore less realistic than it presents itself or as the author himself would like. It is precisely, in fact, the policies that the hegemonic country promotes that lay the foundations of systemic destabilization.

The military expenditure of the hegemonic nation will increase due to the *free riding à la Olson* [67], which generally develops within military alliances, forcing the hegemon to replace the lack of continuity of military expenditure of non-hegemonic nations. Thus, the expenditure on armaments increasingly increases, in relative terms. The hegemonic nation thus risks being overtaken in terms of expenditure and creation of technological and economic resources by the *free rider* nations or from new emerging nations that tend towards hegemony. A war for hegemony therefore becomes possible. This is what has always happened in world history: the Peloponnesian War between Sparta and Athens, the Thirty

Years' War, the Napoleonic Wars, the First and Second World Wars. This is what is happening today with the emergence of China and the division between the USA on one side and France and especially Germany on the other [68].

Having said this, we can now understand how, at the foundation of this "realistic" theory, despite all its *nuances*, there is not only a conception of the State, but precisely that conception that derives from the great Italian tradition of "reason of State".

States, this enduring theory tells us, are human settlements that can be territorially variable in terms of borders, but stable in terms of the clusters of social, economic, technological, and especially cultural power that they allow to stably aggregate on the territories. In this, realistic and "neorealist" thought come together in a harmonious relationship thanks, precisely, to the re-proposition of the theory of reason of State in the study of power relations that outline the power construct of the world.

The theory of Botero, as Luigi Firpo taught us [69], in the sober halls of Palazzo Campana of the University of Turin, is all focused on the preservation of the State: the most difficult of arts. Criticizing Machiavelli, for whom the goal of the State was territorial expansion, Botero argues that the essence of the ability to govern lies in the "care" for the "preservation of the State", that is, for its "stability", for the "firm dominion over the peoples". Foucault [70] stated that the "theories of reason of State" were a revolutionary, original political laboratory, writing as follows:

> This reason of State, in the full sense, in the broad sense that we have seen appear in the text of Botero, this reason of State, it was immediately perceived at the time as an invention, as an innovation in any case, and which had the same sharp and abrupt character as the discovery, fifty years earlier, of heliocentrism, as the discovery of the law of falling bodies a little later etc. In other words, it was indeed perceived as a novelty. It is not a retrospective look, like the one that would simply be able to say: well, something important probably happened there. No. The contemporaries themselves, that is, during this whole period at the end of the XVI and beginning of the XVII century and everyone perceived that we were dealing there with a reality or at least with a problem that was absolutely new.

And Gianfranco Borrelli has well explained to us why:

> In the face of foreign aggressions - he stated - the Italian regional courts give life to a device with explicit purposes of defense of an enormous heritage, economic, artistic, cultural: therefore its main characteristic is that of putting into play a series of discourses and techniques that have the main purpose of the political preservation of a given situation of powers.

Reason of State is the first modern form of political rationalization as it neutralizes the moral element (even of Catholic religious morality), while still maintaining a character of *ars practica*, of prudential ability of political intervention for differentiated contexts of places, times, and modes of action; it is therefore a complex instrumental device that uses government knowledge aimed at enhancing experimental sciences (economics, anthropology, statistics, urban planning). In particular, *reason of State* experiments with increasingly refined technical codes of dissimulation/hiding and simulation/deception, thanks to which the commanding subject—who in the treaties of the seventeenth century is defined as the Prince—tries to identify, select, and use the context of conflicts and antagonisms he has to face. *Reason of State* is first a device of mediation between the conflicting parties, aimed at resolving, in determined times, international crises—but also divisions and contrasts within states—through the use of diplomatic and military codes. In such contexts, force is also periodically resorted to when no other ways of deferring or neutralizing unsolvable antagonisms are experienced: the exercise of violence, which must always be ready and spectacularly exhibited, is the ultimate remedy to achieve objectives considered necessary for political preservation. In fact, *reason of State* activates particular abilities to recognize the conflicts in the field and to convert them to its own advantage [71].

These statements strike me, as I mentally retrace some classics of international relations (between reality and academic discipline), now that I have finished reading, again, after so many years from the first reading, Kissinger's book on the Congress of Vienna [72]. In it, he boldly proposes as the main path to follow, through the historiographic method, the way of the classics of geopolitics, from the great Halford Mackinder [73] passing through Alfred Thayer Mahan [74] and reaching the still mysterious Nicholas John Spykman [75], who is the true, hidden, hero of Henry Kissinger's fascinating text.

Mackinder, as is known, interpreted world power as a set of isolated areas that nevertheless interacted, performing continuous states of imbalance of the international system, *à la Raymond Aron* [76]. The performance occurs based on the difference existing in the natural and technological endowments that States historically possess.

Europe has indeed built itself over the centuries as an eccentric response to the challenges of population growth thanks to exceptional climatic endowments and personal abilities spread in a unique context in the world [77]. But for Mackinder the deepest challenge was the one that came to Mediterranean Europe from Central Asia, more precisely from what he defined (and we with him) the *Heartland*, where the Eurasian masses were and are concentrated over the centuries: here is the *Pivot* that oversees historical transformations understood as transformative geopolitical developments in which both historical factors and forms of life that continuously give sense to spaces, give meaning. It is no coincidence, after all, that Spykman's very first academic test was on Georg Simmel [78], a great interpreter of the enlightening German sociology that continuously opens new and unprecedented paths of research. Spykman did nothing more, with a magnificent knight's move, than elaborate Simmel's theory of social forms in the cognitive context of international relations with an effort of modeling that surpasses the rigidity of "realism", fertilizing the rigidity of geopolitics with the plasticity of social forms of which Simmel was the unsurpassable cognitive builder [79].

In this context, it is almost natural that Spykman, today, with Kissinger, who naturally could not have been uninspired by him, helps us to embark on a new path, at a time when the West no longer has a hegemonic policy and therefore a unified conception of international politics.

The North American unipolarism of the eighties and nineties of the twentieth century and the first two decades of the new millennium [80] has, in fact, had the effect of greatly increasing the degrees of differentiation and the *cleavages* of the system.

And this beyond the imperial divisions, which continue to exist (*in primis* the French and English ones with respect to the dominant American narrative).

Precisely for this reason, beyond all technological innovations, we cannot but continue to maintain, without seeking a reasonable alternative, that "... whoever rules East Europe commands the Heartland; whoever rules the Heartland commands the World-Island; whoever rules the World-Island commands the World" [81].

Hence the importance of the "inner crescent", or those coastal areas that surround the entire *Heartland* and which are the product of the continuous development of terrestrial spaces, rather than the result of external pressures too intermittent to mark the furrow of the field of history.

Historiography thus forcefully enters the theories of international relations. Rather than the *Pivot*, then, it is the *Rimland*—with its powerful internal transformative force—that plays the role of the area from which the world can be dominated. A result that the historical events of the present confirm more and more.

Whoever commands the *Rimland* commands Eurasia and whoever commands Eurasia commands the world, commands the planet.

What I would like to underline, however, because it is congruent with the central thesis of Kissinger's work, is that the very structure of Eurasia has recently changed tremendously. The Prince of Metternich and his policy of *entente cordiale* aimed at preventing the advent of a Europe dominated by a great Prussia (and this is why the great Talleyrand was indispensable to him in the balance of power game) today becomes the metaphor of the inexorable transformation of the functional principles of geopolitical space in its mutual complementarities. They are dictated by state settlements grown in power not anymore in the heart of Europe, but on the shores of the Pacific, not only more in the Atlantic. Cunning could succeed Castelgeard without deeply influencing the European *entente cordiale* because then the only *Rimland* that had to be governed to preserve British hegemony was the Atlantic. Just as it will be for the USA from the decline between the nineteenth and twentieth centuries, as was evident with the Mediterranean adventure of American power during the Moroccan crisis of 1906 [82]. China and India are today, instead, the determining factors of the transformation in progress and China the most potentially destructive one (a dominion without hegemony), on par with what were Napoleonic France and Wilhelmine Germany and even before the Mongol-Tatar hordes, with an empire as extensive as it was fragile and brief.

According to Mackinderian theories, the three spheres of Eurasia, namely Central Europe, the Caucasus, and Central Asia, are now composed into a new and unprecedented—in terms of demographic and technical intensity—space of power and possible disintegration.

The atomic threat, which has only recently been mentioned again in international politics and studies, due to the North Korean and Iranian insurgencies, completes the alarming picture that is increasingly emerging from the depth of the world's geopolitical history.

Central Asia remains the *Pivot*, but the coastal areas of both India and China contain a power shift because the interconnections that link the nodes of the international system are changing. And this is because the point of fall of this system moves from the central Caucasus to Central Europe itself under the pressure rising from the regions of Central Asia and from powers that are both maritime and terrestrial.

India is about to become a maritime power, and China already is [83].

For this reason, the presence of Europe as an active power force cannot but be essential again. It is because the Atlantic lake of the Mediterranean has become a decisive segment of the *Rimland*, just as the Atlantic has returned to be. For this reason, the creation of a new *entente cordiale* between the USA and the European states of an integrally Atlantic Europe becomes the decisive reason of state for the "care of the preservation of the state", that is, of the "stability" internationally threatened by the Chinese hegemonic attempt.

CHAPTER 5

The Reason of State and Russia

The Russian government is an absolute monarchy, tempered by assassination; now, when the prince trembles, he is no longer bored; he therefore lives between terror and disgust. If the pride of the despot wants slaves, the man seeks equals: but a Czar has no equals; etiquette and jealousy vie to guard his lonely heart.

Astolphe, Marquis de Custine, in *Russia in 1839*

An extraordinary confirmation of the theories of the "reason of state" of Boterian memory is today in the history of the new Russia emerged from the collapse of the USSR, thanks to the role of Vladimir Putin, a clear example, also, of the role of personality in history.

In this geopolitical context, we must not forget that the relationship between history and the person is still an immense theme and pregnant with infinite meditations.

If we stop at antiquarian and monumental historiography, we cannot but fall into the error of making undue generalizations that distort both historiography and the person.

It is essential to always distinguish between history and historiography. The former exists independently of us and historiography.

The latter does not exist without history and is its fruit, even if too often it is transient and fleeting.

G. Sapelli, *States, Markets and Wars in Global History*,
https://doi.org/10.1007/978-3-031-26716-1_5

And all this comes to mind when reading the flood of journalism dedicated to Vladimir Putin, and therefore, here is the connection, to Russia in recent times.

Putin as a person is not understood unless he is placed in the decline of the USSR and is not understood as an anthropological segment of that nostalgia or that pro-Soviet revenge that pervades not a few of today's observers and not a few people who live and survive in Russia.

They belong primarily to the category of the desperate, that is, to those who think that history exists to be denied or rethought or reproduced, deluding themselves of returning to being the non-returnable. They do not understand what time is.

Augustine and Bergson had already warned us not to fall into the typical error of the phenomenology of being, in which time is everything and only the existence of being, and not instead the full unfolding of our subjectivity, the subjectivity of the self. And this is because the self, indeed, said Saint Augustine, "measures 'my feeling' in the present existence, not the things that pass so that it may arise".

The "things" pass, indeed, and the USSR cannot return. Our self changes with being and with history, even if too often historiography does not record such change. It could never: it should, to do so, make historiography of millions of souls.

Non-phenomenological difference between historiography and history. It is history that surprises Putin, who is everything but a demiurge of the same.

The USSR collapses when he was still very young and while he was working, as a secret service official, in the GDR, on the furthest frontier of that monopolistic state regime to terrorist dictatorship that was the USSR.

It is on the front line that everything is clearly visible and palpable, where the failure of a system that has wanted too much from its means can become evident to all those who face reality.

Putin well understands like few others that the collapse of the USSR is a new world that opens up before his generation, which must find its roots in the future and not in the past.

The transition that marks his emergence in public life as a character of great importance in the arena of power, Russian, first, and global, then, is significant.

It is the handover that takes place between him and Yeltsin the fundamental historical moment, when he understands that only the defense of the elderly ferryman, now lost in himself after the heroisms he was capable of, now weakened by his and his family's corruption, can signify a new era of the *State building* Russian.

Well, for Putin, Yeltsin must be defended and his legal safety must be guaranteed, before physical, to historically differentiate his figure from those who Yeltsin has favored, but who now must be fought and stripped of the situational power of fact they have appropriated.

And so he will.

The scenario is that of the struggle for the division of monopolistic-bureaucratic resources that has quickly transformed, thanks to the processes of privatization, into a violent and wild plundering of energy, natural and even administrative resources, because the patrimonialization of the Soviet state was also a process of unheard-of violence in a political space that had now collapsed in pre-institutionalization. Any form of rationalization was precious.

With Yeltsin, Russia had changed from Leviathan to Behemoth, that Behemoth so well evoked by Franz Neumann in his studies on the Nazi regime [84]. Now the Yeltsinian Behemoth wallowed in the mud of the absence of law and in the barbarity of force. All of Russia, the very existence of Russia, was in danger.

Of Behemoth, Putin will keep for himself, after having in fact defeated it in its Yeltsinian forms, only the principle of administrative patrimonialization, that is the homophilic and violent control of the state apparatus.

In this way, he gave life to a historically unprecedented form of semi-authoritarian and charismatic political-administrative institutionalization.

In fact, the years in which Putin is formed after the experience in the secret services are those of the de-institutionalization of the USSR through the plundering of national resources and those formed in the bureaucratic-international division of labor of the Comecon and the Warsaw Pact [85].

An international division of productive specialization that, with the loss of the empire, will be fatal to Russia when it is stripped of its vassals, often much more modernized than Russia itself and much richer in natural resources than the nation that was once both the "socialist" mother and the guiding power in a regime of unequal, economic, military, political exchanges.

It is no coincidence that the new ruling and dominant class in formation, after the years of *perestroika* and Yeltsin, tries to oppose the international plundering that has taken the names of "privatization" and "globalization".

The cities and their representatives, initially not democratically elected, but co-opted and only later territorially elected, are the cradles of future political-economic power, especially in the distant provinces.

These are often selection processes that use the weapon of the vote as a trinket to justify co-optation, strong—these territorial ruling classes that shelter themselves and in the meantime withdraw from an increasingly decrepit central power—of the mechanisms of circulation of the elites of which they have become aware and have learned the art in the midst of the decline of Soviet power.

Putin finds in St. Petersburg the arena to position himself in the de facto situational power of the new institutionalization, strong because of the ties previously established in the secret services of which he was a leading part.

Putin knows that it is necessary to ensure a transition from the monopolistic oligarchy of the party to a new form of polyarchic political power, holding together economy and politics in a ring of power still fragile and uncertain, because the stochastic threat of the exercise of Behemoth's force has not been and cannot be totally destroyed.

Nor can "western" democracy be imitated: it is impossible to be realized in a Russia unprepared and hostile to any form of democratic transparency due to the lack of organic, or national, formation of both mass parties and unions, or the intermediate bodies that are the very essence of the reconstruction of a polyarchic pluralism that composes the weights and the weighted relevances of territorial representation and the situational interests of fact.

Putin understands that transferring local administrative experience to the central level can only be done in a system of verticalized polyarchy, or in a succession of rings of power in which parties and intermediate bodies are configured not so much as an expression of a still non-existent civil society, but, instead, of a verticalized polyarchic power, which replaces civil society.

As is typical of every *octroyé* mechanism, it ends up preventing the strengthening of the civil society that it would temporarily replace, coming to fear its very development, as the Russian experience of recent years teaches.

This is because the pushes to return to the mechanism of spoliation in the time of financial globalization are very strong.

Dmitrij Anatol'evič Medvedev, for a long time vice-prime minister or president, alternating with Putin, in the dual composition of the Russian apex power, is the representative of those who believe that the fastest way for institutionalization is the rapid realization of a so-called market economy that acts immediately, even in the absence of a legal-rational legal system and a state apparatus that gives life to a real *State building* classically understood [86].

But experience teaches that by doing so, power can only transform into the return of the oligarchs.

Hence that game of mirrors between the two demiurges of Russian power who hid their real conflicts for years and used corruption to measure the strength and weakness together of their respective alignments that aimed at a very different future of Russia on the economic and political level. For some years now, Putin has won the game.

Putin is engaged in the most difficult task: building a market economic system that is not unfettered, but regulated and open only as much as it serves the power of the nation.

The problems that this power struggle raises are many and they are enormous.

It is worth dwelling here on a theme always neglected, but also strongly characterized by the intertwining of nation and internationalization as always essential more than ever to understand Russia and Putin with it.

An essential issue still open and to which very few pay attention is indeed that of land ownership, which constitutes, especially now in the period of sanctions against Russia, an essential point of international friction and a front of action to weaken the power of the new Putinian oligarchy in power.

Once the USSR was defeated, the entire kolkhozian property was distributed among the peasants; however, not having financial resources for investments, the entire agricultural infrastructure remained unused and soon fell into ruin.

And here is the crux of the matter: "the sell-off of Russian land". In 2013, nine foreign companies still controlled a complex of about two million hectares (ranging from the "just" 50,000 ha, for example, of the Anglo-Swiss mining company Glencore, to over 600,000 of the Kazakh agro-industrial Ivolga-holding), of which about 20% in private ownership; and this without considering the Russian *offshore* accounts.

In short, if the cancellation of the collective management of agriculture was the first and necessary step on the road dictated to Yeltsin's

Russia by international financial institutions to sanction its "capitalist normalization", the resurrection of private property on the land definitively returned the country to the conditions in which, if not the *pomeščik-dvorjanin*, the noble landowner, overtaken by history, his direct descendant, the big capitalist landowner, the *kulak*, returns to rule.

Not surprisingly, "solving" the agrarian question was one of the highest priorities of the "new" Russia that emerged from the table-top disintegration of the Soviet Union [87].

The question of property on the land had been one of the first steps of Soviet power. Immediately after the Decree on Peace, the very first one, adopted on the same day of the October Revolution, the second was the Decree on Land, approved the following night. That decree sanctioned the immediate abolition of all private property on the land and was followed, just three months later, by the law on nationalization. This, as Lenin stated in his polemic with Kautsky [88], constituted a revolutionary democratic-bourgeois measure—of an "ideal capitalism"—that responded to the demands of the huge mass of small peasants, on the egalitarian use of the land, and represented a first step to fully carry out the democratic-bourgeois revolution, before moving on to the socialist revolution in the countryside, strong from the mobilization "of the proletarian and semi-proletarian agricultural masses".

Today, the concentration of huge extensions of land in the hands of large industrial groups, Russian and foreign, and the attempt to stimulate the formation of a class of small and very small farmers who, inevitably, will divide into a narrow circle of large owners and a mass of small debtor cultivators, thus realign Russia to the needs of internal capital and make it available for the exploitation of its resources by transnational groups, agricultural and not.

The paradox is that while there is nothing more stable than the land, Russian power, and Putin with it, are instead forcefully thrown into the complex plexus of global geostrategic instability.

CHAPTER 6

Instability

The element that characterizes the international system today is indeed instability. An instability that is generated, before the existing relationship between states, by the states themselves, as all are shaken by a peristaltic deconstruction of their institutional systems or by the unfinished institutional realization.

Regarding the second aspect, consider Africa, from north to south and from east to west. What cannot be built is the *State building*, that is, the autonomy of the State from civil society. The bureaucratic legal-rational order does not materialize and clanism and tribalism rule.

Congo and Nigeria are two clear examples: mechanisms of succession to power do not materialize and not certainly due to the lack of democratic-electoral processes, but due to their neutralization by a disruptive and anthropologically devastated and devastating civil society.

It is no coincidence that the only territorial complexes that we could call nations where this happens are either the crystallization of millennial processes, such as the militarized Egypt heir to the empire of the Pharaohs, or the emerging Tunisian democracy built on the Carthaginian legacy, or the Moroccan monarchy, sacred and direct descendant of the Prophet, like the Hashemite one that survived the expulsion from Mecca by the Saudi-Wahhabis, and its transplantation by English hands in Jordanian land.

G. Sapelli, *States, Markets and Wars in Global History*,
https://doi.org/10.1007/978-3-031-26716-1_6

And then there is the use of violence, chilling and crystallizing in institutions, like the *apartheid* in South Africa, which has now charismatically flowed into democracy.

But everything is unstable, the Organization of African Unity is just a clearinghouse and the wounds of the African division between the West and the Soviet Union are still all there, with the Somali and Eritrean wreckage and the collapse of a centuries-old empire like the Ethiopian one.

And now even the Gulf States are beginning to divide and question Saudi dominance. The attempt to overthrow theocratic Iran by Iraqi hands has failed. And that failure could only elevate Iran to a threatening power, upsetting the Saudi alliance system and creating that Mesopotamian division of the Shiite crescent that goes from Tehran to Damascus and threatens Beirut.

It is in this context that Putin, together with Foreign Minister Lavrov, following the teachings of that great politician, Foreign Minister and then Prime Minister, Evgenij Maksimovič Primakov, gradually rewrites the entire Russian foreign policy, effectively returning, on the basis, precisely, of Primakov's teaching, to a specific form of return to Eurasian tsarist politics. Primakov's career is significant, without which one cannot understand the guiding thread of Putin's current foreign policy, which arises not from the isolated brain of the president, but from a whole cohort of young people who formed during the years of decline and then collapse of the USSR and later committed to the rebirth of Russia.

Primakov was a senior researcher at the Institute of World Economy and director of the Institute of Oriental Studies of the Academy of Sciences. President of the Soviet Union from 1989 to 1990, he was a member of the Presidential Council of Soviet leader Mikhail Gorbachev and in this capacity special envoy to Iraq. After the failed attempt at a Russian coup in August 1991, Primakov was appointed first deputy chairman of the KGB and then director of the Foreign Intelligence Service from 1991 to 1996.

Primakov worked for a Russian foreign policy based on mediation and a simultaneous expansion of influence towards the Middle East and the former Soviet republics. This policy is known as the "Primakov Doctrine", which is based on the belief that Russia will be great and secure only by dominating the *Heartland*, from the mouth of the Indus to the warm Mediterranean seas. Hence the historical work—today more than ever rewarded—of Primakov to create the strategic triangle consisting of Russia, China, and India, as a counterweight to the United States. This move has been interpreted by some observers as an agreement to jointly combat the "colored revolutions" in Central Asia and the increasingly expanding expansion of a coalition defined by Samuel Huntington as "anti-hegemonic" [89]. Primakov's policy is nothing more than the conscious return to the policy of Aleksandr Mikhailovich Gorchakov, Foreign Minister from 1856 to 1882, Chancellor of the Tsarist Empire until his death [90].

The Crimean War had ended in 1856, leaving Russia prey to a recurring sensation that cyclically pervades its ruling classes throughout its history: the syndrome of isolation and encirclement, from east to west, from the warm Mediterranean seas to the Pacific.

The Crimean War had uncertain results in the Near East, but decisive in Europe: it had shattered the myth and power of that Russia that had defeated Napoleon.

The traditional alliance between Austria and Russia began to waver and the order sanctioned by the Congress of Vienna was questioned: the demilitarization of the Black Sea and the cession by Russia of the area of the mouth of the Danube (southern Bessarabia) in favor of Moldavia was the central issue undermining Russian interests. As is known, Russia was then obliged, certainly not to forget the need to regain the vital Mediterranean space, but at the same time to rework a policy of that expansion that was necessary to consolidate the empire towards the South of Asian Russia, from the Khanate of Kokand to Chechnya and all of the Caucasus, continuing to Bukhara, while thanks to the Opium War it obtained from China those "concessions" that will become strategic to expand to the Pacific. Only the defeat suffered by Japan in 1905 forced Russia to pause in its expansive policy, consolidating its oceanic presence with the base of Vladivostok: but Russia was now a global power.

The redemption line personified by Prince Gorchakov thus came to fruition.

In the seventies of the nineteenth century, Russia saw its Balkan aspirations downsized by the help given to the Ottomans by the European powers led by the United Kingdom and the newly unified Germany. Panslavism had already ignited those hearts that would then trigger the Balkan crisis that will lead to the First World War and from there to the Leninist Revolution.

This historical background is fundamental to understand what was the ideal drive that guided the Russian leadership group educated by

Primakov when all the contradictions raised by the failed partition of the world between Russia and the USA, after the fall of the USSR, emerged as never before, starting from the same Russian lands torn from the empire (Soviet, this time) when it had dissolved, as happened in Ukraine and Crimea.

But they also emerged, for what we have said, where the points of fall of the vital necessity for Russia to control, or better share, the Mediterranean, thus tearing it from the sole North American dominion, which had succeeded, after the Suez crisis of 1956, the uncontested British dominion.

The first signs had already been felt in the change of the rifle shoulder during the repression of the Greek Revolution in the first half of the twentieth century, when the bold US armed forces had replaced the exhausted British forces in the war against the Greek communists who had disobeyed Stalin and followed the hegemonic aims of Tito, thus voting for physical massacre and political marginalization for more than thirty years [91].

But the North American dominion of the Mediterranean was as unstable as ever, as demonstrated by the last thirty years of the history of this geopolitical plexus.

Mediterranean means Middle East, or rather, Mesopotamia: this is the archetypal point that holds together the *Heartland* and the Mediterranean, and it is no coincidence that all the contradictions of today's instability are discharged in the Mediterranean and the Indian Ocean and the South China Sea. Russia is fully experiencing this instability, and it is precisely this instability that gives its foreign policy, which pursues, with Putin, the national interest, an unprecedented strength.

The Mediterranean is no longer a bend of the Atlantic, but the quintessence and emblem of a political void: migrants from Africa and Mesopotamia rise from the Mediterranean and from the Balkan states to Southern Europe to head towards Central and Northern Europe. But here they find the other, striking process of deinstitutionalization. That is, the growing fragmentation and disintegration of second-degree institutions, i.e., supranational, of the European Union.

Here the greatest failure of the second half of the twentieth century is consumed.

The attempt to hold together the complex of nations from which everything originates in the world, i.e., the Enlightenment-Masonic myth of pluralistic rites that functionalist secular theocracy could not only and not so much create law and currency, but also systems of meaning and legitimation, thus forever subtracting Europe from representative democracy, has failed.

Rousseau and Montesquieu had to die.

And it is this sought-after death that creates the international imbalance that emanates from Europe, because the culmination of the process of institutionalization has always resided in the creation of military bureaucracies. As is known, they continue politics by other means, and this is why Europe cannot create them, because it has killed politics. And without politics, there is no threat of war and without the threat of war, there is no dreamed and celebrated Europe.

Hence the international void caused by Europe with consequences that can be devastating. The only two European nuclear powers, Great Britain and France, pursue long-term strategic designs *stand-alone*, that is, they want to go it alone. The United Kingdom with Brexit is, in fact, a return to the fifties-sixties, when the same Kingdom refused to enter the EEC.

Now the plan is that of the Anglosphere, the grand design of a government of military and economic power refounded on the lands of the Commonwealth and the nineteenth-century strategy of the "American economic system" that Henry Clay advocated, arousing the admiration of Lincoln and laying the foundations of American economic nationalism.

From Russia we have come to the USA and then to Germany.

What was, *in primis*, an anti-English design, because the nascent American Republic did not want to end up like India with British rule, became an international model of neo-industrialism and selective neo-protectionism that gave institutional form to what was happening at the time of the foundation of the North American republic in world trade then dominated by the *free trade* of the United Kingdom imposed with gunboats.

And this is what is happening again in world trade for about thirty years, with the end of multilateral treaties and the collapse of global logistics companies.

But if the United Kingdom, in this context, tends again to a new global perspective, France tends, instead, to a deep intensification of its role as a great power in Africa. From North Africa to sub-Saharan Central Africa to Djibouti, not only goods and services, but French weapons are at work for the realization of an imperial design. All this does nothing but exacerbate the friction, all Wagnerian, between the economic delirium of superpower and the military inanity of the great German cultural power.

It has realized an ideological hegemony with the *Ordo-liberalismus*, has achieved economic hegemony in global trade with its surplus, but is struck by the syndrome of impotence because its horrendous history forbids it from transforming all this into military power.

The first consequence of this is the castration of NATO, which was supposed to realize the transatlantic alliance between the USA and Europe and which is today the first point of friction between a great power in search of a new identity (the USA) and a Europe that has never possessed just one.

The European void can only project both Russia and the USA onto the world stage.

It is the European void that will once again create the inevitable US-Russia duopoly: it is an inevitable centrifugal force caused by the absence of a specific role of power, including military, of Europe, which is neither united nor armed.

But being attracted by the void rather than by coexistence experienced as self-awareness is the very fulcrum of instability.

What has been happening for years now in Syria and Ukraine is nothing more than the consequence of having once been unable to design a new Yalta, after the fall of the Berlin Wall.

The most aware of this are the US imperial-military bureaucrats, although divided between thalassocrats and terrestrials, who today control Trump without being able to prevent him from making gestures that the president does not fully control, and this certainly avoids immeasurable trouble.

See the *one shot* in Syria: more a representation for internal use than an attack on the Syrians and the Russians.

See Ukraine, where Minsk continues to remain a dream and Russia continues to hold on tightly to the base of Sevastopol.

See Sweden, a nation that returns to military conscription, the people's army that calls to arms against the age-old enemy, as if we had returned to the times of the first Tsarist Russia.

In all this tormented horizon has arisen for about twenty years, like Atlantis, the completely transformed China of Xi Jinping, which no longer relies on Deng's rule of not killing each other among bureaucrats of Asian state monopolistic capitalism, but—as well as on the pragmatic mass acceptance of the intermediate and popular layers of the nation—on terrorism deployed disguised as a fight against corruption and on the return to Maoist politics of power that is at the tip of the gun barrel.

China has thrown all theories and practices of world domination off balance. With its demographic weight, it has deluded everyone that it would dominate the earth by threatening India and Russian Siberia.

In reality, it has confirmed the theories of the North American admiral Mahan for whom world power is either maritime or it is not. Let's not delude ourselves about the terrestrial Silk Road: a Russian cannon shot is enough to destroy a train. It is not through that route that China wants to dominate the world.

The world is dominated from the sea, that sea with the pearls of the "necklace" that goes from Shanghai to Ceylon to Djibouti up through the Suez Canal to Piraeus, or from the Philippines and Sumatra to Perth in Australia.

The entire power system of the *Pacific Realm* has been questioned starting from the stolid and reassuring solidity of South Korea and Japan.

In this light, the atomic madness of North Korea is nothing more than a game of mirrors to make us forget the danger of the pearl necklace and exhaust the small and great world powers in a negotiation and containment as exhausting as it was, is and will be with Iran.

Trump's USA is located in the center of this stormy ocean and it is natural that they have Russia as their first reference.

But while the USA does not have a strategic thought, but only impulses contained by the imperial military bureaucracy, Russia possesses strategic thought.

It is Primakov's, I remind you again, the brilliant Prime Minister and Foreign Minister before Yeltsin and then Putin, upon whose death Lavrov ascended to the command bridge of a great power that from the Crimean War onwards had a clear strategic end.

It is a story that begins in that half of the nineteenth century that still today underpins the balance of world power.

After the Crimean War, Russia indeed learned that it can only be what its spirituality and culture destine it to be, namely a Eurasian power, but only if it dominates the *Heartland*, that is, it sinks its roots as much in the warm seas of the Mediterranean as in the turbulent ones of the Pacific.

A strategic and powerful design, perfect, exciting, as weak and frail, after the collapse of the Comecon, was and still is the economic body of the Russian Empire that should verify that strategy.

Another factor of instability and permanent global fibrillation.

The solution to this global problem will also be the unraveling of the enigma of Vladimir Putin.

An enigma that is increasingly emerging as essential for the future of world power relations.

And one of the first knots will be that of the relationship with Germany.

The meeting between President Putin and Chancellor Merkel that took place in August 2018 was primarily an act of political realism that can rise to an extraordinary event with very significant consequences in world power relations.

A silent struggle is underway conducted by the segment of the US establishment that has chosen to follow that policy of geostrategic rebalancing embodied by Trump against Germany on the one hand and Iran on the other.

The belief is that carved in the US economic trend of the last twenty years: a growth in fits and starts supported by an increasingly growing financialization of the economic system with the equally growing disintegration of the foundation of North American polyarchy: the urban and rural middle classes increasingly socially distant from the ideal-types of the *new economy* the *bohemian* managers with *stock options* and ultra-technological lowering of general labor productivity (the *total factory productivity*) resulting in mass unemployment and industrial desertification.

The geopolitical consequences are in front of everyone's eyes: the decline of North American power unable to dominate the world alone, while China, freed from the shackles and fetters prior to its disastrous Clintonian admission to the WTO, grows in aggressiveness and military and demographic power (not economic).

Kohl's Europe and then Merkel's has gradually added to the power imbalance in a pro-Chinese and anti-US function with devastating power: that of secular deflation that spills everything towards social crisis.

Putin's Russia continues in this situation to be the object of attacks promoted by what remains of the pre-Trump establishment: the great financial and presidential families together that have destroyed both the American dream and the *American exceptionalism* on which Seymour Lipset [92] wrote the unforgettable pages of our youth.

Germany, in this global context, finds itself between the two perennial fires of its history between West and East: the USA and Russia.

Bismarck had warned the first Kaiser: you cannot have two enemies to the east and west together: the United Kingdom would benefit, which was in fact, before the USA, the mortal enemy of Germany as a great power.

Now Chancellor Merkel reflects this constant of German history: she has chosen to ally with China against the US and therefore has the new America of Trump as an enemy, but she cannot also have Russia as an enemy. Economic interests, led by the Baltic-German North Stream pipeline, do the rest, including the acts of the EU, which to "soften" Trump allowed the importation of the very expensive US liquefied gas.

With Russia, European states must find an agreement, despite US sanctions. And Russia needs the German shoulder like air, primarily in the Balkans, where the fire smolders under the ashes, as well as in Turkey, which from an Atlantic bulwark—especially when it acquires new Russian missiles—is transforming into a bridge of Russia's new return to the Middle East.

All this while Russia cannot abandon the design of the duo-polar dominance of the world with the US in an anti-Chinese role, under penalty of losing the role of dominator of the *Heartland* and its seas: this will be the new battle.

But this is precisely what the US does not want. They have unleashed the usual local economic war (in Syria) against the rebellious power of the seas of the *Heartland* and its Atlantic lakes: Turkey.

Just as they do with Iran at the head of the Shiite crescent that can overlook that Mediterranean which is now an Atlantic lake as contestable as ever. All this while Europe is losing ground in the Mediterranean and in Africa, with only the French and Chinese presences truly active.

The Putin-Merkel meeting of 2018 was therefore full of implications and everything suggests that if a variable geometry relationship (the only possible geometry) between Russia and Germany were to solidify, it would fill the power gaps that the two interlocutors bring with them: Russia is still Paul Dibb's USSR [93], a superpower incomplete, very strong militarily, but very weak economically, while Germany continues to be what we did not think was possible: very strong economically, but very weak, I say! Non-existent militarily.

And without being able to wage war in power, one can only obstruct the balances of power and always instead determine crisis situations.

World power can suffer from the lack of regional power balance. And that's why all over the world the return to the principle of "reason of state" that most call "nationalism" is unleashed.

The role of North American power could not and cannot change.

In some ways, it has been waited for too long. But the international system is a living system. And so nothing is ever mechanically written in history.

Customs policy also supports this thesis: it was the consequence of a power situation called the "Cold War". Multilateral trade agreements, on the other hand, had to ensure the circulation of goods in the West in a system of variable exchange rates and after 1971 no longer based on the dollar as the reference currency. US dominance remained, but it was increasingly weakened. The free-trade wave was moderated by the creation of islands of continental or para-continental protectionism where goods and symbolic goods (currency exchanges) circulated freely among states, but at the same time erecting high protectionist barriers against other areas of the world. The EU (already with the European Common Market since 1957) was one of the first of these areas, paving the way for the customs union between the USA, Mexico, and Canada (Nafta) and Mercosur (Argentina, Brazil, Paraguay, Uruguay, and Venezuela). A movement that also affected Africa and is deeply underestimated, especially today. Think of the Sacu, which is the oldest customs union in the world in the twentieth century, founded in 1910 as the Customs Union Agreement between the then South African Union and other British colonies such as Bechuanaland, Basutoland, and Swaziland. And let's also think about the customs union established with headquarters in Bangui (Central African Republic) in 1964 by Cameroon, Chad, Gabon, Central African Republic, Republic of Congo which was joined in January 1984 by Equatorial Guinea. All states that are part of the French franc area, or the Cemac (Economic and Monetary Community of Central Africa).

All this composition of power agreements and attempts to balance them began to fade about thirty years ago, in the 1980s, with the much-vaunted rise of China as a global economic power, not coincidentally a few years after the collapse of the USSR.

A collapse that was not followed by any international assembly that would redraw the world map along lines of renewed power with the brush of politics.

A new Yalta was necessary. It was as if Napoleon had been locked up in Saint Helena and the Congress of Vienna had not been celebrated, with the construction of a century of *entente cordiale*, until the emergence of unsustainable maritime Germany.

Politics was lacking, politics which is nothing more than the prelude to military and economic agreements. Not surprisingly, in fact, the expansive movement of free trade on a global scale through multilateral trade agreements gradually comes to a halt.

Let's think about what happened in Southeast Asia, an essential point of the *Rimland*.

Southeast Asia's dependence on the USA and Japan is slowly waning, even though these two nations remain the region's main economic partners. The problem is that China has seen an exponential increase in trade growth compared to the two major players mentioned earlier and all other nations on the planet. Its demographic weight transforms and shapes the economy, once again folding the "dismal science" into the lap of historiography, of which demography, with sociology, is a handmaid.

Today it can truly be understood, if one wishes, that globalization has largely been a game of mirrors. The only truly globalized commodity has been money and capital as flow and not as investment. All this while, by decision of the fractal and composed apex of deregulating finance, which alternately governs the US political class with a unique lobbying system in the world [94], China was allowed to enter the WTO without any real counterpart. The consequences have been terrible.

In this sense, and only in this sense, the fundamental thesis of Henry Kissinger is still truthful and prophetic, because it illustrates in what disaster the planet can fall without *international politics based on the art of diplomacy* [95], which is the preforming cause, ultimately, of how the lives of men associated in the struggle between geopolitical spaces are organized and therefore of the so-called international system. It forms and preforms among the constants we discussed earlier.

This substantial invariance of the main axes of the global power struggle does not imply the absence of a short cycle between and of the relationships between the forces that confront each other in this long-term permanence.

The relationship between major world powers has been changing for years according to short cycles of transformation.

For the first time in two centuries, the United Kingdom is splitting from the United States on one of the decisive points of the great cultural involution that has occurred in international relations in the last twenty years: the emergence of China.

I am referring to the twenty years that followed the end of the Kissinger era after the collapse of the USSR.

The general rehearsal of theoretical and practical change began, however, not in the Pacific but in Southern Europe, with the Balkan wars that marked the transition from theory to practice of the end of the Westphalian era. It had never ended except in the illusions of the *Internationalists* we have already mentioned. Under the veils of the 1928 Briand-Kellogg Pact, the power struggle continued relentlessly, stronger than before.

In the salient points of geostrategic interests, each nation could once give itself the political regime it wanted, even if it was chosen by a handful of bloody dictators, and when any sacrifice could be celebrated on the altars. Only areas of the world considered uninfluential in the global balance could see local wars and *intelligence* troops of the more or less clandestine Westphalian armies of the balance of terror being exercised.

Che Guevara in Congo and Colonel Taylor in Sierra Leone behaved like the fantastic characters in Le Carré's novels.

Then came the sad time of the so-called, hypocritical, "humanitarian intervention".

The preparations were still made in the Westphalian period. Arming the *mujaheddin* and the Taliban against the USSR and once the USSR was defeated not worrying if the *mujaheddin* and the Taliban dominated the country just as the Pakistani secret services (ISI) became the real regulators of relations between the USA and India: well, all this could only lay the foundations for chronic instability in very delicate areas of the global balance always in danger.

The historical roots of this change already lie before the fall of the USSR, in the disastrous period for the USA of the Carter presidency, which suffered the first major defeats from the new revisionist states that are emerging in world history, like "snakes against dragons" [96] effectively destroying the policy of exporting security pursued with military intervention in the nations of the Greater Middle East. Iraq, already armed by the USA in the war against Iran, became, just as happened with the *mujaheddin* armed against the USSR, the Trojan horse in the unipolar international disorder of the USA.

The response given to Carter's defeats was the construction of a new American foreign policy, which met years later with the change "via financial liberalization" in the UK and again in the USA with Tony Blair and the Clintons. The change in perspective played a very important role for the entire international system, which was still not able to grasp the transformation of China from an introverted power to an extroverted power.

This new policy was gradually developed first by George Bush's CIA and then adopted by the Reagan presidency, profoundly changing international intervention policies with unprecedented audacity. It founded a change in the very tools of intervention policy, deepening the role of private mercenary combat and *intelligence* agencies in outlining international interventions, foreshadowing the same Reagan-era economic policy that made history.

In October 1980, a foreign policy intervention took shape, based on the fierce internal power struggle between Carter and challenger Reagan, heralding the return of a cohort of *intelligence* men who found in the esoteric ideologies of a great intellectual like Leo Strauss [97] the justification for abandoning all Westphalian ideologies to embrace the assertion of human rights ideology. This was masterfully used as a cover for the profound transformation that would occur in American foreign policy, aimed at defending energy resources in the Greater Middle East at all costs. Noteworthy is the competitive and cooperative relationship with France, which saw in this emerging transformation a bulwark to be used for operations aimed at defending its interests in that same area. Italy will be the nation that will pay the highest human costs, with the massacres of Ustica and Bologna: the darkest, most obscure price of this policy. It could no longer accept, as was once possible, that ongoing negotiation with Palestinian and Libyan terrorism pursued in Italy *in primis* by Aldo Moro and Giulio Andreotti and then by Bettino Craxi to defend Italian energy interests in Libya and the Middle East and Vatican interests in Jerusalem, with the use of an *intelligence*—the Italian one—perhaps second only to the French one for diplomatic wisdom, but much more fragmented and multi-headed in its continuous subordination to the party machine. The issue of nuclear proliferation took on, moreover, at the end of the 1970s, together with Soviet aggression in Europe with the surpassing of NATO and the USA in medium-range missiles, a fundamental importance in relation to the Iraqi nuclear armament projects, to which France and Italy made a now irreversibly documented contribution. And this upset the entire previous way of understanding relations "between Western allies", as they had in fact been outlined after the end of the Second World War. Between the end of the seventies and the beginning of the eighties, a new world of international power relations began.

The memoirs of Ambassador to Italy Richard Gardner and some high-level scientific works allow us to provide one of the most comprehensive pictures of this transformation in such a difficult and multi-layered field of study [98].

The moment of change appeared even more clearly with the Balkan wars among the South Slavs.

In the last years of the second millennium, they provoked the first war after Yalta: twenty years ago, in a crumbling Yugoslavia, they once again posed to humanity the terrible problem of genocide. Then genocide became intra-ethnic struggle in a geographical entity without a state from which nations emerged trying to define state borders with each other by massacring and exterminating each other.

Therefore, the *nation-building* was also at the same time an anti-genocidal humanitarian intervention and was carried out by various actors: NATO, the USA, Italy as an agent of the USA bombing the genocidal Serbs, without ever the much-vaunted "United Europe" showing a sign of life. The conflicting European states lived.

The bond between the United Kingdom and the USA was strengthened from then on around the theory that united both the followers of Leo Strauss [99] of the West and East Coast (the neocons), both the Blairian theorists of the London School of Economics, and the followers of the great French international jurist and constitutionalist Roland Dumas [100].

Kissinger became an old iron, Westphalia a word to forget, and the "just war" entrusted from time to time to the prevailing balance of power to justify both the partition of the world and the fight against international terrorism and nuclear proliferation in violation of treaties.

The link between the UK and the USA became a necessity to continue to have a transatlantic relationship between Europe and the USA just when Germany and France, in 2003, with the war of the USA and UK against Iraq, refused to shed the blood of their soldiers in Afghanistan and Iraq.

France then attempted a rapprochement with the USA during the North African wars, but the contrast had been too deep: trust relations were not reestablished and returned, moreover, to those inaugurated by de Gaulle in the fifties of the twentieth century between France and the USA.

And such they are today. To these, however, the German pro-Chinese schism has been added, which can only be economic, as Germany does not have an army.

The Arab springs exacerbated international divisions, with the USA losing a perspective of power: wars between the faults created by divisions between Sunnis and Shiites and deep internal conflicts in the Sunni world, thanks to the clumsy North American intervention of disavowal of Mubarak, support for the Egyptian Muslim Brothers, consolidated as "Gulf-North African wars" in a context where hybrid armies have state authorities of reference: for the Shiites Iran, Saudi Arabia for the Sunnis.

North Africa's Germany, Egypt, has never needed reference states, but has lost its archetypal role of mediation.

Yet it had that role: we know it from the age of the Mamluks, during the Ottoman Empire, we know it from the Napoleonic campaigns that not by chance took place in Egypt and not elsewhere, we know it from the '56 crisis with Nasser at Suez.

The only one who didn't know was President Obama who mistook the Muslim Brothers for a humanitarian group. The Muslim Brothers, cosmopolitan by definition, as was the old Caliphate, how were they supposed to lead a secular nation like Egypt, instead of its secular guardians? Re-read Anouar Abdel-Malek [101] and his seminal book in the sixties of the twentieth century, still a point of reference.

All the knots came to the comb and everyone lost their heads.

The French forgot that from the Sykes-Picot agreement of 1916 was born what was the most powerful point of balance in those areas, with Egypt, after the First World War, namely Syria for its relationship with Lebanon and—after 1957—with Israel. Israel, despite all the terrible conflicts and wars, from the Yom Kippur War onwards, has miraculously held up thanks to the stabilizing role that the Alawites, to which the Assad family belongs, have guaranteed to Syria for about a hundred years. The very term "Alawite", which denotes an ethnic and religious group of esoteric inspiration whose origin is still the subject of debate, was coined by the French. It was France, in the name of *divide et impera*, to encourage, after the First World War, Alawite aspirations in order to weaken the Arab nationalist project of the Sunni Muslims. At the beginning of the first decade of the new century, France forgot this glorious colonial past and, in order to replace the United Kingdom in its relationship with the USA—Hollande continues Sarkozy—went to war against its historical allies that it, France, had helped to create.

So the triangulation that has been created between Russia (which supports Syria and Iran), Israel and Saudi Arabia (enemy of the Shiites and Alawites)—thus challenging a centuries-old hatred against the Shiites for the sake of the region's stability, guaranteed by the Alawites (Shiites)—risks falling apart.

The neo-Ottoman Turkish intervention only triggers a return to the period of the First World War.

The real difference is that now it is Turkey, with Russia leaning towards Mediterranean contestability, that is dealing the cards of power redistribution in the Greater Middle East.

Only the weight of the American and British military and *intelligence*, and of course also French and Italian, seemed at first able to stop the intervention in Syria. But it was, instead, Russia with an exceptional diplomatic maneuver that marks, indeed, its irreversible return to the Mediterranean, to overturn the table. With an agreement worthy of the great school of Ponomarëv and Gromyko, Lavrov, the Russian Foreign Minister, induced the UN to issue resolution 2118 of September 27, 2013, which still frames in a well-articulated legal context a Russian-American plan for the dismantling of Syrian chemical weapons. A plan that in fact did not prevent military intervention in Syria, but allowed Assad to stay in power, thus rebuilding the support base for a grand return that strikingly recalls what the USSR achieved in the 1950s with the creation of communist parties, and with Baathism in the Greater Middle East [102].

But this meant risking weakening the US dramatically on the world stage at a time when China was becoming increasingly aggressive. The French, blinded by the imperial dream, did not perceive the immense dangers of this isolation and, indeed, pushed not only Africa, but the world to the brink of chaos with the proposal—irregularly formulated by their Foreign Minister Laurent Fabius, with an article in *Le Monde* on October 5, 2013—to effectively dismantle the veto power of the Security Council in the turmoil unleashed by humanitarian problems, overturning the decision-making power on the General Assembly.

In this way, the principle of majority would have applied to the international order and it would have been chaos, as is inevitable in democracy applied on a global scale through the count of states.

The principle of power would have been lost. Fortunately, this did not happen due to the Russian veto, while the US was paralyzed by indecision and internal conflicts.

This sign of US weakness had immediate effects in Asia. These effects were multiplied by the ongoing schism for many years in the US between Democrats and Republicans.

The federal state is on the brink of disintegration whenever similar events occur.

Obama had to give up visits to Asia that were supposed to prepare the work of the TransPacific Pact. And this, after the emergence of Chinese power, had propagating effects of instability especially in those nations always uncertain about their strategic destination (think of Indonesia and Myanmar for example). The Chinese in the same years inaugurated an infrastructure bank in Jakarta, a bank that was in direct competition with the Asian Development Bank, traditionally dominated by Japan and the US.

In Asia, the threatening and warlike Chinese dominance can only be remedied by first rearming Japan and aggregating around it a crown of equally armed and developed states. But in Africa, in all of Africa, there seems to be no remedy for instability.

Europe is divided and the French only give vent to an imperial culture without the means to pursue continental dominance. It was and is essential that the USA continues to maintain its relationship with the United Kingdom, which not only symbolically, but also militarily, represents for them the only ally to bring into play in the chaotic system of international relations.

This in a context where however also the *intelligences* of the United Kingdom and the USA—and especially the military elites—were opposed to an intervention in Syria because they knew that the domino effect would have reached not only all of North and Central Africa, but also Russia and as far as Pakistan and India where the Shiite-Sunni and internal Sunni world fault lines are more than ever at work.

Now we can say that the wave of collective mobilization that hit North Africa was like a huge flock of birds that came to cover the sky. From afar, the compactness strikes and oppresses us: it seems like the gray sky of Permeke's paintings. But as soon as we look closer at the flock, the perspective changes.

The compactness transforms into the scales of a complex and continuously asymmetric fractal.

Let me explain: the reason for this is that North Africa is one of the most diversified vital worlds on the globe with very evident fault lines if we look immediately at the state dimension. It is present in the majority of areas affected by revolts, but with unequal intensity and articulated institutional configurations.

However, the Egyptian and Tunisian events have shown that the State has been configured and does not depend—its existence—on the physical person who holds power. Its physical or symbolic disappearance (the expulsion from power) does not coincide with the death of the institution, which reproduces itself. For the continuity of affairs and state apparatuses, this is essential. Everywhere it is the army that guarantees such continuity, constituting the very backbone of the State. But with two variants. Here are the armies in their post-colonial pan-Arabist culture: either revolutionary (Algeria and Egypt) or monarchic-sacred (the royals in Morocco and Jordan are of hereditary lineages that claim descent from the Prophet and therefore the loyalty of the army is twofold: to the monarch and to the Prophet). Both armies, Algerian and Egyptian, are of revolutionary origin, but now have little national autonomy and are characterized by high dependence on the West (the USA and France *in primis*). The army, and therefore the very continuity of the State, coincides with the continuity of affairs as much as the Western influence on the army will be felt: Egypt *docet*.

The moral of the story is that any transition to democracy (?), any continuity of economic relations, will have to deal with the tip of the rifle, that is, with the relations that the *business community* will have with the army.

Another relevant issue is the clear inability of these countries to give life to economic development and therefore to a growth that is only moderately unequal and only moderately unbalanced, even though they are endowed with great natural resources, *in primis* fossil hydrocarbons and certain mineral resources (I think for example of Moroccan phosphates).

A contributing cause of this lies not in the economy, but in the social stratification and the outcome of the postcolonial political struggle. It has given rise to a class of *rentiers* and bourgeois intermediaries between national resources and their international exploitation: hence the family and clan wrap that parasitically clung around the armies and state bureaucracies. Egypt is a textbook case in this regard, with the immense state-family-clientele proliferation of its bureaucracy.

Finally, there remains the most explosive problem, which is the fuse that was lit in Tunisia and was at the root of the revolt at that time: the formation throughout North Africa of an intellectual underclass that constitutes the true interclass novelty of the revolt itself and is at the same time the unexplored wealth of the area: knowledge combined with youth can foster a passion for development if it is given an outlet in the dignity of work. The danger is that this may not happen, with devastating consequences for the instability of those societies. Work must be the first commitment for those who will act in those countries, under penalty of the crisis of all their projects.

Then there is the Libyan case. It is a case unto itself: tribalism, archaic social relations, absence of the Western-style state, personalistic continuity of a power that has gone from revolutionary to saturnine, even to the point of devouring the tribal children of the revolution. The first task would have been to prevent the Somalization of Libya and prepare for a possible division of the area and fully understand the specificity of the case. In short, to move from economics to anthropology.

And the living anthropology of the Mediterranean crisis is inscribed in the global economic crisis. But the global economy is hanging by a thread of madness. The financial crisis is nothing more than the snowball that triggers the avalanche on the little houses of the national states gathered down in the valley. Even the USA, which dominates the valley, is subject to unheard-of internal tensions over public debt. Devastating for anyone who thinks with their own head is the spectacle of the proposals implemented or announced to deal with what is a profound restructuring of global capitalism based on high-risk financial dominance. In the face of this restructuring, thousands of highly paid economists, locked in international institutions, can do nothing but compile recipes that we now know and recite by heart: liberalize and privatize, especially the labor market; reduce the costs of politics; cut public spending; do not put any brakes on the transferability of capital; do not touch the incestuous structure of the big global banks that leverage excessively with depositors' money, producing continuous massacres of the innocent, but regulate them, instead, from above in a new edition of the ineffective Gosplan. It is not known whether they are fools or cunning: all these remedies have not advanced growth by one step, without which public debt does not structurally reduce.

This question assails us even more when we hear proposals such as banning short sales on the Stock Exchange, when everyone knows that the majority of immediate share transfer contracts are composed in millionths of a second through so-called *dark pools*, i.e., unregulated electronic circuits that investment banks update with extreme and refined care. This plethora of "experts" is divided into two large cohorts. The proponents of the *take over* of Germany over Europe thanks to the lucid madness that says that the danger is not global deflation but inflation: and they are the chorus of the ECB that contribute to fuel and not to extinguish the flames of the crisis.

The followers of the Fed have another design: to support growth by inflating debt to exploit to the unbelievable the real competitive advantage of the USA, their global power, and thanks to this global power to spread growth in the world thanks to the expansion of liquidity and a slight recovery of what can only save us: inflation (the *targeting of inflation* by Bernanke).

Greenspan's memoirs [103] are exhilarating in this light and make us understand that at the center of his thought was not only North American growth, but the continuity of Western dominance. For Greenspan, this can only be achieved by creating the basis for a new global growth and therefore also in Europe and Italy.

But the rates of world trade, from this point of view, are not encouraging: they are slowly descending in absolute terms and the BRICS are losing propulsive thrust in this regard.

Many knots have come to a head, we said.

And all over the world, in a sort of *redde rationem* that starts from the global horizon and ends in national crises, proving the correctness of theories that make the link between nation and internationalization the fundamental connection to understand the red thread of history.

First of all, we look at "the world" through the lens of the economy intertwined in the ring of international politics. There are two most relevant phenomena.

The first is that of the turn taken by halved globalization, that is, mainly financial, towards a slowdown in interdependencies. The sustained growth rate of the BRICS has not come to an end, but to the end of the first phase of their growth, as the Kaldorian theories [104] of development and Myrdal's reflection [105] taught us.

The rapid growth based on capital goods and the creation of urban proletarian and middle classes has ended. In non-communist countries, this has given rise to a class of peasant and agrarian bourgeoisie that allows the overcoming of growth based only on the accumulation of capital goods, but which must also be based on consumption thanks to the agrarian reforms that have characterized nations such as Brazil and India, although to a lesser extent and much less articulated in a private property sense, as in India for example, still dominated by a very strong community culture.

India's backwardness in relation to the domestic market and monetary circulation exploded in pandemic times to the surprise of all those who think that the economy is understood by reading statistics and not studying history and anthropology.

The majority of Indians do not exchange money but goods and even money is not mostly hoarded in banks. The increasing degree of interrelation in the world economy shows all the limits of this backwardness in the field of monetary circulation.

It is the same growth that highlights the problem and causes in this situation the depreciation of a currency so poorly hoarded. We expected it, we who do not believe that everything is always in balance, from the USA to India to Papua...

China, on the other hand, is in a real *cul de sac* because the agrarian bourgeoisie has not formed and the cities are filled with "non-citizen" illegal immigrants who cannot consume as the urban masses should, and in this way China falls into all the traps of countries with a bureaucratic economy and state capitalism directed by terrorist dictatorships: the decline begins due to the overcapacity of capital goods enlarged by the disastrous financial revolution that has upset centuries-old balances, while creating global asymmetries thanks to the entry of the Middle Empire into the WTO in 2001.

This has caused the unequal "post-Bretton Woods" relationship between global metropolitan economies and peripheral world economies to collapse.

Asymmetric competition now becomes an obstacle to the growth of China itself, which fails to create a domestic market, while—paradoxically—it exports forced labor all over the world to seek energy and arable land that it cannot produce at home due to the bureaucratic-terrorist directed economy.

The chaos of Russia is different: it suffers from the isolation of a great nation, prisoner and lonely among a hostile Europe that wants its energy resources, but does not allow it to expand thanks to competitive rules that are leading the entire European industry to decay due to falling profit rates and absence of consolidation—accused of sinful monopoly having forgotten the sacred text of Sylos Labini on *Oligopoly and technical progress* [106].

At the same time, an aggressive China emerges, whose power of pressure increases more and more due to the refusal of both the USA and the dominant nations of the EU to reformulate the overall face of the post-Cold War world with stable alliances. NATO can no longer unify the USA and Germany and France, creating a geopolitical instability built by "voids" of power—and not by "full" of power—both in the variable geometry space of European nations and in the equally variable geometry of nations overlooking the Pacific: power voids that China is eager to fill.

It has been imagined, both by the USA and by the nations of the EU (from Germany with difficulty and only after the de facto annexation of part of Ukraine by Russia, which interrupted the centuries-old historical relations between Germany and Russia), that it is possible to continue to produce growth by excluding Russia from Europe and the world market.

The case of Russia's slow readmission to the WTO, which more than ever makes explicit the disorientation of the USA and the EU not towards Russia itself, but towards China, is exemplary.

Only on December 17, 2011, in Geneva was Russia's entry into the organization formalized. Thus ended a long negotiation, which began in 1993 with the request for membership of the Russian Federation, a request, moreover, submitted years before the dissolution of the USSR. The situation was unlocked by the agreement between Russia and Georgia. Incredible but true. Georgia had already been a member of the WTO since 2000, with the non-compliance of the gentlemen's agreement stipulated by Reagan and Gorbachev, according to which no nation bordering Russia would ever be part of NATO or the EU, let alone bodies like the WTO. Georgia, after the conflict with Russia in the early years of its refoundation, had imposed a veto on the acceptance of the Russian request since 2004, hardening its position after the "Five Day War", which in 2008 led to the breakdown of relations between the two countries.

A fundamental role in the affair was played by the very young Mikheil Saak'ashvili, born in Tbilisi in 1967 and of Ukrainian-Georgian origins, appointed after the bombing of the Georgian capital by the cannons and planes of the "revolutionary" nationalists supported by the USA and France. After being installed as president of Georgia from 2004 to 2013, from 2015 to 2016 he was appointed governor of the Ukrainian region of Odessa, always imposed by the USA. After the never applied Minsk agreement, which saw a Germany as active as it was ineffective in containing Russia, Saak'ashvili himself was deprived of Ukrainian citizenship in 2016 (in 2014 he had already been deprived of Georgian citizenship), becoming stateless.

It should be noted—to highlight the low levels to which both diplomatic and intelligence incapacity has fallen—that this last citizenship was returned to him, publicly announcing it in May 2019.

Here is clearly displayed what were and are the consequences of the failure to stipulate a new Yalta. A catastrophic decision undertaken by American Democrats fascinated by the financial income that could be built in and with China, too tied to the past of the Cold War and forgetful of Kissinger's lesson.

Russia was admitted to the WTO thanks to the pressures exerted on Tbilisi by the EU and, above all, by the USA. By joining the WTO, Russia had committed itself to lowering (up to a maximum of 7.8%) import tariffs (then estimated at 250 billion dollars), to reducing subsidies to internal sectors (in particular agriculture), to defending intellectual property, to opening its banking sector to foreign capital. The agreement, however, did not touch the strategic sector of the Russian economy, the extraction of oil and gas.

Hostilities between the USA and Russia persist despite the mediating role of Germany, which continues to compete with US liquefied gas thanks to the very close ties of France and also Italy with Gazprom.

Despite European pressures, the US and EU sanctions on Russia remain like threatening landslides on the road to the new redefinition of a stable anti-Chinese balance, thus not pursuing the Gaullist goal of a Europe from the Atlantic to the Urals—a tool to prevent the same European decline.

This pushes a great Eurasian nation towards a disastrous embrace with China.

The BRICS will grow less and at ever slower rates after the pandemic and this reclassifies all the growth of South America, except for Mexico and Colombia, which have chosen a path not so tied to the cycle of *commodities*. Which, moreover, is now collapsing, dragging with it the "commodity-dependent" nations... All the others will be forced to reclassify the relationships between mining and *oil and gas* industries and the global cycle, turning more and more towards both the domestic market and new foreign markets. This is what their middle classes, which have been mobilizing in recent years all over the world, are asking for and which well express the theories of Tilly, Haimson, and mine when we studied the phenomena of collective mobilization [107]. Phenomena that only occur in ascending phases of economic and political cycles and to impose changes in the consumption agenda. Now the middle classes of those countries want infrastructure, immaterial goods such as culture, quality of life and thus rediscover every tradition (the political cycle) that can lay the foundations for creating their organizational solidarity.

Here emerges secularism in Turkey and indigenism in some South American countries, as has already happened and as will happen soon in much more widespread forms: see the case not only of Bolivia, but especially of Peru, the epicenter of all South American political cultures.

This will have profound consequences regarding the exploitation of mineral resources, opening a new chapter in South American energy history.

Naturally, the world is now dominated by the North African conflict which sees the return of a revisited and reclassified Nasserism due to the changes that have occurred on the international scene with the fall of the USSR and with the re-emergence of the military as a stabilizing force in a different form from the past.

With Nasser and with Baathism and therefore in Egypt and in Syria and in Iraq, the local bourgeoisies built the nations and capitalism [108]. Today they defend themselves from the terrorist cosmopolitanism of the destruction of the New Caliphate to which the Muslim brotherhoods have given life, endangering the same relationship with the West, between what remains of the Ottoman past and the new hierocratic formations that are trying in various ways to assume power.

After the fall of the Shah in Persia, transformation forces were set in motion throughout the Greater Middle East that still last today, despite the fall of the USSR.

Russia remains, as do the Arab and Persian bourgeoisies, even if disguised as Islamic sects. The terrorist sects of Daesh enjoy the support of powerful state forces such as Iran on one side and Saudi Arabia and Qatar on the other; Saudi Arabia and Qatar which are, in turn, engaged in a tough conflict for hegemony over the Sunni world, which is also reflected in the field of pan-Arab satellite information in the duel between al-Jazeera, the broadcaster of Qatar, and al-Arabiya, which expresses the interests of Saudi Arabia and the United Arab Emirates. This is before us all thanks to the so-called Arab springs which soon revealed themselves for what they really were and on which I too have written extensively:

a revolt of middle classes, both secular and Islamic, armed against each other.

And yet, encouraged by *moral suasion* of the USA, determined to renew the Egyptian command block founded on saprophytic but efficient military in maintaining aggressive praetorian order both internally and externally, primarily towards Israel.

The misunderstanding of the changes that have occurred in the Arab, Persian, and Turkish world by the USA has been catastrophic, preventing the evaluation of the instability of the institutional rooting of the Muslim Brotherhood.

It is not enough to have constitutionalized one's behavior as has happened in Jordan [109] and in Morocco (sacred monarchies, however, let's not forget, due to their direct descent from the Prophet!) for about fifty years; all this is not enough to be able to govern a country like Egypt or Libya, overcoming ties with Islamic roots based on the identity of Islamic law and state law. It was forgotten that Salafism enjoyed and enjoys strong support from Saudi Arabia, while Qatar supported and supports the Muslim Brotherhood. It was therefore not enough to replace the military with those who were thought to have constitutionalized to transform the system of weights and relevancies in the Middle East and North Africa.

The mechanism of defusing military dictatorships with a political reform entrusted to forces like the radical Sunnis had the same effect that was produced in Iraq and well before in Iran, effectively bringing to power the most intransigent Shiism that now constitutes the factor that has destabilized Lebanon and Syria and now commands in Iraq. The risk of a vast "Islamic civil war" fought between Shiites and Sunnis, but also within the same Sunni world, is always concrete.

It is good to remember that internal conflict characterizes Islamic civilization from its beginnings: the first Islamic civil war, the *fitna* (a term that recalls the concepts of divine trial and disagreement), emerged following the death of the third caliph Uthman, between the supporters of the right to succession of one of the Prophet's companions and those who claimed the rights of the members of his family (the *ahl al bayt*, "the people of the house"), who sided with Ali ibn Abu Talib, cousin and son-in-law of the Prophet. The conflict between these two groups, around which different socio-economic formations were structured, gave rise to the fracture between Sunnis and Shiites, which today constitutes the fault that divides deeply different countries such as Syria,

Iraq, Lebanon, Yemen, Bahrain, and Pakistan. Alongside this millennial split, deep internal conflicts in the Sunni world are developing with particular virulence, between secularists and Islamists and also within the same heterogeneous and composite Sunni Islamist galaxy. To the clash of civilizations between Islam and the West feared by Huntington [110] is superimposed a molecular clash within the Islamic world that risks overwhelming nation-states, as evidenced by the disintegration of Syria.

A tragedy that risks striking with particular ferocity the ancient Christian communities of the Middle East, a historical bridge between the West and Islam.

Traditionally, Arab Christians were protected by the caliphal authorities who, by conferring on them the *status* of *dhimmi*, legally sanctioned their subordination to Muslims, but also guaranteed their lives and their properties.

The current crisis of the precarious Arab nation-states, dubbed by the media as the "Arab Spring", is instead causing a proliferation of radical Sunni Islamist movements that identify Christians, but also secularists and Shiites and therefore Sufis, as a tumor to be eradicated at all costs.

A profound and tearing internal crisis within the Islamic world that is spreading in Central African lands, for example in Mali and Nigeria, also putting the stability of the Congo at risk. Precarious states that had painstakingly built themselves after the "great lakes wars" and the genocides that had given way to a territorial partition so far unusually entrusted to the African elites directly negotiating; both with the increasingly invasive China, and with the old colonial powers, France and the United Kingdom *primarily* [111].

But the reclassification of powers in Central Africa will have to deal with the stabilization of Nigeria as was immediately evident from the end of the regalian dominion of the Commonwealth [112]. This is the *nation-building* fundamental to understanding—together with the Congo—what will be the fate of these lands and these cultures.

The problem of the entire area from Morocco and the Gulf to Iran, which constitutes the new land of confrontation in the Islamic world that once saw the hegemonic role of the USA increasingly distancing itself, with devastating consequences, is even more complex. A void that, after the agreement between the United Arab Emirates and Israel, only began to be filled from 2020.

The energy issue is fundamental but not sufficient to understand the situation. Even in 1956—during the war unleashed by Israel, France, and the United Kingdom against Nasser, who nationalized the Suez Canal—the USA seized the opportunity to replace the decline of English hegemony with a ruthless fight against Soviet influence that saved Egypt and Israel, together, from ruin. Now the game is more complicated. Of course: the *shale oil and gas* which are of short duration in the dynamics of the energy world due to the scarcity of North American deposits, determine a growing weakening of OPEC, as denounced by the Saudis with prompt denials and phenomenological evidence of divisions in the royal family. But the confrontation with OPEC is much older. It starts when, in the mid-seventies, the *proven and unproven* reserves of *oil* began to concentrate not in the hands of the *majors*, but instead in those of the NOCs, or the national companies mainly non-OPEC that today own 90% of them. And this has generated an impressive technological revolution, in the disintermediation of the *majors* themselves who have contracted the disintermediation by selling to the NOCs the *capabilities* to face the new technological horizons that have gradually outlined. This has led to an increase in competition and a crowding of new independent presences in the global energy oligopoly. This exploded with the realization of the dream of the great George Mitchell, who, after years and years of difficulty, managed to make his dream of extracting gas and *oil* from *fracking* operational, a project he had worked on all his life (1919–2013) with a utopian generosity that is, alas, now disappeared in the global energy world. But the revolution of the *shale oil and gas* produces powerful but short-term geostrategic and macro and micro-economic transformations. Precisely for this reason they can be devastating as the first twenty years of the second millennium have shown us. And these last ones materialize in the ephemeral transformation of the energy industry, because they give space back to small independent companies for the number of *wild cats* needed by the *shale oil* and for the deep drop in the price of gas caused by the *shale* discoveries, with an increase, however, in the cost of transport that can only threaten intermobility strategies on a local and global scale.

Macro-economically, the role of coal and oil is set to increase in areas not affected by *fracking*, because the USA will intensify their presumed energy independence by importing much less *oil and gas* than they used to, even reaching the point of exporting it.

This has called into question the level of prices, with a reclassification of the profitability trends of the *majors*, which while seeing an increase in extraction and transport costs, see a decrease in the price of *oil* and gas both due to *fracking*, and due to the global economic crisis that has been ongoing for twenty years. In fact, it is intensifying precisely in the BRICS countries, which are the most affected by the processes of *fracking* due to their low degree of anthropization.

But the most significant consequence is geostrategic.

There may arise an illusion in the USA that it is possible to do without control of the Greater Middle East, with the constant loss of interest of the USA in the domination of the Gulf area and in general North African and Middle Eastern. A dangerous power vacuum has already opened, at the time of the proxy war in Syria, because Europe is not able to fill this vacuum due to its internal divisions: due to the absence of a European army, due to the devastating consequences of economic austerity that has destroyed industry in its southern European strongholds and that in some of its strong areas is subject to risks of collapse of *procurement* and internal markets and errors in *governance* due to Franco-German divisions.

The imperial impulses of France do not have behind them the economic strength to be militarily and economically sustained. Only a Europe that integrates Russia into itself could perform the hegemonic task suitable for placing under guardianship and stabilization—alternating military interventions and diplomatic play and commercial agreements—an area destined to be central for Europe's own survival, both from the point of view of internal security (due to the possible penetration of terrorist cells that proliferate within Islamic diasporas due to lacerating identity crises), and for its development due to the *reservoir* of energy present in the area. It risks ending up in the hands of a China that is indeed in decline, but, precisely for this reason, increasingly dangerously aggressive. The fact that an alliance between Saudi Arabia, Israel, and Russia had been outlined to control the Syrian situation by supporting Assad and supporting the Egyptian military who saved Egypt and the West from the creation of a huge Salafist Islamic state destined to threaten both Europe and Central Africa, was a positive fact: but its institutionalization still has to overcome enormous difficulties today.

First of all, intellectuals, due to the fall of Westphalian culture—which I have already mentioned—and due to theories of humanitarian intervention and human rights, without any regard for the compatibilities and cultural specificities of nations and peoples and elites on which the hegemonic powers exercise dominion… or try to exercise it.

All this has plunged the West into an anti-Kissingerism of which we are only now beginning to evaluate the enormous prices to pay.

The military rupture between Shiites and Sunnis is only the beginning of the long inter-Islamic war that was mentioned earlier (which continues that between Iraq and Iran that we have forgotten too soon), which can only be resolved by putting the three fundamental cultures of the area back into communication with each other: the Arab one, the Ottoman (and now Turkish) one, and the Persian one. The West must play this role. The United Kingdom is the most culturally equipped to carry out this work.

In this context, however, Europe is falling apart. And everything will worsen, from the point of view of stabilizing the Mediterranean areas of the Greater Middle East, when the economic and cultural crisis hits Germany even more than it is today. This is because the unequal and cyclical accumulation of capital is stronger than any liberalist-monetarist ideology, especially that of Merkel's own weak homeland.

She won the elections in September 2017, thus leading Europe to ruin. The coalition with the SPD will see the latter subordinate and now devoid of autonomous cultural dignity in the face of liberalism and deflationary politics.

But the most serious problem remains the conflict between the USA and Germany. Europe does not exist, but Germany does and has powerful geostrategic interests in areas at risk of implosion in the Mediterranean.

In this torn context, the event that allowed the start of rebuilding a fabric of diplomatic relations was the Syrian war. Wars are nothing more than the continuity of politics by other means. It should be said that today they often replace the politics of international relations, after the end of the realistic theory of the power mechanism on a global scale.

A counterintuitive result that we must carefully study.

How do we get there?

With historiography and therefore by studying history.

A fundamental turning point, in addition to the SykesPicot agreement, was the replacement of Franco-English hegemony in the Middle East in 1956. The USA sided with the new regional middle powers led by an Egypt leaning towards an alliance with the USSR and at the same time, however, they clearly manifested the will to intervene militarily in defense of their interests in the area. A decision that must be read in conjunction with the turning point of 1967, that is, the "Six Day War", fought between Israel on one side and Egypt, Syria, and Jordan on the other, which turned into a rapid and total Israeli victory.

At the end of the conflict, Israel had conquered the Sinai Peninsula and the Gaza Strip from Egypt, the West Bank and East Jerusalem from Jordan, and the Golan Heights from Syria. The outcome of the war, the legal status of the occupied territories, and the related refugee problem forever influenced the geopolitical situation of the Middle East [113].

Faced with the initial resistance and then the Israeli victory, both Shiite and Sunni powers renounced the clearly expressed will to destroy the State of Israel. Until the Iranian theocratic revolution arrived, which again ushered in the season of military destruction of Israel, a geopolitical season that did not present itself again until 2003.

With the destruction of the Iraqi army after the unipolar US war against Saddam Hussein in 2003 and the green light given by the Saudis to the fundamentalism of Isis, that season of war for the annihilation of Israel began again.

The energy relevance of Mesopotamia and North Africa, moreover, does not escape anyone.

Only fools can believe that the USA have achieved and will maintain energy self-sufficiency thanks to shale oil. All those who reason with their heads and do not chase millenarian philosophies based on ignorance know that the geological plexus of the Greater Middle East constitutes the largest energy reserve in the world. The recent discovery of large natural gas deposits in the Qara district, on the border between Lebanon and Syria, is nothing more, from the point of view of the geostrategic energy struggle, than the rallying call of the "Shiite crescent" to build the large pipeline that will connect Iran and Syria and will reach the port of Tartus controlled by Russia, thus rendering the Nabucco pipeline, heavily sponsored by the USA in an anti-Russian function, inactive. Thus, one can better understand the Syrian issue of the last fifty years, with the decline of the Baathist regimes and the emergence not of classic Arab nationalisms but of the new "fighting patriotisms" of the "Shiite crescent" and of Sunni Islam that has accepted the presence of US armed forces on the territory of the sacred Mecca, but which has at the same time unleashed war on Shiite regimes and their allies, *primarily* the Alawite rulers of post-Sykes-Picot Syria.

In this context, the Syrian issue increasingly becomes the Turkish issue.

With the collapse of the USSR, falsifying all theories of the "end of history", what no one had predicted happened. The end of the USSR, in fact, did not coincide with the decline of Russia as a historical power in the area, but instead with its return.

Unipolarism could not but be countered by the inevitable plurilateralism implored by China, Turkey, and Russia, with all the medium European powers in tow.

This is, as demonstrated, especially after the division between the USA and the UK, on the one hand, and Germany and France, on the other, from the inexhaustible activism of France and the United Kingdom that culminated in the assassination of Gaddafi, not by chance thanks to the realization of France's powerful mediation capacity, which on this point achieved a victorious mediation and involvement, for its African interests, of the USA.

An activism that aims to prefigure a "zone of respect" for France's domination in Africa and—even without an army—of Germany, shared with an increasingly aggressive and declining China.

In this context, the role of Turkey has undergone a profound mutation.

One of the consequences of US unipolarism is precisely the growing weakness of the ties between NATO and Turkey.

The non-recognition of the historical specificity of the Kurdish issue by the USA was crucial in this transformation of power alliances or in their weakening. Certainly, the Kurds have been great fighters against ISIS, but they also constitute, since the Treaty of Versailles (which failed to find a solution to the Kurdish issue between Iraq, Syria, and Turkey only because of the ever-flaming armed conflicts between the agnatic Kurdish families), an important protagonist (multiple and divided and more divisive than it appears to most) of the history of the Greater Middle East.

Hence the glaring contradiction between the need to continue the policy of alliance with NATO on the part of Turkey and the deep contradiction between such loyalty and the active and fighting presence of the Kurds in the Syrian and Turkish area alongside the USA.

Here, then, is Syria, the "great Syria", which forcefully returns to world history.

A role that is very little understood by the "Eurocentric" thought of too much "Mediterranean" analysis, and which must instead return to constitute the starting point of a new reflection aimed at understanding the historical roots of the Syrian tragedy.

The USA decided after much uncertainty to intervene militarily in Syria, against the strong opposing opinion of Germany. On the other hand, Sinai, the focus of a violent jihadist insurrection, would have become even more ungovernable if it had not intervened, as well as Syria itself and the entire northern area of Africa.

Not only desperate and humiliated people would land on the European shores due to poverty and terror, but also ideologically and militarily armed cells that would certainly not rely on the miserable boats.

The coasts of Sicily, Calabria, and Puglia would become the extension of a bloody ideological war in a state, Italy, which has been without a polyarchic head for about thirty years.

It is in this dramatic context that institutional stability must be imposed. The problems, in truth, are much more dramatic than those of the European semesters, however important. Once again, national stabilizations need, to come true, an international power movement, as always in the most tragic and troubled moments of world history.

CHAPTER 7

Increasing Global Divergence

The dramatic events just evoked reflect the end of what I would call "the old global convergence", now lost. Let's try to explain the concept.

For many decades in economic and historical-economic analysis, global growth has always been thought of as a converging process. That is, we have asked ourselves what were the factors that determined—starting substantially from the mid-twentieth century—a global trend in labor productivity, trade, lifestyles that gradually became, not so much homogeneous, as increasingly intense and porous from the periphery to the center.

For some decades now, converging growth has shattered.

The superimposition of graphs has been replaced by a fractal design, that is, variable geometries, mobile, quickly superimposable in their composition. It seems that there is no longer a peak to converge towards. Europe is undoubtedly in a fearful decline. Military, first of all, because it has not been able to transform the Franco-German armies and those surrounding them into a new European army.

The global military dominance, still in the hands of the USA, is being redefined. The clear turning point is not, however, as many thought for some years, in the North American oil and gas, certainly extracted under common law (let's not forget: I exploit my land without asking anyone for concessions as I must do in Roman-Germanic law regimes) and therefore better adaptable to "entrepreneurial spirits" [114]. But it could not be

G. Sapelli, *States, Markets and Wars in Global History*,
https://doi.org/10.1007/978-3-031-26716-1_7

the redefinition of the world treasures of gas and oil deposits. The old primacy of the Gulf does not become evanescent compared to the new routes of the gigantic deposits just discovered: from Canada, to North Dakota, to South Texas, to end up in French Guiana and Brazil and reach Perth and all of Oceania.

In any case, the USA is again at the center of the new energy power map.

The new global energy layer changes its vector: from being only transatlantic, it also becomes, not only, transpacific.

It also goes, in addition to the always central Greater Middle East, from the USA to Australia and disrupts the price regimes and the relationships between now truly alternative energy sources based on price: North American coal will always arrive in a Europe that will be induced to use it in its power plants to replace Russian gas that will soon no longer be competitive. The effects on Gazprom are already evident and Rosneft's strategic move towards shale gas, for example, makes Gazprom's crisis clear.

The main element of the specific European situation in relation to natural gas concerns the structure of the offer. Europe is still characterized at this time by a structure of rigid contracts, take or pay, on the supply side towards Russia, not internally, while at the same time experiencing a moment of difficulty on the demand side, dictated not only by the economic crisis but also by the structure of the so-called renewable energies in the electricity sector. A comprehensive rethink is needed. The solution proposed by the European Commission in the tens of the second millennium, opposed by many Franco-German operators in primis, was that of the realization of new structures for the importation of regasified LNG gas.

The real strategic question, however, is another: where could an LNG operator truly invest in Europe? Which area of the world, moreover, is more profitable, at least in theory? Europe is not among the most suitable areas, if only because it has less interesting prospects in terms of growth volumes and because the margins are less interesting than in other parts of the world. Moreover, the issue of a *hub* in southern Europe has been circulating for more than thirty years, while the countries of Northern Europe have already quickly equipped themselves with adequate structures supported by a network of long-term contracts. This implies debunking the assumption that it is no longer profitable to invest in Europe. Everything will depend on the formula that will be chosen. Just think of the *terminal gate* in Rotterdam and the fact that in Dunkirk in 2015 a new terminal was put into operation, only marginally intended for internal consumption. All these large plants were based on long-term contracts. Having said that, it is important to ask whether there is an economic convenience for investments *green field* of regasifiers or of expanding existing networks. The convenience of entering the European gas market with new energies is linked to the possibility of signing a long-term contract with a large producer obtaining a price that is such as to knock down on the market a part of the offer available today. This is only possible if you have an offer that is alternative to the Russian and Algerian one, but it must be equally powerful in terms of availability and geostrategic influence. What we must be certain of is that we must change the representation of our model of global growth, moving from the one characterized by the symbol of the highest and unreachable and distant mountain, to the symbol of the mountain range, where one peak is certainly higher than the others, but it is no longer unreachable and those who want to climb the highest and farthest mountain share the "base camps" of those who want to climb the mountains that surround that peak.

Liquefied gas—LNG—is the phenomenological paradigm of this new global geostrategy of the supply of this increasingly indispensable energy resource given the cultural changes regarding the environment.

It is naturally a great transformation that has attracted everyone's attention, but which has not been, in my opinion, connected with the already mentioned attempt at a transpacific agreement promoted by the USA between some Asian nations and the South American nations that overlook the Pacific Ocean.

Of course, world trade expands its borders. But trade volumes do not increase: indeed, from 2006 to 2010 they had constantly reduced, with a more significant decrease after the global financial crisis of 2007. What happened? Until 2006 in Europe and Asia the growth rate of exports exceeded that of imports; and this because, until that date, a sustained demand at the global level allowed to keep the rhythms of trade at a decent level. After 2007, after that global crisis, everything changes, because the demand for imports decelerates strongly and simultaneously both in the United States and in Europe and Japan. Starting from the fourth quarter of 2008, world trade had a strong reversal of trend: in Europe, it fell by 16%, in the USA by 7%, and in Asia by 5%.

The world gross domestic product in 2009, as is known, dropped sharply, but even stronger was the contraction of world trade which was ten points higher than the collapse of trade. It is for this reason, and only for this reason overlooked by most, that China became in 2009 the world's leading exporter surpassing Germany, occupying 9.6% of world trade.

On this situation, in September 2008, the failure of Lehman Brothers struck, with the fall in real estate prices, the value of family assets and the increase in savings to the detriment of consumption and investment. The global financial crisis broke out, which still has profound direct effects on world trade due to the reduction in the supply of credit and indirect effects due to the reduction in global demand.

It can be said that we have been and still are facing a significant decrease in the sale of all forms of goods that are traded in the global market: those for immediate consumption, those for durable consumption, those aimed at supporting investments in machinery and technology. All of this results in a vertical drop in international trade. The pandemic crisis of 2020 has only accentuated the process that had already begun [115].

In response to deflationary pressures, households respond by not consuming or consuming less. Companies, on the other hand, respond by integrating vertically. That is, they return, as in the years from 1950 to 1980, to produce internally the majority of the intermediate goods they need to develop production chains.

The 2020 pandemic has been superimposed on a process already underway.

And this means causing a vertical drop in interstate trade and breaking global production chains, which are the backbone of so-called globalization. Companies try to respond to the credit crisis that grips them, but this has devastating effects on trade between company and company and also between banks and company, in a sort of reborn mini-local autarky. Finally, it should be considered that all this has increased mistrust among established partners in world trade: all companies, in fact, respond to the credit crisis by contracting the volume of international trade. Consider that the contraction of world trade has even exceeded the rate of decrease in world gross domestic product.

It is a miracle, in some ways (and here lies, so far, the difference compared to the "great crisis" of 1929), that in the face of all this, with about 200 million unemployed in the OECD, states did not respond with strong and decisive protectionist policies. On the contrary, there are still trends opposite to protectionism, those trends that I mentioned at the beginning: Russia's entry into the WTO and the sought-after, albeit futile, transpacific agreement.

Yet the appointment in September 2013 of the Brazilian career diplomat Roberto Carvalho de Azevêdo as head of the WTO (the organization whose purpose is to develop world trade) was a very important event. In trade policies, Brazil not only, like Japan, does not hesitate to always conduct a premeditated currency war, but also follows what were once, when the economy still had a theoretical breath, called the "principles of the Cambridge school" of the Thirties and Fifties of the twentieth century, that is a targeted protectionism aimed at supporting national industries and agricultural production based on the economic policy chosen by the government.

As is known, these are the principles that, in one way or another, with slight nuances, all the so-called BRICS follow, despite the military and financial efforts that especially the USA put into motion to change the trade policy of these nations in their favor.

First of all, it is very likely that the trend that has emerged in the last forty years in the globalized world to pursue bilateral trade agreements rather than multilateral ones will continue, with inevitable consequences on world trade, which will have more obstacles and therefore more opportunities to be slowed down. Not only is there a lack of aggregate demand, that is, internal markets, but international demand will also decrease, fractally, with the reduction of export spaces and the increasing difficulty of always finding new niches for export.

In short, the archetypal point on which the global economy rests begins to shift from the shoulders of the liberal giant to the shoulders of the neo-protectionist giant. Of course, there is no need for integral neo-protectionism. We would never get out of the recession. But anyone who knows the history of the world, especially that of Latin America, knows that the first response to the crisis has always been the *inward growth* and not the *outward growth*.

It's an old story, now coming back into the spotlight with profoundly new aspects: those of nations that are now medium or large regional powers and with which the USA will have to deal. Europe, of course, will continue to stand by, due to its internal conflicts veiled by the neo-Kantian ideology of peace, as perfect as commerce.

Therefore, there are contrasting trends underway and the face of our future industrial, consumer, even our own vital horizons, is still uncertain.

In this situation, the only response to strategic divergence can only come from the resumption of global leadership. The crisis of political leadership is a universal phenomenon. It is not a problem of national systems: it is indeed a geostrategic problem dictated by the existence of multiple nations in a leadership crisis.

Consider Australia. It is a nation destined to play a very important role in the future because the decisive economic-military game with China, which has formally opened with the attempted transpacific agreement between the USA, some Asian states, *primarily* those of the Indochinese peninsula—Vietnam at the forefront (the age-old adversary of China)—and the "Pacific" states of South America: Chile, Peru, and Mexico.

Australia makes us understand that antipodal points, which are opposite each other on the earth's surface passing through it, really exist, and not only in geography. That is, there is a focal point through which one completely loses the vision of the world that goes from the Equator upwards and reaches the North Pole. It is that dimension, facing Europe and under the starry sky, that was magnificently described by Les Murray, the greatest of Australian poets, when he wanted to represent the relationship between Europe and the antipodes in front of the beauty of a painting:

> In the middle of the river are cobweb cassowary trees of the South Pacific, and on the far shore rise dark hills of the temperate zone. To these, at this moment in the painting's growth, my course is slant but my eye is on them. To relax, to speak European. [116]

It's true: there is a vision of the world that the ongoing depression sharpens and makes even clearer: a vision that pushes us beyond the usual generalizing assumptions and makes us see how the geographical, economic, and social path that goes from Australia to Africa, passing through the Indian Ocean, is much more varied than it appears from above.

In Australia, this is clear: the political and social change that has occurred in the last fifteen years in Thailand and Indonesia has been decisive for economic development. The former appeared as a pearl of Asian growth, with endless flows of indirect foreign investment in financial markets and enviable political stability. Then came the crisis of 1997, the first harbinger of the one now underway: foreign capital withdrew, social crisis flared up in the streets, the difficult balance between monarchy and armed forces, on the one hand, and economic wealth transformed into political power, on the other, broke down and the country plunged into the de facto dictatorship in which it is now immersed, with continuous clashes between the supporters of the opposing factions and the collapse of the illusions of guaranteeing a nation—central to the geostrategic balance between Laos and Cambodia—a stable structure. Conversely, Indonesia, which seemed never to be able to recover from the disaster in the slow and ruinous fall of Suharto's more than thirty-year dictatorship, has found a prodigious political stability, with the parliamentary dominance of a moderate Islamic party that ensures a nation of about three hundred million inhabitants a future that seems among the most serene in the entire Southeast Asian and broadly understood Oceania area, with profound repercussions on economic growth marked by interdependence. Yes, from the antipodal point, we can still talk about interdependent growth—and not just interdependent crisis—despite the current global situation. Just reflect on one fact. The interdependence between economies has certainly hit Australia, it cannot be denied, even if with rates of GDP fall much more limited than ours, which in fact suggest stagnation rather than depression (it is predicted that the economy will grow around 0.5% in the coming years). But the fall in Australian exports, for example, which collapsed at the beginning of the second millennium between 20 and 30% towards Europe and the USA, was balanced by the unexpected but more than real growth of exports to China, *primarily* those of processed coal, which have risen with a prodigious leap forward. And this is due to the impossibility of Chinese state monopolistic capitalism to reactivate old mines, small, uneconomical, very dangerous, which caused only in the year 2002 ten thousand deaths at work, and the impossibility of opening new ones, even in the presence of still immense unexplored deposits, in front of which, however, there are no technical skills and economic resources to intervene. Therefore, to meet energy needs, coal is imported from Australia. China is developing a neocolonial policy all over the world, especially in Africa, but cannot cope with the technical and scientific and human capital bottlenecks on its own territory, with consequences that can be very serious for its overall economic stability and favor nations that are indispensable in the chains of companies for the Chinese chains of instrumental goods, such as energy ones.

This is not seen from the North Pole, if you only read the aggregate statistics… And all this while the battle always and forever rages in the triangle that is drawn in the field of the Stock Exchange and the struggle for the acquisition of *assets* of Australian mining companies.

On the one hand, the central state which issued—one of the first measures of the second Labor government of Kevin Rudd in 2016—a list of rules aimed at protecting the national interest. On the other hand, the shareholders of Rio Tinto who were not sure what to do in the face of the Chinese purchase offer: tempted, in fact, by the profit achievable thanks to the immense liquidity of Chinalco, which wanted to acquire one of the most powerful mining industries in the world, but subjected to unprecedented political pressure not to sell. And from the last and no less important side there were and are the Chinese themselves, who act with immense political-diplomatic coordination in support of energy expansionist aims not only through de facto territorial occupation, as in Africa, but also through action on financial markets, as happens in Australia. It is striking, in this context, the inexhaustible vitality of the Australian stock exchange even in periods of stagnation, of secular deflation, and of constantly threatened global financial crisis.

Of course, public investment also plays its part.

But at the antipodes, everything is socially different. It is the diversity that the old theorists of growth, who are no longer read today because everyone is specifically trained on financial texts, had taught us to understand: we are in a part of the world, at the antipodes, where Australia is the epicenter of economic areas that often overlap between nations different in history, customs, and political constructs, but all are united by the binomial: low population and immense endowment of natural resources.

Just think, to understand what I mean, that Australia owns a quarter of the world's uranium…

Therefore, growth in such areas, provided that one does not rely on a model of parasitic rent exploitation—like many of the oil states of the Gulf, for example, or Nigeria, and I could go on—is guaranteed as long as it is provided for through the distribution of wealth in the least unequal form possible, thus promoting the creation of a solid domestic market that can protect against the uncertainties and inevitable fluctuations of global export flows, always possible in a world with open economies, but interdependent. In short, from the antipodal point of view, instability is always present and yet, unlike what happens in the other hemisphere, it invites caution, not to rely too much on the logic of risk, as has happened and stubbornly will still happen in Europe and the USA.

From the antipodes, a global trend, which I had already described in my comparative studies between the Enron case and the Parmalat case [117], appears to emerge more and more clearly: the increasing homogenization, unfortunately, of the USA to Europe, with collusion of markets and their increasing imperfection, contempt for the rules of good *governance*, fall of the capacity for self-regulation, continuous creation of *inner circles* in which to rally to prevent any change of the dominant personnel [118].

We are witnessing, in short, the disintegration of the establishment: one of the foundations of Western civilization. But from the antipodes, everything is different. We look to Asia, where these evils of capitalist development, which intermittently appear in the USA and continuously in Europe, are instead inherent to all its diversified histories: even if varied and distinct, the *crony capitalism* is a dominant matrix. And yet it moves: the fall in growth has been less strong than elsewhere, this is also proven by what I said earlier about Australian coal and China. Of course, the *Pacific Rim*, as Eric Jones [119], the great Anglo-Australian economic historian, called it, is a world unto itself. Australia does not belong to Asia, to the Asias: it looks at it, they look at them. And from this antipodal perspective, it is understood that the future game for world domination will be played on these shores. That is, the great game will be the one that will decide whether the innovative impulse that continues to come from Australia and New Zealand will be able to domesticate Asian capitalisms and make them more transparent, less clientelistic and less dominated by corruption and the threat of the use of violence. In this sense, the Anglo-Saxon antipodes are truly the last platform for the hope that it is still possible to support and even create in the future a set of nations governed by the *common law*, virtuous not only because judges are less imperfect than parliaments, but also because the *moral suasion* and the civilizing work of old Europe and *in primis* of the British Empire have not yet been extinguished.

Want proof? Just look at how the parliamentary battle in Canberra—and politically throughout Australia—over the Budget, that is, the budget proposals through which the first Labor government after more than a decade of conservative dominance found itself, in the second decade of the 2000s, having to face the crisis. The deficit, due to the public spending that was intended to be promoted, was expected to reach, for example in

2009–2010, the record figure of about 58 billion Australian dollars, with no possibility of returning to a *surplus* for about five to six years; and this in the face of a collapse in tax revenues that has already reached, due to the crisis, the figure of 210 billion. The government debt, therefore, was expected to grow up to 13.8% of GDP, which, compared to about 80% of the debt that was expected for the other strongest world economies, is a real record of public accounts' health.

The strategy to revive the economy was based on a series of infrastructure projects in a nation where historically labor, up to the era of liberalizations (which, moreover, were the same Australian laborers to inaugurate worldwide, well before Blair, with Prime Minister Hawke, a powerful union leader), has been the quintessence of the culture of production and nation-building. That culture and history were resumed, with the forecast to invest billions of dollars in roads, railways, ports, and broadband networks for internet connections. Significant increases in pensions were also planned to revive the domestic market, a drastic reduction in taxes on small and medium-sized enterprises, and monetary transfers to families, whether extended or single. Of course, there is no lack of support for integrative (or alternative, as it is commonly said) energies.

But the most innovative measures observed now from the antipodal civilizing point—the European one—were those aimed at keeping together the reduction in spending on salaries in the public administration, for which a not yet well specified but deep cut was expected and which caused quite a few protests, and the expenses, instead, expected, of about 5 billion dollars, to increase the quality of public hospitals and increase free care for long-term cancer patients, which constituted and constitute a very felt problem. And above all, it was expected to increase by 5.5 billion dollars in the expenditure for tertiary education: universities and research centers... The *tax free threshold*, moreover, that is, the income level below which no taxes were paid, rose by about 5,000 dollars: it was 25,000 dollars a year for those under fifty and 50,000 dollars for those who, instead, exceeded them. Finally, taxes increased for those who earned more than 150,000 dollars a year. The conservative opposition insisted that these measures did not reduce unemployment and protested the abolition of tax exemption for those who took out private health insurance and proposed to replace it with a tax on smoking (while the government had been defeated in parliament on the idea of increasing taxes on alcohol), but, in fact, it was unable to oppose an alternative to the government of Kevin Rudd and then Julia Gillard, who succeeded Kevin Rudd to be, then, ousted by him a few months before the September 2013 elections.

In short, politics is a personal struggle all over the world… Naturally, the conservatives won the elections and sought a dangerous rapprochement with China without caution and without limits, putting the very existence of the nation at risk. The inevitable, and already minutely predicted, was the tightening of measures, already very severe, on immigration. These heavily affected especially the potential well-qualified immigrants, to defend the job market of those who were already working in these sectors in Australia. The qualifying element of the situation, however, was not and is not only the predisposition of these measures to face the crisis. Essential was the concurrent prediction, stated in a truly explosive white paper, published by the Australian Ministry of Defense in the last years of Julia Gillard's Labor government. In this substantial and very detailed study, carried out with impressive scientific seriousness, it was argued that from the year 2009—the year of publication—and until 2030, a good 25 billion dollars a year would be needed to rearm Australia, in the face of the Chinese military threat, as Kevin Rudd (former Labor Prime Minister), who had a long diplomatic career and spoke excellent Chinese, had already stated. China was indicated as a power determined not to limit its territorial ambitions to Taiwan alone. Taiwan, which Australia already considered part of current China, supporting the thesis, in the diplomatic arena, of the existence of a single China. The publication of the white paper (which was taken up again in 2016 and 2020) shocked public opinion not only in Oceania, where reflection on Chinese influence has been ongoing for years. Consider the fact that the Fiji Islands, where a military dictatorship is in place, have long been the subject of massive investments and attention from China, as is the case in all the islands of the Oceanic archipelago. But, I was saying, the publication of the white paper shocked all Asian diplomacies, reigniting a debate that seemed to have been overcome for years and whose echoes have reached Europe very lightly (also in the USA, for that matter). A debate that had and has at its center what we should expect from China's growth as a great power that aspires to a role not only regional, but global, even if it does not yet absolutely have the means. The first warning of the resumption of the debate, moreover, occurred on the occasion of the deployment of naval forces that in December 2018 and then—in the midst of the pandemic—in March 2020, China proudly and with great "clangor of trumpets" made manifest, before the whole world, with parades worthy of the Middle Empire and typical, as was once the case with the USSR, of a great power with hegemonic global aspirations. The demographic power of China is combined with the manifestation of what is the true nature of that regime: a military dictatorship that is not afraid to reveal itself. And that holds, however, and that in this is different from all other dictatorships in history, a very powerful force within it: the creative growth, often carefully managed, of new middle classes and new forms of political integration that continuously compensate for the serious social cohesion problems that inequality causes, starting from the countryside and the medium-sized industrial cities [120]. On the international level, however, China behaves like a dictatorial-military state, exporting forced labor and state capital in a composite nexus between state monopolistic capitalism and a return to the apology of territorial dominance with settlement colonies. For this reason, dissent and adversity against its behaviors are growing primarily in Asia and Africa, where it has most strongly settled. And now it is also growing from the antipodal Australian point, which nevertheless has a different relationship with China than any other part of the globe. From this point of view, the trip that Hillary Clinton made to Beijing in September 2009, the first trip after her appointment as US Secretary of State, to meet President Hu Jintao and which centered on disputes over borders in the Asia–Pacific region, Syria and Iranian and North Korean nuclear issues, was seen by Asia and *primarily* by Australia as an act of unforgivable weakness.

China cannot rid itself of the burden of US public debt because it is this burden that allows it to survive in the crisis and is, moreover, a component of only 4% of US debt. Consider, for example, that the Chinese dragon cannot feed its people without cooperating to create a modern industry that it does not currently possess and that only the capitalist West can give it.

And from Australia and New Zealand, this is seen every day: you do not compete with China, you work with, for, and in China.

In the face of Chinese power, the crisis from which the US is far from being able to free itself looms worryingly.

Obama already had to face, during his presidencies, a very difficult situation. The ongoing economic depression played a decisive role in his second victory.

And a decisive role must now be played by the industrial and agricultural forces of the North American giant.

It is a very precise message that comes from the antipodal point and that pierces the same optics of ethnocentrism and geostrategic North Americanism.

It is necessary to build a new world order to face the unstable and uncertain, in its aims, Chinese growth.

In fact, the US will be able to face the challenges that both the economic crisis and the emergence of China clearly outline in the global horizon, only if they re-establish strong ties with Russia and Oceania, as well as with India, as they have already tried to do.

It is not a paradox: the global recovery of the economy can only come from the recovery of the North American economy in a framework of cooperation with that Russia that is slowly emerging from the collapse of the USSR, and with the medium oceanic powers, as well as with Japan and India. This is why international cooperation for a new world order that points on the oceanic compass to describe a horizon of growth in Southeast Asia and not only in Oceania is the decisive challenge that awaits the whole world. Europe will have to understand that it must, in the face of this scenario, find a unity that now seems impossible, with the ever-increasing divisions, instead, between France, Germany, and the United Kingdom.

An important lesson, compared to the international disorder we have described so far, comes from the global fossil hydrocarbon industry.

Until about the mid-seventies of the twentieth century, the US was the largest producer and consumer of oil in the world. A unique case of energy self-sufficiency, considering the fact that until that time gas did not have the extraordinary importance that it has assumed today. But for most Western countries, that oil self-sufficiency did not exist. All nations had to seek oil, the *oil*, as we called it when we were young, outside their borders. The *oil* is extracted like gas from the bowels of the earth and is transported and refined from Borneo to London, from the Arctic to Amsterdam and Rome.

The gas industry is a global oligopoly that lives on cooperation between nations: I can transport it in various forms only if I can buy it from the nations that own it and only if they decide to sell it to me when such sale does not harm their power interests. Sure: it's a matter of price. Today there are fewer refineries than thirty years ago, yet there are two giants, China and India (where all new refineries operate for environmental law reasons), which are huge consumers and very poor producers—and an *over supply* of gas is forming at a global level, with consequences that can be unforeseen given the coincidence of this technological revolution with the global recession. Obama's decision to allow the export of *oil* and gas extracted with *shale* techniques in 2014 reflected the crisis in which the US is still immersed from a manufacturing point of view, not in services, with heavy consequences on the European gas market, as well as on the Asian one.

Investments are communicating vessels. If there is no communication, prices rise. If the vessels communicate thanks to investments, prices fall.

The *shale gas* has stimulated immense investments, building from scratch a global gas industry different from the one of the past, even causing deep divisions within OPEC itself between the Saudis and everyone else. (They argue about *oil*, but problems will also arise on the non-OPEC gas front...).

The world today is turning its peristaltic axis even more towards cooperation in the global gas industry.

The *shale gas* and the *shale oil* will last the space of a morning. The world's *reservoirs* remain in the Greater Middle East and Oceania.

And this despite the fact that globalization is changing pace. It is no longer that linear and contradiction-free path that was glimpsed after the fall of the Soviet empire, the quiet emergence of China as a counterweight power as imagined by Kissinger, and the unfolding of the market which could not have missed the construction of democracies where the market itself needed them most. That is, in the Gulf States, in those of Central Asia, imitating the (presumed) achieved democratic and economic stability of Latin America.

However, everything has gone and is going differently: the market does unfold, but among a thousand faults and cracks, and the forgotten theory of Seymour Martin Lipset and Steve Rokkan [121] on the *cleavages* that the whole world suffered and suffers in the processes of change comes to light with unusual power. First it was terrorism: today it is still the latter, but it takes a quasi-state form and is located in a fault that risks dividing the world in the area of crisis with the highest disintegrative intensity [122].

Where the densest fossil hydrocarbon energy reserves on the planet reside.

A fault that runs splitting North Africa in two and reaches as far as the Persian Gulf and risks disintegrating the Middle East and Central Asia like a taut and cutting cloth. At one end of it is Saudi Arabia and its Sunni-Wahhabi hegemony threatened by Qatar and, at the other end, Iran and its Shiite ideology: both leopard-spotted, divide, jagged, oppose all the Gulf States, the Middle East, from Lebanon to Persia.

Syria has violently disintegrated, like Libya, and these faults risk swallowing up the Hashemite monarchy that reigns over Jordan [123], as well as exacerbating the never dormant inter-confessional conflicts in Iraq and Lebanon (in a very deep socio-economic crisis), naturally also threatening Israel.

Jordan and Morocco are the "sacred bodies", along with Saudi Arabia, of a world that relies on very delicate balances. They have been reproduced not only by the stabilizing role of Syria, but also by the decisive one of the Egyptian military (Egypt, as it was said, is the Germany of North-Saharan Africa). This was eloquently demonstrated by the unfolding of the political crisis from the mass mobilization of young middle classes in future abstinence that had impersonated the scene from the "Arab revolt" after 2011.

The Libyan crisis is an indirect consequence of this general process, with evident distinctiveness for the failed *State and nation-building* of that tribal aggregate dominated for fifty years in a Bonapartist manner by Gaddafi after the armed downfall of the Senussi monarchy [124].

A tribal balance in full disintegration that has not yet been restored and that only the return of the USA to the Mediterranean with an anti-Russian and anti-Turkish military deterrent (with indispensable French consent) will be able to contain, preventing the first North African war a few kilometers from the European "Kantian peace".

In fact, this crisis stems from the aggressive Anglo-French pact that destroyed Gaddafi's Libya, a pact that was the preview of the military and strategic evolution of a strategy not European, but diplomatic with strong neo-national characteristics of alliance in the fight for control of the real object of future contention: sub-Saharan Africa outside of any consensus or collaboration with the USA. And this while all of Africa was moving towards disintegration.

The Great Lakes region is Conrad's heart of darkness and the energetic, nutritional, and industrial heart of the future. Surrounded by the states that crown the new Congo after the "first world war in Africa" [125] fought precisely to redefine post-colonially the Great Lakes region, the Congolese question will become the question of the future and the conflict with a China already very active and with penetration strategies very different from those colonial of the past and post-colonial of today will have to be contained and for this reason the topic must be studied carefully.

Yet, despite the ongoing institutional disintegration, the next fifty years of world economic history will be the story of the emergence of black Africa: whoever will exercise with the Africans the dominion over those lands, will dominate the world.

Mali is an ancient French colony, independent since 1960, which boasts an ancient imperial tradition and a cultural development among the most remarkable in sub-Saharan Africa. That is, of that complex of states that go from the shores of the Pacific, with Senegal, to those of the Indian Ocean, with the Horn of Africa.

In Europe, we were every day so breathless for the decisions that were gradually being made regarding the Libyan crisis, that we never remembered that in that area of the world south of Libyan Fezzan lies the largest sediment of non-ferrous minerals in the world and immense reserves of oil and gas. We forget that every movement that is created in one of these "emerging states" affects all the others.

Mali, with 15 million inhabitants—80% of whom are Sunni Muslims and the rest in fact animists—borders to the north with Algeria, to the east with Niger, to the south with Burkina Faso and Ivory Coast, to the southwest with Guinea and to the west with Senegal and Mauritania. Its strategic centrality is immediately apparent: it is the gateway to black Africa. And the anti-gate is the "Libyan" Fezzan, over whose dominion the French have always aimed. On their way, they have always found "the blue men of the desert": the Tuareg, who claim independence from Mali.

One of the reasons that determined the intervention of France in Libya was the control that through the war could have been more extensively exercised over regions like Mali and beyond.

On March 22, 2018, international correspondents announced that a military coup had been triggered by the troops of a well-armed but poorly paid army, that of Mali. An army imbued with a nationalism that smolders especially among the most numerous ethnicity, the Bambara (whose language is, along with French, effectively the national language of the country) who have been fighting the Tuareg for centuries and who consider the intervention of the central government too weak. The Tuareg want independence and have always sought the support of Algeria and effectively blackmail the mining companies operating in the area. The Tuareg were the most loyal supporters of Gaddafi, until the end. Moreover, their family and tribal network extends to Niger, a country that has played and plays a central role as a rear territory of the power of the Gaddafi tribes.

The rebels deposed President Amadou Toumani Tourè, who was holed up in the capital Bamako protected by troops loyal to him. The leaders of the revolt (among whom stood out Captain Amadou Sanogo, who called himself trained by the marines) declared they wanted the return of civilians as soon as the Tuareg revolt was crushed. After all, it is true that there was a separatist attempt, as was also emerging in Libya.

This fragmentation worries the large companies working in the region, first and foremost Randgold Resources, which is a real interstate power that had already expressed strong concerns about the fall of Gaddafi in Libya, fearing chain reactions among the different ethnicities and tribal powers south of Libya itself. A prophecy that came true. Naturally, the neighboring states united in an interstate association without intervention powers—Ecowas—and the European Union, whose ineffectiveness is glaring, confirmed their support for the deposed president, who resolved the military situation in his favor.

However, the unresolved question remains: How to stabilize an area that risks, once Gaddafi's power is over, exploding among a thousand fragmented identity realities, all the way down to Congo, where not by chance fighting has resumed on the borders of Rwanda?

It seems that a pile of bricks once held together by the autocratic but non-Islamist regimes of North Africa, with the collapse of Libya, is slowly decomposing, dragging into decomposition the power systems that had stabilized after the "war of the great lakes" that ten years ago had brought peace and "normality" to the new Congo. Also in these cases, as in Iraq and Afghanistan, armed intervention proves to be the harbinger of serious unforeseen consequences, deluding all those who think that resorting to arms solves every problem.

Let's go back to Mali: it borders Niger, and Niger [126], since the end of the ancient Swasi empire, on the borders with the Boer state, and in its dissolution due to the action of the large mining corporations, is the gateway to what remains, divided, tormented, marked by new conflicts, of the great former Belgian Congo. The disintegration of Libya, with the sinking of Fezzan and Sinai into chaos due to the fall of Gaddafi and the replacement of Mubarak's military with the Muslim Brotherhood, has caused entropy and disorder to spread like an oil stain beyond the borders of the great Saharan deserts.

It seems to me like reading the sublime pages of Hegel on the construction of European states, a construction that appeared to the great philosopher, at the beginning of the nineteenth century, uncertain and very difficult.

Imagine Africa, you might say.

And you will also say: Is there nothing new, then?

There is a lot new, instead.

The delicate formation of new African states is now threatened by a formidable enemy without a state, that is, without borders. I am talking about the new imperial project supported by currents of radical Islamism, which surpasses everything with advanced technologies and a supranational geostrategic vision unknown to Africa for the last two centuries. Those who fight the infidels who have destroyed Gaddafi's Libya and who risk spreading if Alawite Syria ever falls are now the supporters of a new post-colonial African imperial regime: they are the radical Islamists, Salafists, and jihadists of various sects, who, if Mali were occupied, would expand more rapidly both to the west, towards Algeria and Niger, and to the south, towards Burkina Faso and Nigeria and then, from there, the Congo.

The stake is the control by a new—in fact—Islamic caliphate of Central Africa of the energy resources of the entire continent.

With China that has not yet decided who to side with. The attack in 2011 on the oil facilities shared by BP (British), Statoil (Norwegian), and Sonatrach (Algerian) was not at all or not only a retaliation against the Algerian decision to allow French planes to fly over the territory of the Republic, but a precise symbolic action of neo-Islamist claim of African energy resources. With the rise of armed political Islamism, everything changes, in fact. The Europeans have noticed it, even if rightly in a low voice. Even Germany, always so hostile to military commitment, in this case did not hesitate to side with France, which has a very long experience of war in the African heart. The energy resources of the African colossus are rightly seen as the heart of growth; indeed, I say, of future survival. An era is over. Today, post-colonial African politics cannot be conducted as it once was, by intertwining ties with dominant African groups. Today even the power of neo-clan and post-tribal organizations is challenged by a geostrategic and political actor that until now in Africa we had never known: radical political Islamism that does not limit itself to territorial control (Somalia, Sudan, etc.), but aspires to a supranational neo-caliphate dominion that disrupts the very fragile interstate relations that in Africa in the last two decades have been laboriously built.

It is, therefore, a battle that must be fought with different strategies, without being able to exclude war, armed struggle, as the French and Anglo-Saxons have long understood under false pretenses (the owl states of Rwanda and Burundi from which the attacks on Kabila's Congo start). The great faults of history between the Mediterranean, the Persian Gulf, and the Indian Ocean have always been decided by the meeting or clash, as harsh as ever, between the three great civilizations that have dominated those lands for centuries: the Arab, the Persian, and the Turkish. Only the collapse of the Ottoman Empire obscured this truth, with the treaties already stipulated during the First World War that gave birth to a set of states with no relation to ethnicity or history. States without a nation, that's the Arab problem. And, on the other hand, nations with strong states and built by modernizing elites: this is the secret of the Persian tradition and the Turkish invention. But this balance could only hold because between the two world wars too much was involved in Europe in building the bases for the destruction of Versailles, including the Kurdish state built on paper at Sèvres and destroyed by the same Kurdish factions in a couple of years. In the immediate post-war period, the construction of the two bulwarks to Stalinism was carried out: to the east, Saudi Arabia, a North American construction between tribalism and the sacred dominion of religious tradition; to the west, Egypt, which after the tear pursued with clamor by the US against post-colonialism aimed at the conquest of the nationalized Suez Canal, will be, with Sadat, the faithful guardian of North African Atlanticism, once British hegemony in the Mediterranean was over.

All unified strategically, even from opposite fronts, in a single strategic thought, in short, and not made divisive, as most think, by the Cold War.

Indeed, this gave meaning to Turkey's role as NATO's southern flank and allowed for a balance of power to be established in Syria as well.

And the old Hafiz al-Asad, a great political and military leader, a high-ranking Baathist and Alawite, president of Syria from 1971 until his death in 2000, did it magnificently.

I had the opportunity to meet him and he impressed me for life. Thanks to the Alawites, "created" by France and strongly supported by the USSR and the Christian Churches in order to moderate Baathist extremism, a state backbone could be formed in Syria which, as we understood after the end of the USSR and the destruction of secular nationalist alternatives to both Westernism and communism, unfortunately overflowed into a sort of localistic neo-imperialism that reached its peak in the Iran-Iraq conflict for a good ten years. The fall of the Shah in Iran and even earlier the unfortunate fall of Muhammad Mossadegh (who tried to nationalize Iranian oil by expelling the British from the area) due to a poorly conceived and foolish Anglo-American coup, paved the way, years later, for a theocratic regime unlike anything ever seen in Iran or the entire Arab and Turkic world.

In this context, in my opinion, neo-Islamist terrorism with a jihadist matrix challenges what was the great turning point that matured at the turn of the nineties in the international horizon.

As globalization opened financial markets to the tragic absence of regulation, the abandonment of the firmly Westphalian Kissinger perspective opened the way for a series of military adventures without strategic thought.

These have been the black hole of international disorder for the last thirty years.

A hasty, episodic, and sectarian reading of Leo Strauss, who knew everything about the Bible but nothing about Machiavelli [127] (Hegel's pages against Frederick II, critic of Machiavelli, come to mind, if tragedy did not turn into farce), did the rest. But as the absence of regulation triggered the most terrible financial crisis of the last three centuries (only Hyman Minsky [128] foresaw it), the intellectual and then diplomatic overcoming of Westphalian conceptions in foreign policy burst onto the world stage, unbalancing all the mechanisms of weight and relevance that had built the world order according to Kissinger's strategy of global trilateralism: China, USSR, and USA.

Europe, from this design, had always remained absent because the Adenauer and Gaullist project had never materialized and the efforts of Mitterrand and Kohl to follow up on the 1963 Elysée Treaty had dried up when it inevitably had to face the role of the *force de frappe* nuclear, in the actual absence of the English interlocutor capable of balancing with France the preponderant weight of Germany in a Europe then dominated by the Cold War. Then people started wanting to have people vote who had never voted according to territorial representation, but always according to lineage, strength, the disorder they artfully provoked and then declared themselves winners and rose to leaders, or through corporate power rather than personal.

And so it began, also in Ukraine and Georgia, springs… springs to illustrate which would require the pen of Alberto Arbasino or the *cartoonists* of the *New Yorker*, so cloying and fake… except then they do not become tragic and dramatic when a young man, harassed and humiliated, sets himself on fire and the prairie blazes with fury…

What has been happening in Africa over the last thirty years, first in the North and then gradually down to Black Africa, is primarily the result of a failure to stabilize transatlantic relations between Europe and Russia. A Russia, let's not forget, that, after the collapse of the USSR, was humiliated, strategically isolated between Europe—with missiles pointed and the stubborn liberalist anti-Gazprom policy on one side—and the aggressive and increasingly armed China on the other side of the Urals.

The Gaullist ideal of a Europe from the Atlantic to the Urals was the only international counterweight to oppose what has now become, without Europe and without non-communist Russia, the loneliness of the USA in a global situation that sees the great North American nation leaning towards its Asian destiny or rather its Pacific destiny (in the *Pacific Realm*) [129].

But it must—despite the fact that it is the world's leading energy power in 2020—still linger to guarantee the essential energy sources to its grudging, tired, non-belligerent European ally.

France has grasped the problem; it still has what is necessary today: an imperial mentality, a culture! From this point of view, the collapse of Egypt dominated by the *clique* of Mubarak was a disastrous event. Only the foolishness and ignorance of an *intelligence* now devoid of the outstanding intellectual characteristics it once possessed, could think that Morsi's Muslim Brotherhood could replace Mubarak, with Russia no longer among the strategic allies not of Egypt but of the stability of the area.

No: Russia had to be humiliated and weakened in Syria, a Russia weakened and humiliated by American mistakes. Russia, which suffers from a strategic isolation that prevents it from exercising that role of moderation and of *intelligence* and mediation that it has always exercised, once British hegemony in the Mediterranean ended, replaced by that of the USA.

The role of the USSR was decisive for the maintenance of the balances of the Mediterranean and all of Africa, even though the bloody wars for the domination of Congo that involved the Cubans and that kept, in any case, Islamist extremism at bay. Once the USSR collapsed, the humiliation of Russia and its strategic isolation emerged, identified by Sergey

Karaganov as the *pivot* to understand post-Soviet Russian geopolitical behaviour [130], the USA embraced the dictates of post-Westphalian democratic interventionism which proved disastrous, even more amplified and dilated by the monstrous events of September 11th (it was the only response not possible but intellectually conceivable by an American mind, Allan Bloom would have said [131], which had already tragically closed…).

What still interests Russia today is to be able to reach the warm seas steadily, thus preserving its Mediterranean base of Tartessos, in Syria, and therefore be able to sell its gas and its *oil* without which its economy does not exist and simultaneously exercise its historical role of pressure on the warm seas of the Atlantic Mediterranean lake.

If it is threatened, the entire global balance is in danger. North Africa has been and is the first test bench of this imbalance of power relations that has led the USA to an illusion of self-sufficiency and strategic and military omnipotence together.

Today, Russia's strategic solitude prevents any containment of the aggressive impulses of all medium-range regional powers: they can now exercise a role superior to their possible one, but allowed by a strategy of containment of the ever precarious disintegration of the North and Central African area. Consider Turkey, which pursues neo-Ottoman imperialist designs and endangers the military pact with Israel that was one of the archetypal strengths of the area's balance, which began with that pact, continued with the stabilizing role of Syria, continued again with the neutralization of the Palestinians thanks to the role of the Hashemite monarchy's gendarme in Jordan, and finally ended in Egypt with Mubarak's ironclad armed control of Sinai.

Now everything has been called into question due to the greed of military personnel who, however, prove irreplaceable. Egypt was abandoned by the USA during the time of Mubarak and Obama because it was believed that the absence of the USSR could allow a changing of the guard between the greedy Mubarakians and the normalized Muslim Brotherhood who could succeed the military in power without affecting Egyptian secularism.

This meant not understanding anything about the transformations of the symbolic Islamic continent.

The Muslim Brotherhood has a rich tradition of ingenuity, patience, cunning tactics, which had its test bench in a Jordan [132] that made them fit for an operation of penetration into institutions without losing their character as a mass movement—and like all mass movements, they retain a great variety of articulations, of political souls within them. And they also retain that ability, as the works of Gérald Bronner [133] teach us, to be open to discussion, elaboration, implementation, and terrible enactment of the most extreme theses, precisely because they are not the dispossessed, the Muslim Brotherhood like the Salafists, like the jihadists; they are not the hungry of the earth as the third world rhetoric never dead in today's world claims, but refined intellectuals, technicians, experts, entrepreneurs, professionals, builders of multi-faced networks, as the experience of Bin Laden shows. The fall of Gaddafi and Mubarak has shifted the geostrategic power balances in Africa downwards. If Assad had fallen, it would have been an incalculable disaster for the ensuing proliferation of warfare and terrorism, since entire areas of the country were already controlled by jihadist groups. Far from springs: they would have been horrific winters... There are weapons, trained troops like the Tuareg, interracial conflicts, inter-European conflicts (just think of the conflict around the Great Lakes between the French and the English and North Americans). There are attempts at coups in Eritrea and Ethiopia and troop movements, armies that only have the name of an army and that must be supported, armed, directed by European and North American powers. In Africa, going on the ground is then essential. There is no room for any Rumsfeld doctrine. The supranational design of the jihadists and the Salafists and the increasingly enigmatic and mysterious role of Saudi Arabia, willing to do anything—let's not forget—to destroy Iran and eradicate Shiism everywhere, raise disturbing questions about the future.

We must return to the Peace of Westphalia intervening only in case of attack on the energy sources that are everyone's heritage regardless of ownership. It is the only possible "rational" strategy and must be pursued thanks to an agreement between the African Union, Europe, Russia, the USA, and China (a silent but always present interlocutor who has not yet revealed his cards). This can be done by creating a technologically advanced rapid intervention force equipped with sophisticated *intelligence*—or the risk is to chase the proliferation of an infinity of local wars and genocides like those between the Hutu and Tutsi that are already about to ignite in many areas of the continent.

This is in a context where the North American decline is not as inevitable as some think, but is transparent and more visible than before due to the economic crisis and the strategic uncertainties of that great power that must once again choose at any cost to position itself as the leader of the West. Of course: it lacks that European transatlantic relationship that is essential to guarantee world order. The USA must find another strategic pillar to align with itself: Europe can no longer be it in a unified way. Hence the importance of the contrasting confrontation with China and the strategic alliance with emerging countries that want to continue on the virtuous path of growth.

In the global context, the USA still has to delay to guarantee the multiple bases of power indispensable to their grudging, tired, non-belligerent European ally, incapable of finding itself and building a self-sufficient military force that can guarantee security, not peace which doesn't mean anything, on the southern flank of NATO and in North Africa.

Until when will the USA continue to play that role, which extends to the Mediterranean and Israel, protecting that astonishing North American-Sunni institutional-tribal construction that is Saudi Arabia?

Here is the most dramatic of those questions that strategic reflection poses to us today.

Thinking about contemporary growth on a global scale as a convergent process was, in fact, first of all an essential element of a geostrategic approach to world history.

Here is the decisive point.

We have asked ourselves what were the factors that determined, starting essentially from the middle of the twentieth century, a global trend in labor productivity, trade, lifestyles that gradually became not so much homogeneous as increasingly intense starting from the periphery to reach the center.

Moreover, this interpretive model was a reflection of what led David Ricardo to question decreasing returns and how to curb this decrease by gradually expanding the new cultivated lands.

This model had been transposed from England to Europe when the "peaceful conquest" (to use Pollard's words) [134] of industrialization had crossed the Channel and had come to mark like a leopard's spots the three Europes: the Scandinavian, the continental, and the southern [135]. Across the ocean, the United States had made a transition to indigenous industrialization, generating a very specific and particular model that had qualified to be so convergent with the English and European one as to surpass it in wealth produced. Later, as I was saying, after the Second World War, we began to question the possible convergences of growth.

The starting point is not economic, but political: namely the 1955 Bandung Conference of non-aligned countries that sees two future territorial giants such as Egypt and India emerge among the protagonists of the same growth. The growth of regimes with monopolistic state capitalism, that is, of countries with "real socialism", was not taken into consideration except to demonize or exalt its characteristics. A process, the latter, which is repeated today with China and which will disappoint the followers of that model, which in China presents itself in a terrorist version of Asian despotism, just as it disappointed the singers of the Soviet Union. What matters in any case is to underline the fact that the emphasis was on convergence. Towards what? Towards the mixed economy of European countries and the less mixed and more market-oriented economy of the United States. It is no coincidence that this reflection on growth took place in a context of international dominance of capitalism and the military force of the Anglo-Saxon peoples: first, in history, the gunboats and flags of the United Kingdom, then the aircraft carriers and flags of the USA.

The transition from one leadership to another was, in fact, immediate, and without excessive contradictions, between those who were leaving and those who were taking the baton, except for the conflict that arose between the United Kingdom and the USA during the Egyptian campaign, when Nasser nationalized the Suez Canal: American paratroopers did not accompany the French, English, and Israeli ones, because the USA wanted to repeat the move they had made in 1945 in Saudi Arabia to the detriment of the United Kingdom, that is, to exchange military support for a certain and long-lasting energy supply. Egypt, more than energy, provided the bulwark in defense of American hegemony over the Gulf States in order to counter the dangerous hegemonic attempt of the Soviet Union. Everything was held: military leadership, economic leadership, with Europe in an ancillary role, the process of convergence of the former colonial countries, India at the forefront, towards the Anglo-Saxon and European peaks. As Kissinger tells us in his *On China* [136], even Mao and Chou En-lai aspired to converge towards those peaks and not towards the Soviet peaks. This was already known from historiographical research, especially American: now we know it from the account of the only intellectual of the twentieth century who saw his theories realized on a global scale, which allows us to read the records of the conversations he had mainly with that giant of Chou En-lai, preserved thanks to the prodigious work of the *desk office* of the *intelligence* American who followed the greatest diplomat of the twentieth century.

For some decades now, convergent growth has shattered. The overlap of graphs has been replaced by a fractal design, that is, by variable geometries, mobile, quickly superimposable in their composition. It seems that there is no longer a peak to converge towards. Europe is undoubtedly in a fearful decline. Military, first of all, I repeat, because it has not been able to transform the Franco-German armies and those armies that surrounded them into a new European army. From this point of view, the disarmament of Germany, strongly desired especially by the Soviet Union, for obvious reasons, has been disastrous not only for the global political hegemony of Europe, but also for its economic growth which has been mutilated by that threatening, but formidable propulsive force that for centuries and centuries, even before national unification, was the German army. Moreover, those, who are old enough to have belonged to the time when good readings counted for the formation of the person, will remember that the thesis of Otto Brunner in that masterpiece which is *Land and Power* [137] is that it was the formidable intertwining of military force and feudal land ownership that laid the foundations especially of Prussian power, but also of the most powerful pre-unitary German states. It could be said that without a German army, whether we like it or not, Europe has lost all global influence. We have not even been able to try to transform the poisonous volition towards the Fourth Reich into a harmonious and united continental army that perhaps would have delayed the European decline on a planetary scale, which not by chance has become irreversible after the Second World War. I have always considered it symbolic that the only armed forces that did not withdraw either from Berlin or from Germany in the fifties, as the French and English did, were the Soviet and American ones. North America began its global deployment in hegemonic forms also in Asia, even here with the disarmament of Japan, despite the tremendous threat of the Chinese communist revolution. To fight in the Korean War were not the Japanese or the Europeans, in fact, but only the Anglophone soldiers, Americans *in primis*. Of course, this military decline has been masked for decades by the creation of NATO, but it was more of a diplomatic operation than a military one, as was made clear by the war in Libya: the intervention of the USA was decisive and that of the French, English, Italian armies, only ancillary. This military dominance is being redefined.

What has changed is something deeper than the economy. It is the capacity for strategic direction and hegemony: the Gulf-North African wars are a clear demonstration of this. This is the real danger that the West and therefore the entire world face: menacingly.

After the failed Congress of Vienna, which needed to be done and was not done following the fall of the USSR, the international system slowly began to disintegrate, inexorably.

The reason? The reason lies in the fact that the United States believed they could dominate the world alone, with a unipolarism destined for defeat from the start. The defeat was certain from several perspectives, and I will try to list them briefly.

Financial deregulation, caused by the ideological and practical capture of the European and North American socialist international (the Blair and Clinton families) by the financial oligopoly, had laid the foundations for increasing instability of markets and large *corporations*, threatening the compulsive power of national states. To this was added, here is the second variable, the weakening of the sixty-year pact between the USA and Saudi Arabia, determined by the weakness of that unipolarism and therefore by the fall of hegemony in the complex of world energy power. The Saudi system could not withstand this fall and released the Salafist variants of Wahhabism, up to Bin Laden of September 11, 2001.

A new protagonist of the international system was looming on the horizon and, not by chance, had made his general rehearsals within the USA itself, engaged in battles against the Red Army in Afghanistan, arming the Taliban with those deadly weapons that would then turn against the Americans.

The latter would respond with a further disintegrating factor, declaring war, a war fought on the ground, on this terrorism, culturally favored by Saddam Hussein's aggression against Kuwait.

The latter caused not only the fall of one of the historical leaders of Middle Eastern Baathism, but also the physical and institutional destruction of his armed forces and his police, which, when Obama later unleashed the Arab springs in his neo-Wilsonian democratist, would be ready to provide the international armed army to jihadism. The same happened in Iraq in 2003, let's not forget.

Another factor of disintegration, which has occupied the world arena with unexpected speed, has been the growth of a new and renewed Maoism in China, with the unprecedented aggressive protagonism of China on a global scale, well beyond its South Sea.

A further factor of disintegration emanated and emanates from Europe.

The US unipolarist illusion was accompanied, in fact, by that of a new Germany's globalist one. It had unified due to the end of the European civil war and had overturned Adenauer's design to unify Europe first, defeat European communism, and only then unify Germany.

Germany was unified, instead, in the system of European states weakened by the subtraction of sovereignty carried out by the European Union, a subtraction of sovereignty that multiplied exponentially with the euro and a ECB that in fact were and are a disguised mark and Bundesbank. But German power and Chinese aggression, combined with great deflation and low growth, which followed the recession of 2007–2017, broke the charm of unipolarism.

Trump's victory in the US in 2016 was, in fact, the rejection that the American people, not its establishment, made manifest towards the rampant globalized liberalism, the exacerbated anti-Russian unipolarism, the inertia towards the Chinese threat.

There had already been a glimmer of this when the US had insisted on proposing and imposing a cosmopolitan Italian intellectual at the head of the ECB, Mario Draghi, so as to be able to counter, at least on the monetary level, the *Ordo-liberalismus*.

But if everything was not useless from the financial system's point of view, it was from the international one.

Germany slowly disintegrates and devours all of Europe, and the USA cannot allow this, but, nonetheless, they cannot stop its disintegrative force. What England once did for the balance of European power, the USA should now do, constantly and anxiously seeking to strengthen the economic base and strategic objectives of NATO as long as they continue to consider Russia a dangerous power, while, in fact, it is not.

On the contrary, it is the only force that, with the USA, can counter the threat to the very life of the world embodied in China and its culture.

The French developed from the mid-nineteenth century, with the Restoration, the same effort to rebalance anti-German power from Sedan to Versailles, from de Gaulle to Macron.

On the contrary, Italy—or rather the Italians—continues to be what it has been for centuries, excluding naturally the Savoy state: a land of dominion, in the last seventy years, first to a greater degree of North American and English influence and then, after the creation of the European Economic Union, primarily Franco-German. The Spanish, having lost, with the defeat of Cuba at the end of the nineteenth century, any domination over the world, also lost it in Italy.

If we add to all this that from this disintegration of the international order—which begins in Europe but cannot end in it—the only Eurasian power in the world, namely Russia, could not fail to emerge, we understand that the disintegrative trends continue, thanks to the non-collaboration between the USA and Russia, while, thanks to this resurrection, they could, instead, find a barrier.

Why? Because Russia is forced to deal with the *Heartland* and the *Rimland*, namely those lands that flow, precisely, onto the seas of the Pacific and the Mediterranean—Atlantic lake—from which the world is dominated, if we add to this the domination of the Congo, Conrad's heart of darkness, and the next stage of the global power struggle.

It is well understood, then, how the only way to oppose international disintegration could be a new global power pact between the USA and Russia.

This does not happen mainly for two important reasons. The first is the fight that the financial and intellectual-democratic establishment has unleashed against Trump and his providential selective anti-Chinese neo-protectionism, choosing as the battlefield the continuity of the fight against Russia, inaugurated by the Clintons, both anti-Russian and anti-German.

The second reason is the disintegration that Germany is causing in Europe, destroying its cohesion, aided in this by France which continues to be the worst enemy of a strengthening of NATO in Europe.

Turkey under Erdoğan has well noticed this and it is no coincidence that the first two European states to suffer the consequences were Greece and Italy, with the pre-invasion of the Aegean and Libya by Turkey and the fight against Eni and Total in the disputed and never pacified Cypriot waters.

The Russians, for their part, support North Korea, but in such a way that the Korean farce can become a tragedy, with Putin's display of nuclear muscles.

It is an illusion to believe that stabilization can occur technocratically in a polyarchy like the European one that continuously fuels the mirror game of democratic legitimation, electing an institution that only appears to be a parliament, because it is not equipped with legislative compulsion.

The geopolitical foundation of Europe is the concrete historical Franco-German relationship.

It has been almost more than fifty-five years since the signing, on January 22, 1963, of the Franco-German treaty, signed by two countries that were stunned by the end of the Second World War. France, with the defeat of Hitler, Mussolini, and Hirohito, regained its institutional unity that it had dramatically lost with Pétain's betrayal and the Vichy regime.

Because this is what it was about, not just a military defeat of dramatic dimensions, but also a shocking cultural surrender: it was the values of the French Revolution that had been shattered, and with them a wound had opened that, like the events in Algeria, was removed, but instead deeply marked French history.

The fate of Germany was entirely different: it was divided among the victors and even when, already at the end of the 1940s, the possibility of a pacification between the two dominant cultures of Europe began to emerge, well, the wounds of division were very deep.

It was in the midst of, after all, the European civil war that made the historical situation of the humanistic heart of the whole world very complicated and still little understood, that is, of that complex of nations from which the Holy Roman Empire sprang with Charlemagne, and which only the eighteenth-century Spanish succession wars led to a real disintegration.

A disintegration in which we still live today and which the European Union has only scratched, but has absolutely not managed to overcome the fractures created after the fall of the Austro-Hungarian, Tsarist, and Ottoman empires, which occurred following the First World War.

Moreover, the European civil war did not allow to overcome the centuries-old Franco-German divisions.

Yet the Soviet Union was not just a military threat against the democracies that the bourgeoisie and the workers' movements had built since the second half of the nineteenth century, along with an England that looked at the continent with a detached air.

That continent that institutionally detached itself by deciding to apply the Napoleonic Code in that intertwining of love for England and fear of a Prussia loved but always feared, as the tutelary deity of constitutionalism, Benjamin Constant [138], shows us.

The Soviet Union was also an alternative to the capitalist regime of property, and Stalin's brutality, in the years after Yalta, with the defenestration of Beneš and then the repression of German workers in '53, of intellectuals and Hungarian workers in '56, and again of intellectuals and Czechoslovak workers in '68, showed that weapons and bureaucratic dictatorship defended not only a political regime, but also a property structure, a civil society totally alternative to the European and North American one.

France and West Germany (i.e., what remained of Germany and looked to the West) were obliged to cooperate, to collaborate, to hinder the expansion of a property regime that governed the vast majority of the Euro-Asian territory.

Yet, as early as 1954, the failure of the European Defense Community (EDC) advocated, before the advent of de Gaulle, by France to dilute in an integrated European army what was still feared: the rearmament of Germany.

Everything was resolved with the integration of West Germany into NATO so that, with a united France and again aware of its destiny, it gradually began to consider Germany a possible strategic partner, so as to increase its competitive advantage, from the French side, both towards the USA, and especially towards the United Kingdom.

Studies show that France's interest in other European states was what it is today: always very weak, with the exception of Italy, not only and not so much because it, along with Germany, was the site of important NATO bases, but because of its geographical location, combined with its economic power, made it a land of conquest, both for its national potential and for its African presence, as Cavour had very well understood and as all Italians have recently had reason to rediscover with the Libyan events, and even more recently, with those of Niger.

The 1963 Treaty was an important step forward in overcoming historical differences, but it did not mark the beginning of a true form of collaboration between the two nations. And this is because, even in the presence of the feared Russian bear, the Franco-German attitude towards the USA, which effectively kept the bear chained, was very different.

De Gaulle, who had already in 1958, just ascended to the presidency of the Republic, obstructed the entry of the United Kingdom into the European Economic Community, pursued with determination a neo-imperial design: Europe from the Atlantic to the Urals, convinced that, more than military deterrence and dominance, the bear could be placated with hegemony and economic cooperation, up to, not so much being able to do without NATO, but to deeply condition its strategies, directives, decisions, strong in the possession of nuclear weapons.

And the fact that the United Kingdom also possessed it was another good reason why it should be excluded from the EEC, so as not to hinder

French dominance. Moreover, the United Kingdom, incidentally, on the economic level did not know what to do with Gaullist vetoes, as demonstrated by the existence of EFTA (UK, Commonwealth, Scandinavia and Portugal) which lasted until 1973.

The treaty that was signed in '63 at the Elysée contained measures of substantial bilateral cooperation in the fields that are much talked about today and it should be noted that in terms of defense, much more stringent decisions were envisaged, and never implemented, than those of today and of a future as envisaged in the treaty. It is worth remembering that, in the turmoil of the sought-after great German coalition, with a reluctant social democracy, precisely what was supposed to unite divided the Germans at that time. I refer to the fact that, while in France it was ratified calmly, in Germany only social democracy imposed, with its pro-Atlantic vocation, against the will of Adenauer, the so-called preamble, that is an addition in which Germany's support for NATO and the EEC was reaffirmed.

De Gaulle understood the hint and considered this social democratic proposal, which found in Ludwig Erhard, Adenauer's successor, an unconditional adherence, that this was how it was acted, in fact, to make a just signed treaty a dead letter. And in one of his emphatic dialectical exercises he pronounced the famous phrase in which it was said that if the Elysée Treaty had remained a dead letter, it would not have been a tragedy.

A totally new and totally different phase was opening up that saw Germany, rather than France, return to the center of the European destiny. And precisely on the ground of the clash-meeting with the USSR.

These were the years of the *Ostpolitik* that saw the German liberals, with Walter Scheel, write one of the highest pages of their history, together with the role played by Willy Brandt who not by chance received, for this policy, the Nobel Peace Prize in 1971.

As you can see, the situation was very different from today and we must consider whether the deep and rooted Franco-German differences can ever be overcome, especially today, when for decades the USSR has collapsed and the European civil war has ended [139].

But if there is one thing that never ends, it is geography and with it history, whatever the discipline of international relations and historiography may say and think.

And this thought is very important when US policy reveals, since the time of the Obama presidency, a distancing from Germany and a rapprochement instead with France, while the US itself continues a policy of confrontation and containment of Russia and China.

After all, Obama was already clearly stating that the new American horizon was Asia and the Pacific, and that Europe would have to solve its problems on its own.

In any case, a situation similar to that of the second half of the 1980s could not manifest itself. At that time, the growing budget deficits of the Reagan administration and the Reykjavik agreement with Gorbachev, in 1986, on the dismissal of ballistic missiles, without the European allies being consulted—thus overturning a NATO strategy pursued for years—led Kohl to show interest in new Franco-German relations as a possible alternative to NATO itself.

But even then the French did not dismiss their suspicions of Germany and conducted an absolutely unexpected policy, imposing that British and French nuclear forces be included in arms control agreements.

Naturally, it is well understood that what was announced in 1987, with great fanfare, namely the famous Franco-German brigade of about four thousand men who would not be part of the integrated command structure of NATO, was only a fig leaf that hid, in fact, the continuity of suspicions.

Just as well it was expressed in that bilateral defense and security council, based in Paris, in the official protocol of the Treaty of the Elysée in 1988, which was ratified by Kohl and Mitterrand.

With the second decade of the 2000s, we return to a situation similar to the one previously described: rather than cooperation, competition is underway.

Today the world, in economic spheres and in the political spheres of associated life, is pervaded, in fact, rather than by cooperation, by national competition: and on three fronts of stable human settlements.

The first is that of the relationship with the USA, with opposite attitudes, of positive cooperation with Trump on the part of Macron and of deep conflict on the part of Merkel.

The second is that of sub-Saharan Africa, where the French are the masters and where the Germans count almost nothing because they did not intervene in the Mesopotamian wars, still being deprived of an army.

The third is towards all of Europe and its institutions, with Macron climbing the Pyramid, while Mrs. Merkel is left without the apron.

Good Franco-German treaty! The game of mirrors will continue in a united Europe that will be increasingly divided.

But it is precisely here that the duopoly could crack: to continue with this miserable policy of the miser means to impose also on France, in the absence of competitive devaluations, only internal devaluations, lowering wages and mortifying domestic demand and, again, cutting public spending which would instead be greatly needed when some rebound is felt in the world and European economy.

From the dominant economic policy emanates effects that increase the gap between economic results and total factor productivity among the various nations.

In this regard, the statements of the European commissioners have always been truly chilling. If there are economic gaps between nations, and there are, praising the fact, as is often continued to be done, even in the post-pandemic world where forms of fake mutualization of debt and public spending are flaunted, only masks new clashes of Teutonic and Scandinavian power. Now 22 out of 24 European countries have reached the insane goal of drastically reducing public spending and this does nothing but spread deflation throughout Europe, now dominated by an ideological impulse to balance the budget, whatever the economic conditions of the individual nations: this could not and cannot but lead Europe to economic and social catastrophe.

While Europe groans under the Teutonic heel, Asia sees its geopolitical relations change.

And this is because President Trump's actions in Asia have always been a spectacle of fearful amusement. He clumsily imitates Kissinger and confuses statecraft with intimidating the opponent, disconcerting them with true illusionist moves. He arrives in Japan and in his speech does not flatter Abe and the Japanese. He accuses them of unfair trade, reminds them of the dictate imposed on them at the Plaza Hotel in 1985, when the US forced the Land of the Rising Sun to revalue the yen, plunging that great nation into a stagnation from which it has not yet recovered. This is how North American goods were defended without screams and theatrics.

The novelty is that after Trump's reprimands, Abe flew to the most infamously famous port in Vietnam to stipulate or rather continue to try to stipulate the APEC in the context of ASEAN, that is, the attempt to recreate a free trade area between Southeast Asia and the Pacific coast of South America. The same thing happened in China, where Abe was greeted with unimaginable splendor.

The problem is that everything is suspended and everything is conditioned by the threat coming from North Korea and therefore from Russia: the danger is real and therefore the stick and carrot must be used with skill.

The fact is, however, that all the parties involved act in the same way and therefore US hegemony seems only rhetoric. The test will be in the Philippines, where it will be necessary to see how Duterte behaves, always balancing between China and the US, as the Thai military, who only ended the funeral honors for a dead king two years later, understand well. And to think that Thailand was a secular ally of both the United Kingdom and Russia, as well as the US!

In short, everything is out of alignment and international instability is chronic: the only certainty comes from the US Congress, which always approves substantial increases in military spending.

The case of North Korea, with its imperfect but dangerous missiles, is exemplary: it is a good cognitive exercise to understand how international politics and the order, or disorder, that can arise under certain conditions work.

Let's get to the root causes.

The world is emerging from a design that David P. Calleo has called "mad" [140], that is, that of unipolarism deployed, without strong powers of counterbalance and contrast, as was hypothesized in substance by the US after the collapse of the USSR until the first Obama administration.

Followed by the three families that have jeopardized the greatest power in the world, the madness of thinking they could dominate the world alone on the wave of the theories of the fantastic dean of Harvard, Professor Fukuyama, for whom after the end of the empire of evil democracy would have immediately come true and with it the uncontested dominance of the US. However, alas, this design was scratched by the terrible attacks of September 11, 2001, and then unipolarism turned into a war deployed against the enemies of security and liberal principles, and it was the war in Iraq and in Afghanistan, with all the mistakes that were made.

Only the last Obama understood that if he wanted to start defusing some of the mines that the Mesopotamian war—started with the break with the Saudis and the approach to Iran—had triggered, it was necessary to rethink the entire foreign policy and then came out, then, that interview with *The Atlantic* [141] which predicted a neo-medieval form of international order with the sun of the US that revolved around the world surrounded by a series of mini-satellites that imitated its path as faithful vassals.

With the sun, the vassals would have had to divide the world, living off the light that reflected on them.

We know how it ended. With the collapse of what was an illusion, unfortunately. An illusion that should, instead, become a constantly pursued international policy.

On one hand, the division between the USA and Germany and France continues, and on the other, the emergence of Iran as a sharp crescent that stretches from the Euphrates to the Mediterranean and the advance of the Russians towards a new Eurasian power from the Mediterranean to the Pacific, confirming their power, capable of giving a definitive turn to the Mesopotamian wars in a strong alliance with Iran and Turkey, thus disintegrating the southern front of NATO.

And meanwhile, the Chinese military power advances slowly and steadily from the South China Sea to Djibouti to the Suez Canal, doubled up to Trieste and the former communist states of Europe, to end with the Anglo-British utopia of the "Anglosphere", which aspires to recreate a new Commonwealth with a strategic alliance with China.

A scenario where unipolarism has been non-existent for too long and the USA, while trying to restore the power system prior to the disasters caused by that insane political line, has been continuously tested and threatened by unexpected obstacles, like the North Korean launcher of Russian missiles, imperfect but frightening.

The design is that of the bullfight, with the *banderillas* and the horses that rotate around the bull until it goes mad, which Hemingway, in 1925, beautifully described in that beautiful novel that is *Fiesta*, where the bullfight and the bull are given so much importance while the senseless, very rich and beautiful Brett Ashley pines for love and disappointment. The USA today is the bull that the Chinese wound, humiliate, and prick thanks to the shapeless and battered *matador* lent to them by Russia, which is North Korea.

Shapeless and monstrous, but which, however, serves magnificently to the purpose because it reminds every day that you cannot govern the world alone even if you are the strongest and that—precisely because you are the strongest—you must choose one or more partners who, without being allies, exchange a controlled rivalry with the common search for a peaceful ground for growth in international peace, that is, sheltered from thermonuclear wars [142].

It is precisely this, instead, that China makes increasingly difficult, after Xi Jinping's thought has been placed alongside that of Mao and Mao's methods of internal control have been revived, with the planned assassination of unfaithful bureaucracy and the mockery of thermonuclear war that is no longer feared, but that must rather be used as a calculated threat against the main enemy, namely the USA.

Trump and the Pentagon, or rather the Pentagon and Trump following, understand that overcoming the troubles of unipolarism is only possible with a stable alliance with Russia. But it is precisely on this point that the American establishment is divided, as can be seen by following the vicissitudes of the *Russiagate*.

North Korea infuriates the bull and Trump risks ending up like Lady Brett Ashley.

In this context, the reflection of Graham Allison on the "Thucydides' Trap" [143], that is, the perverse game of challenge, response to the challenge, mutual distrust and initial aggression to prevent being attacked that leads to conflicts, from the Peloponnesian wars to the challenge between Russia and Japan in the China Sea and in Manchuria after the failed Congress of Vienna, which needed to be done and was not done following the fall of the USSR. The international system has slowly begun to disintegrate, inexorably.

The reason? The reason lies in the fact that today a situation similar to that after the First World War is reoccurring, with the provocation that German maritime growth threw in the face of the United Kingdom, thus triggering unnecessary repeated massacres, ending with Pearl Harbor.

Everything starts, in fact, when a dominant power already in decline sees in the emergence of another power, which is growing economically and arming itself, a challenge not only to its dominance in the world, but to its very existence. And so various forms and natures of nationalism are unleashed.

In this global dimension in which we must question neo-nationalisms, we must ask ourselves: Have global trade wars replaced military wars? It is a question that we must ask not superficially and contingently, but with the perspective of understanding the ongoing and future transformations of the power of nations and together with the large companies that shape their strategies the same States and condition the historical evolution of human settlements.

When the States involved in a trade confrontation are continents like China and the USA, the question can become dramatic and at the same time reveal the true face of history. China reacts to Trump's declarations by expanding the list of goods subject to punitive duties but at the same time makes that move that is primarily in the hands of the State: it devalues the currency. The yuan will lose value to favor Chinese exports and this is an event that truly marks a turning point. In 1985, the USA gathered at the Plaza in New York the central bankers and ministers from all over the world and forced the Japanese to revalue the yen that was devaluing and endangered American dominance over world trade. About fifteen years earlier, moreover, North America had (in 1971) ended the Bretton Woods agreements and declared that the dollar would no longer continue to replace gold as the reference currency of the international exchange system.

Quickly the USA had used the sword to make the dollar a problem for others and not for them.

The same thing China is trying to do today. It is a power challenge unheard of until a few years ago and that still needs to be studied in depth to be well understood. Perhaps it is a desperate act: the Chinese economy seems to be able to count only more on its demographic dimension, but perhaps it is an emphysema, not a state of good health. The Shanghai technological index, the Star, plunged, two years ago, into total chaos due to poor *governance* and the great Chinese entrepreneurial and financial bourgeoisie is increasingly intolerant of the dominance of the single party that despite repression, or perhaps because of this, cannot restart the economic machine.

On the other hand, the USA is a nation divided on everything, but not on China, in which the institutional pillars are wavering.

See Trump's continuous attacks on the independence of the central bank, the Fed, which saw its governor contested in a very different way from the past: with the *tweet* tearing sent to open markets and not with the muffled steps of the *soft power* as it had always been done. Moreover, Trump announced trade wars in this way too in a *stop and go* tearing. The problems, however, are real: a war is underway that, before being commercial, is a confrontation for global technological dominance and the USA absolutely cannot lose the stake at play.

China has launched the challenge not only on the commercial level but also on the military one with the strengthening of the navy (as has always happened in world history when an emerging power challenges existing balances) and with the so-called silk road which is nothing more than debt imperialism and military challenge to the entire West. The USA has a formidable weapon in response to the Chinese threat: diversify suppliers and markets primarily in an Asia that behind the Vietnamese economic miracle is redesigning all the *supply chains* not only Asian, but global. That's why China, with its tough face, is a paper tiger especially towards the USA, which is anything but an exporting power, as industrial economics applied to geography teaches us, being instead a formidable importing society based on the very stable expansion of a huge and varied domestic market. The dangers exist—instead—for Europe, which has pursued a policy of fierce protectionism against the whole world with disastrous results (an exception was the trade agreement with Mercosur, which put an end to a senseless policy towards a South America with which Europe has deep historical, cultural, and economic ties).

The only exception that has always been made was that towards China, confirming above all the anti-Atlantic vocation of the great European powers, Germany *first and foremost*, as the story of our manufacturing systems of the automobile and steel industries, which are now disarmed in the face of openings towards China, and the never really sought virtuous integration with North American manufacturing systems. The same should be said for agricultural and food industry chains.

It is important to place in this global context the issue of the confrontation between China and the USA because today world trade is increasingly a comparison and exchange between business chains and between companies, rather than between States. And it remains and will remain so despite the state monopoly on currency and taxation. That's why today the military confrontation is further away than before.

But not impossible, when technology is the object of contention. For this reason—since the control of technology is nothing more than the control and manifestation of power—world power still risks falling into the abyss of non-localized, but global, military confrontation.

For this reason, it is good not to play with power balances. We have seen what happens with stock indices and it is just a jolt. It is, therefore, good to stop and not challenge fate too much by playing with the fate of the world.

Everything is talked about in the world, after all and not by chance, not so much about the collapse of world trade, but about the need to rebuild it with new rules.

The institutional situation is also dramatic, with the crisis of the WTO, the World Trade Organization, and the disengagement from this organization by the USA, due to the conflict between the USA, EU, and China precisely on world trade.

This conflict is mainly caused by the different positions recently taken by the entire North American establishment on China, advocating a new cold war against it, while the EU, led by Germany, instead makes China the new reference point for world trade, thus exploiting the different structure of German industrial capital compared to European partners, who are thus weakened. The clear and painful proof of this division is in the drama of European steel, which is hit by low prices and the low quality of Chinese steel that bounces off American tariffs and endangers the French and Italian steel industry in the first place, increasingly threatened, when not also replaced, by Indian and Turkish competitors. They enjoy protectionism at home, while exporting abroad goods created with conditions—unimaginable elsewhere—of low wages and pollution (Ilva teaches). The resignation of the director of the WTO, the prestigious Brazilian diplomat Roberto Azevêdo—whom I have already mentioned—in 2020, was another painful consequence of this. It is a dramatic crisis.

The WTO's forecasts of a collapse in international trade between 13 and 37% in 2020, depending on the duration of the pandemic and the health policies to counter the crisis, were all the more dramatic as the production chains were located in different nations to produce and then assemble the goods.

Fortunately, the trends towards so-called *reshoring*, or the relocation of activities previously transferred abroad to national territories, was not a pandemic phenomenon, as was often superficially claimed, but had been underway for years. If this had not been the case, the consequences would have been even more dramatic and unimaginable, especially for health and food supplies.

The pandemic had only accelerated a phase change in global trade and the expanded development of capitalist accumulation. Of course, the pandemic's devastating effects of the virus on global *supply chains* and on the supply of components to manufacturing were very significant. In China, 80% of the national gross domestic product was hit by the virus. But all over the world, companies fortunately retooled to produce locally the components that they had allocated in China over the last ten years.

The relocations, decided a decade ago based on costs by US companies, for example, are no longer convenient, because what changed—well before the pandemic—was technology.

It has reduced the incidence of labor costs and proportionally increased coordination and control costs and especially the "incompleteness of contracts" very serious in a deeply corrupt society like the Chinese one. American companies have invested in new technologies and the last years of prosperous economy have helped improve conditions for territorially reallocating numerous productions. Hence a redefinition of the scenarios of world trade and especially of the large value chains that concern manufacturing and that the coronavirus has accelerated and not caused. Up until the pandemic, the major relocation processes had affected the textile, fashion, and clothing systems worldwide and in Europe in particular. They were followed, due to the pandemic, by other sectors such as medical, which the coronavirus has highlighted the role and need (especially in the USA and UK and in France) for its entrepreneurial actors to remain as close as possible to local suppliers for control costs and for the quality of the supply.

As for the *automotive*, capital goods, electronics, and metal products, their incidence on the total relocations of recent years has been about 40% and should continue. Asian markets will remain a reference from both the production and distribution points of view, despite the approaching Chinese structural crisis that will change the world again.

It is a huge process of exogenous crisis that has hit both demand and supply, the world of production and services to people and companies—both the production of machines for machines, and the production of goods for people. Companies need not only stimuli and tax relief, but, in this context, structural interventions of relocation and investments in fixed capital stock to increase the organic composition of capital and the productivity of both labor and the total system. The United States has reached the global peak of these *reshoring* interventions with a thousand "homecoming" operations from 2004 to today, creating 750,000 new total jobs and starting to recreate—after years and years of maintenance degradation—efficient infrastructures, thus raising the level of total productivity, along with investments in research and development and improvement of the quality of so-called human capital. Public incentives, in the USA, have been and are fundamental. This process has confirmed the theories of the circular economy, which place at the center the belief that delocalized productions cannot compete in quality with those coming from strong territories and well geographically located around the industries and services they supply. The international production system is based on a high productive fragmentation that originated the so-called *global value chains*. With mega-chains of companies from different nations, it has thus been revealed, not only in theory but also in practice, to be intimately fragile. Intermediate goods produced in China rose from 24% of total exports in 2002 to 32% in 2018, and if we consider that the exchange of intermediate goods always forms about 50% of world trade (which the 2008 crisis had already downsized), the decline will become increasingly significant and the growth gap between production and world trade—which is the secular foundation of the internationalization of the production of goods by means of goods on a global scale—is practically being nullified. And this is due to the slowdown in the growth rate of both the EU, afflicted by secular deflation, and China, heading towards a crisis of its already very fragile economy that will be devastating. The phenomena of relocation accentuate these processes.

Germany and the Scandinavian-Baltic nations have in fact also pursued the North American process, despite the absence of a European central bank, thanks to their low rate of internal debt. A policy that France, with its less agile industrial base and too intertwined with functionalist Colbertism, has been unable to pursue, which hinders the aforementioned transformation of the USA.

The nations that are the economic substance of the world, namely the USA, Germany, France, even China, despite being in serious political-economic crisis, but demographic power as well as India, are however moving, showing signs of change. This naturally causes intra-European contrasts, with the EU lacking a constitution and competition between nations also being unleashed in relation to world trade. Between France and Germany who fight each other with temporary alliances within Europe and between the USA and Germany, France, and Russia in the whole world. It is necessary, therefore, to rebuild as soon as possible a shared system of world trade rules to prevent the return of new crises. However, the mistakes made with the admission of China to world trade in 2001 must be overcome, while Russia was only admitted in 2011, thus encouraging its expansionist tendencies and conversely the world power of China exponentially. An indiscriminate admission, that of China, not conducted according to the rules of good *governance*.

These are the rules we need in world trade. Only diplomacy can rebuild them on new bases. Remembering, however, always, that the first rule will be to overcome the obstacle that has prevented since 1995 to today (since the WTO, the World Trade Organization, was founded) the stipulation of a multilateral trade treaty, giving rise to few plurinational treaties, such as Mercosur, for example. The cause of this is the competitive existence of three world powers that are at the same time both agricultural powers and industrial powers: the USA, France, and India. Since the time of the American civil war between the industrial North and the agricultural South, this obstacle, between potentially more protectionist farmers and potentially more free-trading industrialists, governs the fate of the global economy and at the same time hinders world free trade. We should always keep in mind that competition between industrialists and farmers, to create rules more functional to world trade.

CHAPTER 8

Here We Go Again

Here we go again this is the cry that is heard as a new international system completely different from the one that was not established after the collapse of the USSR is slowly taking shape. And this reconstruction follows, together, already well-defined paths and also paths never traveled until now and full of dangers.

For the great Mackinder [144] the historically deepest challenge in the construction of the international system was the one that had come to Mediterranean Europe from Central Asia, more precisely from what he defined as the *Heartland*, where the Eurasian masses were and are secularly concentrated. In this context, it is almost natural that Mackinder (and with him the too forgotten Nicholas Spykman) [145] help us today to embark on a new journey, at a time when the West does not yet have that American hegemonic policy again, which replaced a unified conception of international politics.

The North American unipolarity of the eighties and nineties of the twentieth century and the first two decades of the new millennium (on which David Calleo [146] has written unsurpassed pages) has, in fact, had the effect of greatly increasing the degrees of differentiation and the *cleavages* of the international system, not reducing them as the simpletons imagined by supporting precisely a unipolar system.

Imperial divisions continue to exist (*in primis* the French and English ones with respect to the dominant American narrative). And also the

G. Sapelli, *States, Markets and Wars in Global History*,
https://doi.org/10.1007/978-3-031-26716-1_8

growing divisions in that decisive plexus in world history that was and is the *Rimland*, the *inner crescent*, that is those coastal areas that surround the entire *Heartland* and which are the product of the continuous development of terrestrial spaces, rather than the result of external pressures too intermittent to mark the furrow of the field of history. These are the states of the Persian Gulf and Southeast Asia, up to those of the South China Sea.

Whoever commands the *Rimland* commands Eurasia and whoever commands Eurasia commands the world, commands the planet.

But the structure of Eurasia has tremendously changed recently, that is in the last two centuries, due to the transformation of the functional principles of geopolitical space in its mutual complementarities dictated by state settlements grown in power. China and India are the determining factors and China is the most potentially destructive (a dominion without hegemony), on par with what were Napoleonic France and Wilhelmine Germany and the Mongol-Tatar hordes, with an empire as extensive as it is fragile and brief.

And we're not talking about Nazi Germany...

According to Mackinder's theories, the three spheres of Eurasia, that is Central Europe, the Caucasus, and Central Asia, come together in a new and unprecedented—for demographic and technical intensity—space of power and possible disintegration. The atomic threat, to which only recently reference is made, with the North Korean and Iranian insurgencies, completes the alarming picture that emerges with increasing force from the depth of the world's geopolitical history.

And now let's talk about contemporary changes, taking place before our eyes.

Central Asia remains the *pivot*, but the coastal areas of both India and China contain a change of power because the interconnections that link the nodes of the international system change structure.

And this is because now the point of fall of this system moves from the central Caucasus to central Europe itself under the pressure rising from the regions of Central Asia and from powers as much maritime as terrestrial.

The role of North American power could not but change. In some ways, it was even too expected.

Here we go again! In this context, why is this cry heard everywhere in the world? The answer lies in that secret that many years ago Paul

Dibb [147] revealed by writing perhaps the most intelligent history of the USSR that has ever been written.

It demonstrated that there are great unfinished powers. And that seeking the power profile of a nation cannot be the result of applying an abstract model as happens too often in the discipline of international relations. The international system is a living system, it is not the functionalist one described by Robert Gilpin [148], but rather, the one humanistically understood by Raymond Aron [149].

And so nothing is ever mechanically written in history. It can be, mechanical, historiography; never history, fruit—in the Crocean sense—of the Spirit.

The USSR was an unfinished power because its military potential did not at all correspond to an equally solid, vast, polymorphic, economic system and it was this incompleteness that, with the Afghan war, led that nation, capitalistic-dictatorial in a monopolistic form, to its downfall.

Today this is what happens to China, but in the opposite sense: its demographic and military power does not correspond to an equally deployed economic power and this explains how its national and international history has always been characterized by continuous leaps forward, always disastrous, from the forced collectivization of the lands of the Fifties of the Twentieth Century, up to the "cultural revolution", to now reach the neo-Maoism of Xi Jinping which is the latest transformation of the Chinese social construct.

But China, unlike Russia, whether it is non-capitalistic or neo-capitalistic like today's, China cannot be, due to its weak and unstable economic weight, the protagonist of that unstable balance of power that is the very essence of the international system.

But if there is no balance of power, an international civil war between powers is unleashed, which is far worse than wars between vassals, often proxy wars: there is no middle ground.

Well. A pole that has guaranteed this absence of civil war has been that of the USA.

The USA has exported security and economic growth over the course of about forty years: those of the cold war with the USSR. The North American commitment followed the path of the clash and at the same time the unstable balance of power: it was the effect of atomic terror, of the possible nuclear war.

The game at stake was clear and had its deep reflections in Europe: the division of Germany accepted and based on the role of NATO and on

German disarmament, while the other two nuclear powers, the United Kingdom and France, pursued national power goals in a relationship always critical with the USA. A relationship that has further cracked between the USA and Germany, after the Mesopotamian wars at the beginning of the second millennium, in which the USA was left alone by Europe and after the German diesel frauds [150], which further worsened interstate relations.

Here opens a void in the international power system.

This void is inevitably covered by the USSR, because, as previously stated, Russia is the only nation able to govern the *Heartland* and to deeply influence the *Rimland*. All attempts to question this role of Russia are destined to fail. But the crucial problem is China.

With China's entry into the WTO, the world was invaded by goods with very low value content and a high rate of environmental and sustainability destruction. Deindustrialization was the inevitable consequence of this unprecedented measure dictated only by the financial and speculative interest of the stock option managers of the major investment banks.

The foundations were laid for the destruction of the same US power. The data of world trade in the US-China segment are eloquent and relentless.

China is the United States' top trading partner, with a terrible imbalance in Beijing's favor: in 2017, bilateral trade reached 636 billion dollars, with 130 billion dollars in American exports and 506 billion in imports, with a surplus of 376 billion in favor of Beijing. Trump is determined to reduce this imbalance using the argument of the threat to national security and the violation of intellectual property through massive transfers of American technologies to the Chinese warlike elites.

The European Union, meanwhile, has toyed for years with declaring or not declaring China (hear! hear!) a market economy and feared Trump's measures which were instead aimed at defending Europe itself, which gradually deprived itself of that slender selective protectionism that characterized its founding beginnings, when industrial culture prevailed over financial-speculative culture. Among the ruling classes and among the European technocracy increasingly oligarchically inclined towards a liberalism administered from the top of the procedures and far from the grassroots of healthy competition between companies, fear and anxiety spread in the face of Trump's positive neo-protectionist activism and nothing else was known to do but to pound fists and threaten retaliation, forgetting that Europe without the United States is nothing. Cooperating with the USA is better than competing in the face of Chinese aggression.

The USA started by threatening tariffs on steel. Europe screamed without ever saying what I have been saying from the beginning, namely that the danger for Europe and Italy from these tariffs stemmed from the fact that the steel that bounced against the North American tariff shields ended up in Europe, perhaps permanently damaging its industry. It is no coincidence that Indian investments have increasingly replaced Franco-German-Italian capitals in the steel industry in Europe.

It is, indeed, about the fraudulent competition of Chinese and Asian steel which Europe still does not worry about today, only asking for the EU to be exempted from North American measures!

Instead, it is time to seize the opportunity to redefine all global customs and trade policy, taking advantage of the healthy shake-up that Trump has given to an unsustainable system that leads to the actual destruction not only of industry, but of the same Western social system.

The enemy is China.

Europe must understand this before it is too late.

Xi Jinping is the resolution of an enigma. With him, China returns to what it was: a great power aimed at world domination. However, to expand globally, the country must return to the sources of national power. This is the basis of the thought of the "new Chinese emperor", in which the slogans of Liu Shaoqi are recognized more than those of Mao: the search for social legitimization of the "red bureaucracy" and strict control of the party cadres, accompanied by the development, towards the outside, of a truly global power.

The 19th Congress of the Chinese Communist Party in the fall of 2017 was an event that marks, more than any other assembly, the fate of power relations at the international level. That very long historical period that began in the middle of the fifteenth century has definitely ended, when a great Chinese navigator of Muslim origins was recalled home by a declining emperor and destroyed his ships: thus was raised that insurmountable barrier between China and the rest of the world that lasted until the nineteenth-century opium wars.

The Middle Empire surrounded by barbarians dominated for centuries the situational powers in fact enclosed in its immense lands.

The greats of international sinology, from Needham [151] to Granet [152], racked their brains for decades to define what was the triggering cause of that retreat from the world of barbarians, when China had immense power.

Xi Jinping is the resolution of an enigma, let's repeat it. With him, China returns to what it was at its imperial origins: a great power aimed at world domination. And to do this, he gives reason to those who support the thesis of internal control as a source of expansion abroad: the old Wittfogel [153] supporter of the "Asian mode of production". This paradigm is based on the strict imperial dominion of the potentates who controlled the waters, and in this way the Empire: to achieve this result, internal control of the sources of power was absolutely necessary.

Mao had tried to achieve that control, but with immense social costs. The cultural revolution was nothing more than a way to annihilate the opposing factions of a party that from the beginning had to deal with, after Japanese nationalism, rivalry with Stalin and the international weight of the Soviet Union, starting from the defeat of the revolt and the strikes in Shanghai in 1927. There were not only internal enemies: the great Soviet power had come to create a state, North Korea, to make China's very existence depend on Soviet aid, in the confrontation first with Japan and then with the United States.

Mao physically and morally eliminated the opponents until his death. And then Deng Xiaoping was able to emerge and establish that rule that has been consensually respected by the warring factions until the rise to power of Xi Jinping: among bureaucrats, no one kills anymore. The same, moreover, happened in the Soviet Union with the advent of Khrushchev.

Xi Jinping broke that rule as soon as he came to power, increasingly intensifying a fight against corruption that confirms what we now theoretically know after decades of studies on the subject, in every part of the world: the war on corruption is nothing more—more or less markedly—than a tool for internal struggle among the power elites, in more or less bloody forms depending on the degree of existing democratic legitimization.

China is among the human settlements with the lowest degree of legal civilization: this is understood as long as it is studied scientifically and not to derive economic benefits from it, as happened in the case of its admission to the WTO. A green light wanted by the US Democratic Party, led by the peaks of unregulated finance, which laid the foundations of the global catastrophe in which we are immersed.

History is linear: when he comes to power in 2012, Xi Jinping shares it with the well-active fractions of his most immediate predecessors, Hu

Jintao and Jiang Zemin, but breaks with the rules of collegial leadership imposed by Deng Xiaoping. He quickly takes control not only of the Military Commission, as is customary, but especially of those of Internal Security and Economy.

The congress will be a test of his ability to gather around him factions of loyalists as Li Keqiang has done in these years: a prime minister also capable in international relations who has effectively controlled the Standing Committee of the Politburo. And then also the most important faction of all, like that of Beria in the Soviet Union: that of Wang Qishan, who led the anti-corruption campaign that destroyed the factions gathered around the mayors of the largest cities, in crucial nodes of the army and especially in the party apparatus. Wang's age (69 years) is an obstacle to his reconfirmation, but an organizational solution will certainly be found because, in my opinion, the more than one million trials, which have followed each other in the years since the last congress, have not yet definitively destroyed potential opponents. This is demonstrated by the incessant campaign conducted both on the right and on the left, that is, against the ever-resurgent neo-Maoisms and the still active remnants of the "Shanghai clique" that has been undermining the central power of Beijing for decades. Faced with these internal dangers, Xi Jinping has chosen a path that we could identify in the agglutination and neutrality of any other possible adversary that does not come from the bowels of the party. Hence the opening towards religions, all religions, which reached its peak with the Vatican agreement that will be perfected with the Secretary of State Pietro Parolin and the Society of Jesus that has effectively dominated the Roman Curia for years. And then the opening towards the same Buddhist souls, even in Tibet, as demonstrated by the incessant work conducted by the president's loyalists in those lands. Xi Jinping, to achieve these ends, was able to count on loyalists like Li Zhanshu, head of his staff and director of the Central Committee. The old friend who worked with him in Hebel province was also the invaluable collaborator who prepared all the most important meetings with Putin.

As can be well understood, Xi has laid the foundations over time for a new expert and trusted faction, both domestically and internationally, thus preparing the projection of the great Middle Empire abroad.

This was possible thanks to incessant purges that have never ended. This is demonstrated by the case of the continuous repressions carried out in Chongqing, where Min'er has settled, who is only 57 years old, but is a sure candidate for the Politburo. What Li Zhanshu did with Russia, the young Vam Yang—who should become a member of the *steering committee*—should continue to do with the United States.

It is an agreement that will take years to conclude, but is inevitable unless Europe returns to being, on the French example, what it is potentially and what it must be: a colonial power in Africa, under penalty of its disappearance as a civilization.

What will Russia do? The conclusion of the 2017 Congress holds part of the answer to this question.

To understand what Moscow will do, it will be necessary to follow the career of Cai Qi, sixty-one years old (therefore very young by Chinese standards) who is and will be in charge of the central National Security Commission, an organ that ensures not only internal repression, but also the stages of preparation of international agreements.

The security of the borders with Russia is strategic to guarantee the "new emperor's" China a dazzling expansion. This process cannot take place without an agreement with Russia, following the path of the Shanghai conferences: it would be a new pact capable of uniting both Russia and India with China, thus allowing Beijing to continue its dominance over the seas, conceived in the wake of the American Mahan (studying geopolitics based on maritime power as taught in American naval schools). In Russia, it was the aforementioned great intellectual Sergei Karaganov who hypothesized this post-Soviet way out of the "great Russian" isolation.

In this sense, the resolution of the North Korean crisis is vital. Let's not forget, I repeat, that North Korea was a creation of Stalin, not only to scare Japan, but also to weaken Mao and force him to ask for Soviet help in case of war with the United States. Those times are over, but thanks to the collaboration between the United States, Russia, and China, the issue could also be resolved through the annihilation of the North Korean leadership group—which would imply a number of victims greater than those of the narrow circle of the leadership summit.

This is an inevitable choice, because the path outlined by Xi Jinping is that of the cyclical expansion of China's presence abroad. Once the domestic front is stabilized, it is now the conquests abroad that allow for strengthening at home and vice versa. The result will be an increase in territorial conflicts with India, the Philippines, and especially Vietnam, a historical enemy.

These are conflicts that will effectively decide the fate of strategic nations like Thailand (never colonized in its history) and which not surprisingly see a strengthening of the military regime, as well as throughout Indochina.

From Djibouti, if the hinterland of the South Seas is secure, China can then set off for the conquest of Africa and Australia.

All the declarations about Chinese socialism do nothing but lay the foundations of a strong state where the state has the last word in the economy to guarantee expansion abroad. Jiang Zemin and Hu Jintao were still healing internal wounds with the theories of the "three representations" and "scientific perspectives for development". Today all this is destined to be replaced by a sort of neo-Maoism effectively achieved internally, through the continuous and massive elimination of opponents and the return of economic power in China: less investment abroad, preached in 2017 by Xi Jinping, unless these serve for the path of world domination.

For this reason, bureaucratic phrases will not be carved into the stones of monuments as was done before; instead, what matters will be engraved on the stone of the new bureaucratic state monopoly with a terrorist matrix, namely the thought of Xi Jinping.

The "new emperor" thus seeks to solve the difficult dilemma of establishing an effective relationship between the institutionalization of dominance and the political project; a step that differentiates him from past leadership groups. Xi can only do this by not destroying the need to promote frames with meritocracy, without factionalism and incessant internal struggle clouding the seriousness of meritocratic selection processes. Control over every fold of society is, after all, his primary task as demonstrated by the fight against corruption; but this cannot be at the expense of the vitality of a society like the Chinese one that has allowed ever new leadership groups to fight and survive.

Confirming this thesis of mine is the same story of Xi Jinping and his father, a historical revolutionary and hit by the terrible purges of the cultural revolution. This is a story that has profoundly changed Xi's psychology, allowing him a relationship with the great masses that no longer belonged to any of Deng's followers.

In any case, Xi expresses a neo-Maoist characteristic so far not so fully revealed. The power of the party is first of all, as demonstrated by typical practices of the nomenclature and Chinese communist bureaucracy: self-criticism, mass politics, the return of socialist ideology, and discipline.

In my opinion, the crisis that occurred during the power of Hu Jintao at the top of the state was decisive: a very violent factional struggle broke out and an increasingly difficult assumption of decisions by collegial and consensual means, in the context of ostentatious corruption that deeply weakened the legitimization of the party's elites. The years of Hu Jintao, moreover, were the most disastrous from the point of view of the effectiveness of political direction.

Let's not forget that Xi Jinping was brought to power by the "red princes", namely the descendants of Mao's revolutionary comrades, tired of the barbarization of the party's life and the degradation of society. It is no coincidence that the fight against corruption quickly extended from the party to society and to public and private companies, where extraordinary and imaginative measures were taken—but revealing—such as replacing, in public companies, the clause of state command with that of party command. They have come to arrest those who play openly in the stock market and to limit foreign financial investments in favor of those within, starting a fight never seen before against the *shadow banks* and the *shadow pools*.

And after all, the digital world must indeed establish a new economic power, but always ensure a capillary social control. Only in this way will the "Chinese dream of the great renaissance of the nation" be achieved. A clear and strong message that joins the increasingly strong role of the party and the Red Army together.

Often rethinking the history of the Chinese Communist Party, I recognize in Xi's slogans not the watchwords of Mao but of Liu Shaoqi [154], in the typically Soviet search for social legitimation of the "red bureaucracy" through technological and military achievements, tightly controlling the party's cadres and developing a global power in the international arena.

I have confirmation in the controls to which Chinese universities have recently been subjected, which are now called to develop "Chinese ideology", strengthening themselves to ensure that fewer and fewer Chinese students go to complete their studies abroad.

Expand as a great power in the world, but return to the sources of national power: this is the secret of Xi Jinping in a nutshell. If he wins, a completely new system of weights and global relevance will arise. But the pandemic also works against him, in addition to the statist rigidity of the party's terrorist control that is also exercised on the Chinese bourgeoisie who have pragmatically accepted bureaucratic dominance. Until the economy, like the maintenance of international relations, does not collapse.

CHAPTER 9

The Syrian Crisis: Seeing Through the Mirror Game

It is my belief that the post-colonial disintegration of the Greater Middle East is just beginning. The return to the scene of Turkey, with the neo-Ataturkian resurgence of the capitalist bourgeoisie—which is well composed of religious roots much more complex than it appears to the undeserving public (68% of Turkish religious citizens are Sunni, 30% are Shiite, the remaining 2% includes small groups of Sephardic Jewish, Greek and Armenian Orthodox, Byzantine Catholic and Armenian Protestant communities)—aimed at energy self-sufficiency in the now contestable Atlantic Mediterranean lake is proof of this.

It all starts with the Syrian crisis and with the Italian-French negativity in front of a disarmed Germany and therefore even more dangerous for the international revisionist impulses that it evokes and promotes from the point of view of *soft power* economic and *intelligence*.

A delegation from Alternative für Deutschland, the German right-wing party, went to Syria in March 2018 to meet the Grand Mufti of Syria, Ahmad Badreddin Hassoun, in Damascus. The purpose of the visit was to "Get to know the Syrian situation in person and understand the war from a German perspective".

The AfD deputy of the North Rhine-Westphalia Land, Christian Blex, described the meeting with the Grand Mufti as the "highlight" of the visit to Syria. Stating that "His Excellency reiterated the need for a strict separation between the State and religions to ensure peaceful coexistence".

G. Sapelli, *States, Markets and Wars in Global History*,
https://doi.org/10.1007/978-3-031-26716-1_9

At the same time, he emphasized that the Grand Mufti "is convinced that 70% of Syrian refugees will return to Syria", adding that he is ready to go to Berlin to appeal to refugees who have left for Germany.

"The aim of the trip is to... analyze *on the spot* the humanitarian situation and the reconstruction work in the areas liberated from terrorists, as the information from the media in Germany does not offer the possibility to evaluate the real situation in Syria", wrote *Der Spiegel*.

The German government had harshly condemned the trip of the representatives of the German right, who in this way wanted to find an agreement to favor the return to Syria of the refugees living in Germany. The indignation of the SPD and CDU for the trip to Damascus was not accompanied by indignation for the sale of Leopard tanks used on the Afrin front or for the weapons sold for billions of dollars to Saudi Arabia and the Emirates while the war in Yemen was raging.

Germany announced that it would not participate in any intervention in Syria alongside the USA and this revealed the caution with which this great nation moves when its role in Africa is at stake, mindful of the defeats it has historically suffered on that continent.

While quite different was, as is known, the decision of France and the United Kingdom. Macron declared: "Assad used chemical weapons, we have the evidence", and the British increased the dose, in continuation, moreover, of their anti-Russian action after the spy scandal that had affected for days and days all the world public opinion, in a mirror game that has nothing to do with a spy game, but instead with a game of mass distraction from the stake.

The stake, for the USA, France, and the United Kingdom, was to achieve the reorganization of the world power balance by preventing Russia from asserting an unprecedented power in the Middle East and therefore in the strategic point of the *Heartland* and the *Rimland*, that is in the heart of the world terrestrial power and in the seas that lap it. The Atlantic lakes of the Black Sea and the Caspian Sea are the periphery of the Persian Gulf and the Indian Ocean, and this is why the control of Syria has always been strategic. The French at the time of the Sykes-Picot agreement, in 1916, knew this well as did the British. From the Golan hills, both Lebanon and Aden are controlled.

The USA, which replaced this post-Ottoman dominion in the fifties of the second post-war period, thought with the Bush presidencies that they could support their regional power by destroying the Mesopotamian political system, thus generating that tragically systemic implosion that reached to the heart of world power and that still lasts today, opening the way to the neo-Ottoman dominion and the new Russia heir to Primakov and personified by Lavrov and Putin. The situation became dramatic for the USA and the historical powers of the area (France and UK) when the flag of the Syrian government was raised in Douma, the last insurgent area near Damascus, marking for the Bashar al-Assad regime the resumption of control over the entire Eastern Ghouta. The Russian army announced this and this announcement took on a general historical significance: "An important event for the history of the Arab Republic of Syria occurred today: the flag of the Syrian government was raised on a building in the city of Douma and marks the control of this location and therefore of the Eastern Ghouta in its entirety", said Russian General Yuri Evtushenko.

"The fighters of the Jaich al-Islam group have handed over their heavy weapons to the Russian military police in Douma", reports the Syrian Observatory for Human Rights.

The day after the buses were seen passing the Muhayam al-Wafedin checkpoint, en route to Douma, where they would have loaded the rebels and their families.

In the face of all this, what some independent observers expected happened.

An alleged chemical weapons attack in Douma could not be missing. All serious international sources, however, declared that the attack, the attacks, had never occurred.

The tragedy of Iraq in 2003 is repeated, when an entire geopolitical complex was destroyed by inventing weapons of mass destruction that did not exist. On this fact, a series of highly intense American films were even produced.

The day after the *tweet* of war by American President Donald Trump, Secretary of State Pompeo warned that the *soft* policy towards Russia was over, but specified: "War is always the last resort". The Kremlin spokesman, Dmitry Peskov, stated, for his part, that "the communication channel between Russia and the United States in view of the American attack on Syria is active". He added that a telephone conversation between Vladimir Putin and Donald Trump was not planned.

British Prime Minister Theresa May ordered submarines to be moved within missile range of Syria for a possible action against the Assad regime. From the UN, meanwhile, came a warning to avoid an escalation.

"I never said when an attack on Syria would take place. It could be very soon or not so soon! In any case, the United States, under my administration, has done a great job of freeing the region from Isis. Where is our 'Thank you America?'". Donald Trump wrote this in those fatal days on Twitter.

A game of mirrors began, of solar mirrors that emit signals with languages unknown to the world diplomatic tradition, in a succession of colossal gaffes by all Western leaders.

Only the Russians maintained an Olympic calm because they held the field and the hegemony, making the knight's move to strengthen ties with Turkey in an unprecedented alliance between the Sublime Porte and Great Russia.

In this unprecedented context, the warlike activism of the French is striking, in a sort of new war for Morocco. The French president then reiterated that he is in almost daily contact with Donald Trump and stressed that there will be "decisions to be made in the desired times, when this will be more useful and more effective".

Germany, I remind you again, did not take an active part in any military intervention against the Syrian government and this brings to mind the final outcome of the second Moroccan crisis at the beginning of the twentieth century.

The so-called first Moroccan crisis, also known as the Tangier Crisis, was fatal for Germany.

It was provoked by a visit of Kaiser Wilhelm II to Tangier, at the Sultanate of Morocco, on March 31, 1905, in which Germany took a position in favor of Morocco's independence threatened by France. But Germany was isolated and France improved its position by increasing its influence over Morocco with the Algeciras Agreement of 1906.

In 1911 Germany, in the midst of the growing power of its fleet that so worried the United Kingdom, sent its gunboat *Panther* in front of the Moroccan port of Agadir, provoking the second Moroccan crisis. But this move, which aimed to put pressure on France to obtain greater compensations in exchange for renouncing German claims on Morocco, was interpreted by Great Britain as an attempt to take control of the port of Agadir by the Reich's navy, making it a stronghold capable of countering the routes of the central Atlantic [155].

The Mediterranean turned out to be an Atlantic lake…

Germany was defeated and had to definitively recognize French supremacy in Morocco.

These crises on African soil were of considerable importance for the history of Europe, because, on the one hand, they helped to strengthen ties between England and France, and on the other hand, they deepened the divide between these two countries and Germany, foreshadowing what would later be the alignments of the First World War.

In this context, here is the neo-Ottoman declaration of January 2019: "United States and Russia stop being street bullies" on the Syrian issue. It was a stern warning from the Turkish government, another key actor in the conflict: after the escalation of tension due to the alleged chemical attack in Douma, Ankara is worried. It fears that the instability caused by the Franco-English-North American air strikes will disrupt the unstable balance of power at its borders, giving new voice to Kurdish militias of all factions, disrupting its plan for territorial expansion in Syria and Iraq.

The balance of power between Russia and the USA will, therefore, be decisive not only for redrawing the borders of the new Mesopotamia, but also for re-establishing a balance of power in Europe between France and Germany and between these two powers and the United Kingdom, which acts with strategic intelligence to maintain a global role despite Brexit, which for some marks, instead, the English sunset on a global scale.

Theresa May's action was exactly all aimed at supporting the opposite and at relaunching the western horn of the new "anglosphere", the global agreement with the USA, while silencing the eastern horn, i.e., the relationship with China that does not find the USA on the same power line.

As always, where the *Heartland* plunges into the Atlantic Lake of the Mediterranean, the earth and the seas tremble and disrupt the faults of the state dominions of old Europe and the entire world. The neo-Ottoman revenge could only come true, once again in front of the division between the European powers in the Mediterranean. The Libyan crisis could not but deepen. Bab-ı Ali, the Sublime Gate of the Golden Horn, could not but reveal itself [156].

CHAPTER 10

Economic Madness, Technocracies and the Energy Transition

The world economy, in this geostrategic context that gives the Mediterranean a crucial role, is hanging by a thread of madness.

One of these threads is the tendency, now entrenched in global institutional projects, to solve the major problems of distortions produced by the late prevailing debt capitalism with transnational rules under technocratic direction. One of these examples, the most illustrious, is the destructive utopia of being able to solve energy problems through a "transition" technocratically overdetermined.

Figures 10.1, 10.2 and Table 10.1 encapsulate the challenge that this so-called energy transition contains within itself.

The realization of the replacement of coal in transmission circuits and in global energy generation processes cannot but profoundly transform the geopolitical structure. The energy sector, in fact, historically, does nothing but follow, or often impose, the progressive shifts of weights and relevances of confrontations and power conflicts at a global level. The demographic variable, as was known to the classics of the study of international relations and power conflicts, is a variant, with technology, indispensable for understanding, as far as possible, the physiognomy of social transformations. The emergence of China, India, and some African states as great demographic powers constitutes an important independent variable and therefore determinant in the transformation process [157].

G. Sapelli, *States, Markets and Wars in Global History*,
https://doi.org/10.1007/978-3-031-26716-1_10

A caption should be added for
uniformity with the other two

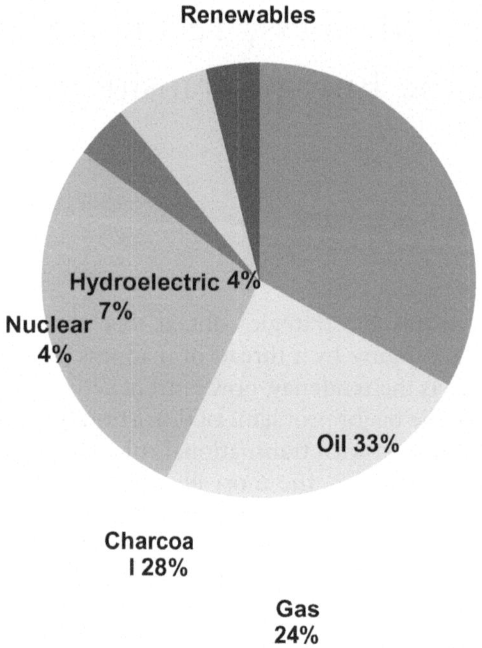

Fig. 10.1 Type of fuel and generation (percentage utilization) (*Source* BP Statistical Review 2019)

We are still immersed in a transition from an era characterized by complex but, ultimately, still stable and predictable relationships between the core of consumer countries belonging to the bloc of Western democratic poliarchies, represented by the OECD, and the relatively small group of producers gathered around OPEC (plus Russia), to a new world characterized, instead, by new areas of production and consumption—especially in Asia—rapidly expanding. Hence a level of fragmentation of energy relations at the transnational level that we have never had in the past.

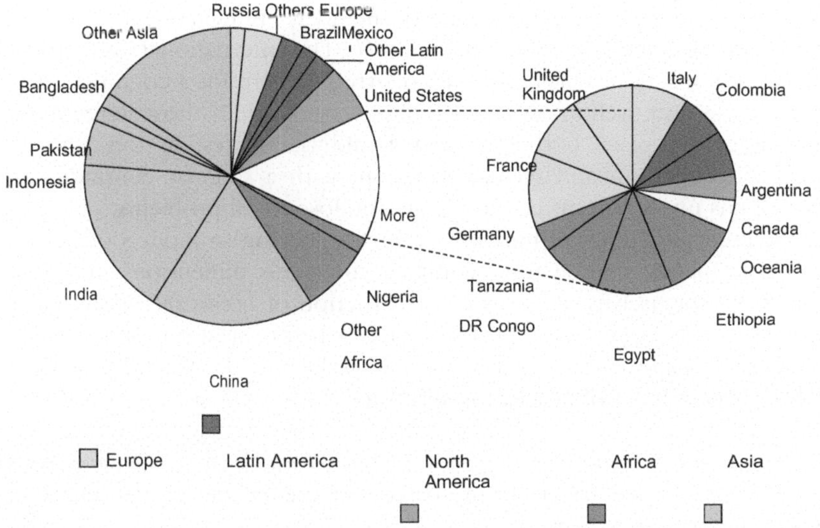

Fig. 10.2 World population (*Source* UN data for 2017)

Table 10.1 Distribution of energy growth and CO_2 emissions

China and India	50%
USA	20%
Developing countries	13%
Russia and Middle East	12%
Other countries + Europe	5%

Source BP Statistical Review 2019

The models of *governance* poliarchic, both among companies and among States, must undergo profound transformations and will be difficult to manage through previous models.

They have simultaneously become manifest, as proof of what I had predicted years ago, those deep faults that are increasingly opening in the global capitalist system between States and *clusters* of companies, between the new interstate complex of spongiform relations and what remains of the States, on the one hand, and the new forms of technocratic-oligarchic relations, on the other. A new face of the State appears without more "reason of State" and increasingly porous and hybridized by subjects that escape the rules of liberal democracy, such as the one that had been handed down to us by the tradition of the great French constitutionalism *à la Constant* and *à la Madame de Staël*. The international agreements on decarbonization, which are only referred to here for a cognitive need as they are now well known to the "universe world", those agreements should even replace both the market and the States, in this time of unfolded liberalism and secular deflation, with a singular contradiction that opens up significant economic and philosophical problems.

We are called upon as humanity to act according to models of behavioral biopolitics that assume complex interstate dimensions and that constitute themselves as forces of construction of *landscapes* ideological, semantic (*à la Appadurai*) [158] like never before seen on the globe.

A new "religion" that is in reality, according to the teaching of Gray [159], a new form of atheism is spreading with a pervasiveness hitherto unknown.

Biopolitics becomes the behavioral whip to which the once dangerous classes are obliged to conform, based on the beliefs of the elites of globalized interstate power.

Are philosophers preparing to change the world?

Are new believers sprouting like forests to replace the old believers? [160].

The conditioning of consciousness goes hand in hand with the continuous dispossession of States of the "reason of State", which has always been, until now, the very essence of their *existence* in history.

Conversely, with difficulty but with impetus, mainly due to US political transformations, a movement opposite to the one mentioned is being affirmed, generated *primarily* by resistance to the financialization of politics and the economy (against its denationalizing and de-statizing effects).

On the one hand, therefore, interstate cooperation agreements on issues once proper to the "reason of State" and freedom of enterprise are increasing (think, precisely, of the commitments made by representatives of diversified interstate technocracies on energy transition, decarbonization *primarily*), and on the other hand, diversified rejections of multilateral cooperation models are becoming increasingly manifest. However, it is becoming increasingly difficult to make any model and implementation process of guidelines, rules, and inclusive and stable behaviors compulsory.

The root of this lies in the fractal world that is primarily taking shape in international relations.

After the collapse of the USSR, a regulatory vacuum was created in power relations that has not yet been filled, because no general agreement has replaced the architectural complex built during the Cold War. This happened due to the absence of a treaty that could rebuild, after the collapse of the USSR, the system of global international relations.

This was not done due to the *madness* (as our great David Calleo [161] defined it in a seminal work) of the "unilateralist" power spirit of the USA and now the whole world is paying the consequences.

A war for hegemony, in fact, becomes less and less possible and it is such hegemony that is instead necessary, essential, to *stabilize* the world, regulating its relational mechanisms with a new *entente cordiale* of which Raymond Aron [162] has forever defined, years and years ago, the essential features. Such hegemonic will was not in the strings of the unilateralist US polyarchic command group. However, it reappeared, with unexpected force, with the election of Donald Trump as president, testifying to that cultural transformation previously mentioned. This has led to a cultural, political, and diplomatic dislocation of American power that is still ongoing, but already decisive and advocated by that segment of the power elites that are currently in command (in an infernal and unstable way, however) in the USA. All this while a new dictatorial maritime power emerges on the world stage (demography, thanks to technology, is indeed transforming into a possible state power profile hitherto unheard of in the Chinese case), disrupting relations between states that had found no settlement after the collapse of the USSR, as demonstrated by the European-Balkan wars and the Mesopotamian wars, with the Mediterranean once again contestable due to Russia's return to the warm seas.

And in the Atlantic Lake of the Mediterranean, the de-vertebration of the same power conflict continues, in continuation of that de-vertebration that is at the center of the reflection proposed in this book.

Not only proxy wars in areas that are on the slopes of Eurasia and in the lakes (the Mediterranean, precisely) that are dominant for the control of the lands, but wars that serve to alternate crucial diplomatic initiatives for the stabilization of the conflict and balanced victory. The example that came from the Libyan wars (as from the Balkan ones) is precisely this. In fact, there was no total clash between Turkey and Russia, but what happened in Bosnia happened: an alternation between military action and diplomatic negotiations. From a strictly military point of view, Turkey was advantaged having managed to drive Haftar's forces from much of

Tripolitania. But such a situation is always reversible, like the unstable balance of fractals.

Libyan power, as Peters' masterpiece continues to teach us [163], is extremely fluid because it depends on the alignment of hundreds of militias, tribes, and local forces that can change sides from one moment to the next. Consider what happened in Tarhuna in June 2020, which fell because the Seventh Brigade aligned with Sarraj left the field and allied with its former rival, Haftar.

And behold, therefore, the continuous fractal in the decisive fault of energy issues.

Similar processes of readjustment have always occurred in world history: the Peloponnesian War between Sparta and Athens, the Thirty Years' War, the Napoleonic wars, the First and Second World Wars are the result of the emergence of revisionist maritime powers, from Persia and then from Athens to Germany and Japan and now to China.

What is happening today is certainly the emergence of China but accompanied by the very dangerous (for any *entente cordiale*) division between the USA on one hand and France and Germany on the other [164]. As you can see, the problem of "decarbonization" is immersed in a great global power confrontation and is a tangle of themes and problems that, once unraveled, require us to look at the world and the power that emanates from it with different eyes than those artificially constructed by the narrative, from the *landscape* ideological today dominant, well defined by Gray. To fully understand it, we need to revisit the classics of geopolitics, from the great Halford Mackinder [165] passing through Alfred Thayer Mahan [166], reaching up to the still mysterious Nicholas John Spykman [167], who is the true, hidden, hero of the times we are going through without most of us being fully aware of it.

Mackinder, as I said, interpreted world power as a set of isolated areas that nevertheless interacted, performing continuous states of imbalance of the international system, *à la Raymond Aron*.

Performance is based on the existing differences in natural, demographic, and technological endowments that states historically possess. Hence, the interconnection between the energy issue and its transformation and the morphology of global power.

Europe has historically built itself as an eccentric response to the challenges of demographic growth and energy opportunities thanks to exceptional climatic endowments and personal skills spread in a unique context in the world [168]. But for Mackinder, the deepest challenge was the one that came to Mediterranean Europe from Central Asia, more precisely from what he defined (and we with him) the *Heartland*, where the Eurasian masses were and are historically concentrated: here is the *Pivot* overseeing historical transformations understood as geopolitical transformative developments in which both historical factors and forms of life (*à la Simmel!*) continuously give sense, give meaning to spaces.

The international system is a living system.

And so nothing is ever mechanically written in history.

To truly understand what has happened and is happening, think about the events in Southeast Asia, an essential point of the *Rimland*.

Southeast Asia's dependence on the USA and Japan is slowly waning, even though these two nations remain the region's main economic partners. The problem is that China has seen an exponential increase in trade growth compared to the two major players mentioned earlier and all other nations on the planet. Its demographic weight transforms and shapes the economy, once again folding the "dismal science" into the lap of historiography, of which demography, with sociology, is a handmaid.

Today it can truly be understood, if one wishes, that globalization has largely been a game of mirrors. The only truly globalized commodity has been money and capital as flow and not as investment. All this while, by decision of the fractal discomposed apex of deregulating finance (which alternately governs the US political class with a unique lobbying system in the world) [169], China was allowed to enter the WTO without any real counterpart.

The consequences have been terrible.

In this sense, and only in this sense, the fundamental thesis of Henry Kissinger's classic masterpiece on the Congress of Vienna is still truthful and prescient, because it illustrates into what disaster the planet can fall, I repeat, *without international politics based on the art of diplomacy* [170] (which is the pre-formative cause, ultimately, of how the lives of men associated in the struggle between geopolitical spaces and therefore of the so-called international system are organized).

But diplomacy, to be realized as a world form creating stability, needs states with the "reason of state".

And this is what is lacking today and continues to be fueled in a vertigo of risk.

The neo-statist, enlightenment *à la Adorno*, and technocratic processes *à la Wright Mills*, with which the so-called energy transition and decarbonization are intended to be realized, are an example of this.

Heteroregulation replaces self-regulation, just when there is much talk of *corporate social responsibility* and autopoietic behaviors of companies and interest associations are invoked.

Madness dominates the world.

In this Shakespearean drama, the United States increasingly manifests itself—fully with Trump, but *in essence* already with Obama—as a revisionist power. It is only apparently a contradiction: usually, in fact, the leading power prefers to preserve the existing order.

But the group of elites currently in power with Trump (military and large old-style energy industries and heavy machinery) consider the preferential relationship established until a few years ago with China (which in 2001 was granted entry into the WTO under extremely favorable conditions) and the unbalanced relationship with the EU, considered in fact a projection of German power, which behaves as a vain opportunist, with little expenditure on security, largely delegated to the Americans; almost exclusive attention to commercial strategies aimed at creating *increasingly larger surpluses* that harm the rest of the world; due to the dominance of the *Ordo-liberalismus* imposed by Germany on the rest of Europe, growing convergence of interests with China; propensity to be the best in class in terms of rights and legal rules.

This "revisionism" does not apply in the form of military intervention (see Bush Jr. and, to a lesser extent, Obama) but increasingly leverages economic (sanctions) and techno-digital (cyber) factors. For some time, the Americans have been uncomfortable on the ground (Iraq, Syria, Afghanistan) and prefer to bend the architecture of international relations to their advantage where their power gap is greatest (but this creates shocks and imbalances whose medium-long-term impact is difficult to assess: see the role of the dollar). Trump, with some isolationist reminiscence, wants to limit as much as possible the application of military force abroad.

The issue of alliances becomes crucial. The revision of relations with the false Chinese friend and with Germany in the EU, an ally mostly in words, thins out American support in the world: the Anglo-Saxon powers (*Five Eyes*), Israel, the Saudi bloc, and Japan remain secure.

However, revisionism needs allies: what would be crucial, namely Russia—also to avoid isolation in the trio of great world powers: now there is a sort of reverse Kissinger 1972—encounters hostility from much of Washington's world and seems feasible only in small steps (as seen in the Middle East and perhaps also in Pyongyang), in homeopathic doses. This makes the mercantile ambiguity of Germany/EU more serious, which is increasingly weakening in strategic uncertainty, weakening Western democracies.

Never as today, now it can be well understood, the idea of a global order based on multilateral institutionalism is deeply shaken.

It is in this scenario that the technocratic interstate processes that have been proposed with multilateral agreements concerning the global energy sector should be read, made up of organizational populations of companies and relations between these companies and states, up to being configured, in the case of National Oil Companies, as state companies and therefore as lumps of "reason of state" embodied in the form of state-owned companies, a segment of the theory and practice of public finance.

The processes of energy transition and decarbonization have been induced—primarily but not exclusively—by the global fight against climate change.

I will return to this later. But I would now like to specify what broad geopolitical changes will be outlined.

The transformation of the energy paradigm on a global scale will involve a redefinition of the balance of power between producer and consumer countries, the emergence of new areas of geopolitical and strategic interest, and the progressive disinterest towards others. It will be necessary to access new natural resources such as lithium, cobalt and rare earths, with the confrontation that will open between *players* global and local elites to ensure their control with a redefinition of the rules that oversee the security of supplies. If the heart of global fossil energy will remain for centuries to come between Arabia and Mesopotamia—the *shale oil* and the *shale gas* in the USA are just a fleeting illusion—that of the sources also necessary to build the carriers of the so-called renewable energies will move towards areas of the Earth different from those of today and will require a predisposition of the containment forces of power adversaries very different from the current one. It is also true that the progressive disappearance of fossil fuels will never occur, on the contrary, their use will grow exponentially precisely to prepare the infrastructures necessary for the so-called renewable energies which (if we overcome the veil of ignorance today dominant even in the world of technocratic elites) are not sources, but instead carriers and therefore will increasingly need fossil sources, whatever the dominant narrative says.

However, the political and social pressures of collective movements induced by the *lobbies* of the interests expressed by the need for state subsidies to finance economically unsustainable renewable carriers and the industries and services linked to these carriers, will undoubtedly have consequences on the political stability before the economic one of the large producing countries. On this, see the fundamental work of Massimo Nicolazzi [171].

And the behaviorist forces of the new atheisms glorifying a nature of new gods, in a pagan and polytheistic ensemble, will do the rest, with powerful symbolic and ideological forces.

But many fossil fuel-producing countries, heavily dependent on oil rents, will feel threatened in their system of state and interstate alliances of the authoritarian polyarchies of which they are mostly part.

The unstoppable development, on the other hand, of the new cutting-edge technologies necessary for the new technologies will create new interests and geopolitical power conflicts linked to the procurement of raw materials and competition on and for networks, with consequences that we already foresee in the ongoing confrontation on these issues between the USA and China. The sub-Saharan African continental situation will be decisive: millions and millions of people do not have access to essential energy services and therefore factors such as technological primacy, together with commercial expansion, will be key elements of the energy policy of medium and large global powers, provided that the assumptions of the dominant world policies of neoliberal limited rationality and the resulting shrinking of internal markets are overturned.

In this context, the current mechanisms of *governance* of the energy sector—essentially based on the dualism between a compact group of consumer countries gathered under the umbrella of the IEA, and the producing countries consortiumed within OPEC (and some of its extensions, see ROPEC) and, albeit with a more limited impact, GECF (Gas Exporting Countries Forum)—are proving inadequate to face the changes underway to face the challenges of the energy transition. We are faced with a clear testimony of the inadequacy of the current international institutional architectures in the energy field.

What matters is to underline that it has been affirmed, in the symbolic construction imposed by the agencies of financial globalization, the narrative construction based on the assumption that decarbonization is the main way through which it is possible to achieve a reduction of CO_2 that is emitted into the earth's atmosphere, ignoring that it is the *complex of sources* of all energy (always environmentally improvable) that, instead, allows the reproduction of the world's economic and social systems.

Coal is an essential element that also ensures that thermodynamic balance through which energy allows the social reproduction of the capitalist system and of those Asian state monopolistic capitalist systems (China, North Korea, and Vietnam) that coexist with different degrees of interconnection with the global capitalist system operating in other lands of the planet. Reducing the percentage of coal and CO_2 produced on Earth is an effort not only complex, but so massive and cyclopean as has never been presented before. And here the demographic challenge and the transformation of international power systems to be overcome emerges in all its evidence, carrying on our shoulders not coal anymore, but everything that can (technologies, *mores*, and narratives) replace its use in whole or in part in the Chinese and Indian demographic powers [172] ...

We must avoid the disturbing oversimplifications that follow incessantly, such as those related to the fact that the greening with global percentage quotas of presence in non-entropic energy circularity will automatically lead to a decrease in CO_2, forgetting the energy generation processes necessary in the manufacture of renewable infrastructures. This issue intersects with demographic disparities with shocking systemic effects...

And it must also be overcome, therefore, the belief that the classic industries of both fossil and mining sources, for example, cannot lead to CO_2 savings even larger than those achievable with the greening of energies not coming from fossil sources.

As stated by a protagonist of the global mining industry (Andrew Mackenzie, Chief Executive of BHP), in an interesting article appeared in the *Financial Times* on July 23, 2019 [173], where it says:

> That is why we must change the current assumption that there are easy, single solutions and acknowledge that there are many competing perspectives that must be taken into account in the purpose of effective responses to climate change. It is also why I believe that those who simplistically call for divestment from all resource companies are fundamentally wrong. The mining industry must play a leading role in this... A range of solutions are vital, from carbon capture and storage to use of renewables and reforestation. The money will be invested in these as well as other innovations and partnerships... Much of the emissions from the resource industry come at

> the end of the value chain, as our customers process our commodities into products like steel... This shows why we all have to be part of the solution and why the divestment movement is misguided... No sector of the economy can do it alone, but it's clear that resource companies and energy intensive industries must step up to take their share of the responsibility and action.

It is, therefore, about the need for a profound transformation of the entire way of producing on a multifactorial global scale. It is unthinkable that this process can be entrusted to interstate heteroregulation. It can only be carried out, instead, through business self-regulation, under penalty of running the fatal risk of disinvestments in those sources that are increasingly indispensable in the global demographic change that are nothing other than the ancient and insurmountable fossil sources.

What needs to change profoundly are the productive processes that use and produce them for any form of energy or manufacturing or services: nothing else.

That said, the issue of regulation must still and always be preliminarily put to discussion: for the first time in world history, in fact, such a massive transformation has been imposed through a series of interstate agreements. This implies a transformation of the practice and the very concept of "reason of state".

Anne-Marie Slaughter, in this regard, has focused attention on this point in her important works years ago [174] on the transformation of international relations and the constitutional profiles that such transformations provoke, increasingly subtracting large areas of compulsiveness from the democratic process. Processes that intervened with unexpected force especially after the collapse of the Soviet Union and the emergence of an increasingly centralized and self-regulated neo-financialized capitalism, to which I have already drawn attention [175].

And it is also undeniable that an *landscape* imaginary and symbolic built over years of *soft power* by the power groups expressed by industries and movements in favor of so-called renewable sources today determines a large part of the economic policy choices of the rapidly transforming capitalist system and imposes as priority choices on the elites who govern the system economic and social policies profoundly different from those of the past.

Politics, as Ulrich Beck claimed [176], even if it disappears from the self-referential technocratic process of the oligarchies well described by

Anne-Marie Slaughter, reappears where it is least expected: in the decisions of interstate heteroregulation of climate agreements, for example, which are nothing more than forms of regulation in view of the implementation of economic policy processes!

The distinctive root of these political forms is the fact that they all move at the boundary between state and market, preforming both with the technical procedure and with the ideology (in our case "climate" and "naturalistic") now one now the other of the elements of the state-market relationship, thanks to the powerful weight exerted by the interstate relations that have settled in this symbolic and social intertwining of the new transnational power.

How to define this new *landscape*? How to classify it among the great transformations of the relationship between companies, state and society that always overdetermines the configurations of the markets and the volitions of the organizational populations that inhabit the markets peristaltically?

A widespread system of beliefs and symbolic reflections has been created, not only ideologically widespread, but which should find realization in forms of fixed capital stock in a form hitherto unusual. And this in the mechanism of capital circulation and production of goods by means of goods, which is typical of the economic system dominant throughout the planet, except in China, Vietnam, and North Korea, where monopolistic state capitalism regimes with bureaucratic-military dictatorship prevail with the presence of extensive but not politically dominant national capitalist bourgeoisie strongly interrelated, after China's entry into the WTO, with the globalized financial capitalism today dominant [177].

This system of beliefs constitutes the new international secularization and spreads with very diversified beliefs all arising from the absence of the sacred in personal relationships: anthropological and axial transformation of formidable importance also for what concerns the issues posed by the problem of decarbonization.

At this point, one cannot fail to remember the most important intellectual contribution to understand this new form of atheism in need of a new sacred, as John Gray might say, which Walter Benjamin offers us imperishably in his writing on "capitalism as religion" [178].

Why? Because capitalism is a cult religion, perhaps the most extreme and absolute that has ever existed.

Everything in it has meaning only in relation to the fulfillment of a cult, not in relation to a dogma or an idea. Consider the little Greta who climbed the altars of the mass media and collective rituals, the communities of NGOs striving for the salvific realization of themselves and the whole world. In fact, this cult is permanent, it is the celebration of a cult "sans trêve et sans merci". It is not possible to distinguish between holidays and working days, but there is a single, uninterrupted holiday, in which work coincides with the celebration of the cult. And the capitalist cult—Benjamin claimed—is not directed towards redemption or the expiation of a guilt, but towards guilt itself. It is, in fact, a cult not of expiation, but of guilt... A guilty conscience that knows no redemption turns into a cult, not to atone for its guilt in this, but to make it universal... and to finally capture God himself in guilt... God is not dead, but has been incorporated into the destiny of man.

This cult, in fact, tends with all its strength not towards redemption, but towards guilt, not towards hope, but towards despair: *it is a religion of despair*.

It cannot escape anyone who has done good readings that such a perspective, which is the one now rampant in the global symbolic discourse woven on decarbonization, is nothing but a return to the vision of nature and God that Spinoza made his own centuries and centuries ago.

Spinoza abolished the distance that, in the Judeo-Christian theological and philosophical tradition, exists between God and the world that God creates: he replaces a God who is the transcendent cause of the world with one who is the immanent cause, since between God and Nature there is a perfect, or unconditional identity [179].

The Spinozian consideration of God and Nature, with the affirmation of a radical immanentism, has in fact led several commentators to speak of pantheism, and some even to consider the expression *Deus sive Natura* "the slogan of Spinoza's pantheism" [180].

Spinoza was convinced that his way of understanding God was the only truly legitimate one, and that all providential conceptions of an anthropomorphic, free and good God, derived from superstition and imagination. Pierre Bayle [181] was the first (of many) who for this accused him of having modified the sense of the word "God" to the point of completely betraying it and therefore, in fact, being an atheist [182].

But perhaps the transformation underway in the symbolic imaginary of the era that opens with hyper-regulation and the creation of highly ideologized interstate institutions like those advocating decarbonization is the one that the old indispensable Hegel had grasped in response to Spinoza and his critics.

According to Hegel, Spinoza, far from denying God, had divinized the entire cosmos, and the error he had committed was to be called rather "acosmism" than "atheism".

It was in fact a radical denial of the autonomy of Nature with respect to God, of which it would only constitute a set of modifications, which was nothing but a reaffirmation of the uniqueness of the divine substance, in relation to which Nature is not heterogeneous [183]. Hegel, who also considered Spinozism the necessary beginning of all philosophy, therefore, reproached Spinoza for not having found a dialectic capable of overcoming the two moments of affirmation and negation and for not having been able to guarantee the autonomy and dynamism of the finite (deprived of its individual reality as it exists in something other than itself and is thought through something other than itself) in relation to the static infinity of divine substance [184].

The world returns as worship and nature reappears as the essence of the world and divinity.

A true "capitalism as religion".

But capitalism as religion has become—if it ever was—something other than a salvific imaginative element, rather a series of terrifying and frightening events. Here is the crisis from pandemic contamination first and then the crisis from possible global nuclear war. Capitalism as religion has suffered a formidable setback on the salvific plane: it has become a telluric element.

The collapse of the economy, not only Chinese, but global, has occurred dramatically, but not following the mechanism historically determined by all classic capitalist crises.

It was, in fact, a dual crisis exogenous to the movement of valorization of global capital. Or rather two exogenous crises, one following the other: first the pandemic, then the imperialistic aggression of Russia against Ukraine.

All in a very short span of time: from February–March 2020 to February 2022, when Russian troops crossed the Ukrainian border.

The pandemic that has affected humanity for about two years has given rise to reflections, analyses, and discussions. All of these have pushed us to question the ultimate purposes of life, because the pandemic has confronted us, as humanity, with the ontological problems of being: the transience of life, the presence of death, the distinctiveness of human experience from that of all other living species on earth, the uniqueness of man in posing the sense of being and of having to be.

The "tragic thought" has been reborn before us.

A thought that still reveals to us today the "truth of the world" because it reveals it to us in an anti-dogmatic way [185]:

> For after all what is man in nature? A nothing in relation to infinity, an all in relation to nothing, a middle between nothing and everything. Infinitely far from understanding the extremes, the end of things and their principles are invincibly hidden from him in an impenetrable secret, equally incapable of seeing the nothingness from which he is drawn, and the infinity in which he is engulfed. [186]

There is, in fact, an "impenetrability" of the "pandemic reason" that preforms the impossibility of answering the question of *why* the contamination is active, of the *why* of the presence of death.

It is the tragic question of this time in which we are immersed: *why*?

What comes to my mind is *Le dieu caché* by Lucien Goldmann [187]. It was Pascal and Racine whom Goldmann also questioned for us, today, to try to understand what was and what is the path that must lead us to the awareness of the tragic that is always present in human history; even if we always, cyclically, forget it.

In Pascal, in the *Pensées*, in the *Écrit sur la conversion du pécheur* and in *Le mystère de Jésus*, and in Racine, we find the paradigmatic conceptual "figures" [188] of the "tragic point of view".

The "tragic thought" is the critical counterpart of the triumph of a bluntly anti-humanistic idea of reason that is so pervasive today.

Indeed: with the weakening of rationalist-scientific paradigms—which have only come to declare, and still declare, even in the pandemic and in the omnipresent death, the immortality of a human who would be exempt from any form of moral obligation—in the decadence [189] of the secularization in which we are immersed, the pandemic event instead calls everyone to the awareness of the transience—along with mortal life—of an Enlightenment reason that wants not only to medically treat evil, but to respond to the tragic question that emanates from it [190].

Montaigne had already foreseen everything centuries before, when he wrote, referring exemplarily to doctors and the "Gascons" (*Vascones, fama est, alimentis talibus usi produxere animas*):

> And doctors are not afraid to use it for all sorts of uses for our health; whether to apply it inside or outside; but there was never any opinion so unruly that it excused treason, disloyalty, tyranny, cruelty, which are our ordinary faults. We can therefore call them barbarians, with regard to the rules of reason, but not with regard to us, who surpass them in all sorts of barbarity. [191]

The reference to "barbarity" is substantive because it introduces us to the otherness of the symbolic universe in which we are today immersed compared to the past. Almost a sort of *Lettres persanes* transmuted over time.

The times of the pandemic are, in fact, a radical transformation of all our symbolic universes. And the most symbolic is that of death.

The late-capitalist pandemic leaves us unarmed in the face of death: death that in the infinite moment of the symbolic present of the magnificent progressive fortunes—which always envelop the capitalist plains of the end of history [192]—seemed, instead, definitively overcome.

Montaigne anticipated, as brilliantly as only great moralists can do, the *landscape* symbolic in which the pandemic of late-capitalist globalization has immersed us all: a "look" *à la Starobinsky* [193], or that look which is characteristic of "literary creation".

Literary creation, or "the act by which the demand of the gaze surpasses and destroys the visible world to arouse, in spirit, the 'vision of the world'... make manifest the reciprocal links of the real and the imaginary" [194].

A non-scientific vision of the world: a vision that raises the problem of human destiny, as can be characteristic of the imaginary.

For this reason, Montaigne still speaks to us today: he places at the center of our symbolic world the relationship between the human and death. A world today dramatically different from the "total social fact" of a pandemic time, which returns to being faced with death.

We read:

> What dream is it to expect to die from a failure of strength that extreme old age brings, and to propose this goal to our duration, given that it is the rarest and least used type of death? We call it the only natural one, as if it were against nature to see a man break his neck from a fall, suffocate from a shipwreck, be surprised by the plague or pleurisy, and as if our ordinary condition did not present us with all these inconveniences. Let's not flatter ourselves with these beautiful words: we should perhaps rather

> call natural what is general, common and universal. Dying of old age is a rare, singular, and extraordinary death, and therefore less natural than the others; it is the last and extreme kind of dying; the further it is from us, the less hopeful it is; it is indeed the limit beyond which we will not go, and which the law of nature has prescribed not to be exceeded; but it is a very rare privilege to make us last until then. It is an exemption that it gives by special favor to one in the space of two or three centuries, discharging them from the obstacles and difficulties that it has thrown between two in this long race. [195]

Montaigne's time *coexisted* with death, or death was an inherent element of life itself: death caused by events similar to the pandemic, catastrophes, and incurable diseases were lived, *lived*, as inherent to life itself, not to the expectation or terror of death: that fear of contamination that today overwhelms us, in the pandemic, and on which I will return later.

To understand how this dramatic presence of death in the ongoing pandemic upheaval is posed before human consciousness, it is necessary to resort to the *Essai sur le don. Forme et raison de l'échange dans les sociétés archaïques*, by Marcel Mauss [196].

In that essay, the reference to the "total social fact" can certainly be assumed as a paradigm to understand today's drama.

And, in my opinion, the most illuminating guide to adequately understand its importance lies in the definition that Lévi-Strauss gave of this "total social fact", in a golden booklet [197], where it was stated:

> The total social fact presents itself... with a three-dimensional character. It must coincide the properly sociological dimension with its multiple synchronic aspects: the historical, or diachronic dimension; and finally the physio-psychological dimension. However, it is precisely in individuals that this triple convergence can take place. If we focus on this "study of the concrete which is of the complete", we must necessarily realize that "what is true, it is not the prayer or the right, *but the Melanesian of such and such an island, Rome, Athens*". [my italics]

It is only in this way, in fact, that it is possible to "relier – continues Lévi-Strauss – le physique (or physiological) et le psychique de l'autre" [198].

And it is precisely this "link" that Ernesto De Martino encountered in his very current research, which powerfully expands our ability to interpret Mauss's legacy, initiating us with unimaginable coherence to the understanding of today's experience, connecting the physiological with the psychic with impressive foresight. Perhaps the writing in which this foresight is most astonishing is the one dedicated to continuing the reflection of Benedetto Croce's *History of the Kingdom of Naples* [199], in the essay "Kingdom of Naples and jettatura":

> Now this enduring power of the negative – De Martino wrote – translates, from the existential point of view, into the recurring experience of the precariousness of basic vital goods, in the insecurity of prospects, in the chaos of clashing particularistic and individualistic interests, and in general in the uninterrupted pressure of non-dominable forces – whether natural or social – pressing from all sides and crushing the individual without the culture as a whole and society in its texture offering the possibility of effective realistic behaviors to face the negative and reduce it to a human measure. [200]

And it is precisely this "reduction" that—yesterday as today, in Milan, in Rome, in Athens, in New York, in Beijing, in Melanesia—is necessary to ward off the individual psychic collapse together with the collapse of the very reproduction of society. A "reduction" that becomes of great relevance.

It constitutes that "fourth dimension" of the "total fact" on which Lévi-Strauss insisted in the already mentioned essay, not by chance published in the years following the catastrophe of the Second World War. A dimension that Mauss had tried to conceptually achieve:

> … the attempt – Lévi-Strauss recalled – that he himself made, about the notion of *mana* [201], to reach a kind of "fourth dimension" of the spirit, a plane on which the notion of "unconscious category" and "category of collective thought" confronted… The unconscious would thus be the mediating term between the self and the other. [202]

In a universe where almost all of the *symbolic landscapes* are performed by what is defined as the *mass media*, with the techniques that perform precisely the same meanings.

And McLuhan's reflection (who, like a meteor, wrote in five years, in the sixties of the twentieth century, three works that are still indispensable today) is always current.

He sensed that the transition from a historical phase of expansion of the mechanical era to a phase of implosion, approach, and "reintegration" of the electric era, would have converged into a new technological-psychic paradigm: the algorithm applied to telecommunications and data collection, thus becoming a very powerful production of symbolic messages. While in the mechanical era the media were extensions of individual functions or senses, in the electric era the human nervous and psychic system would have been transformed, not only extending it, but also creating simultaneity and total involvement at maximum power in the mechatronic era applied to magnetism.

The electric era of the media would have "embraced" the world, our man claimed [203], shrinking it to the size of a village, without any community that was not that of artificial segmentation and no longer "natural", organic, à la Ferdinand Tönnies [204].

It is undeniable that our era—as McLuhan had still predicted—allows political power—which can make use of communication tools—to contribute to the redefinition of symbolic universes, inserting itself into the four-dimensionality of the "total social fact".

To this is added, in a dialectic as contrastive as it is consensual, the immense signifying and significant role of collective *prosumption* that springs from the so-called *social*. They allow the person and people, in very powerful virtual communities, to continuously redefine the symbolic space through forms of collective sharing of time and magnetic space.

With his extraordinary heuristic irony, Maurice Godelier had, in this regard, stated, discussing in one of his seminal texts about *potlach* and the power system it revealed:

> His powers over the invisible [... of the Sumerian monarch] therefore had to prove themselves in the visible world of the daily existence of his people. It is this service factory, some of which appear to us today as purely imaginary and others as very real, which provided the reasons for the consent of the community members to the exercise of his power and domination.

If we replace the "Sumerian monarch" with the peristaltic ruling classes of the differentiated capitalist societies of today, we grasp the concept well [205] ...

This understanding introduces us, before the same personal psychic representation, to the theme of acceptance, variously modulating in collective universes, of the practices imposed or desired by the "Sumerian monarch" of the moment in the face of the danger that strikes social reproduction.

The economic one, of this reproduction, is only a part and not even prevalent; and consequently it affects or can affect the reproduction of the same "monarch".

Always a social and always a political relationship, therefore.

A relationship that only becomes more and more dispersive of energy and therefore always on the threshold of entropy.

Increasingly likely, such entropy, in the continuation of the pandemic crisis.

And this is because

> This social relationship is always apprehended, lived, thought of as more or less legitimate, or even illegitimate, by the individuals and groups that make up the society of which it is one of the modes of organization... the ideal part of a social relationship also consists of the values, positive or negative, that are attached to this relationship, and therefore to the ideal rules and principles that allow it to be generated: "Values" here means both principles and judgments, and representations charged with a force of attraction or repulsion... All this does not imply that the ideal part of social reality is reduced to its conscious part. We have used the term thought, and it goes without saying that, for us, thought largely overflows from consciousness (and language). [206]

And here we come to the crucial point that marks the necessary turning point of this reasoning.

The "conscious part of reality", as Godelier asserts, recalls the rules or values that overdetermine social practices and personal psychic vibrations that define both "purity" and "contamination" in social relations.

Mary Douglas never stops talking to us about these themes; they are, ultimately, an ontology of existence and emerge as such during pandemics.

Purity and Danger [207] began with a reflection on the *Leviticus* that would last a whole long life of a scholar and witness of our time [208], thus helping us to understand how societies have elaborated and continue to elaborate forms of representation, defense and control of contamination: contamination, before being viral, food and epidemic, in an infinite succession of rites, magical and religious procedures of "classification" (think of food practices and ablution) that all societies have elaborated and that were and are aimed at preserving from contamination and preserving and reproducing purity.

A classification that implies the description of the mechanisms and classes of both gradients of authority and control and acceptance of risk and therefore of contamination itself. Durkheim first described myths and rites and classes of liturgical actors of magic and religions, paving the way for understanding not only segmented societies, but especially differentiated societies.

Durkheim still speaks today in a work (that on the elementary forms of religious life) appeared, let's remember, in 1912: in the years of Die protestantische Ethik und der Geist des Kapitalismus by Weber (of 1904–1905) and Totem und Tabu by Freud (of 1923), without forgetting Lévy-Bruhl's *Les fonctions mentales dans les sociétés inférieures* (of 1910).

Durkheim, stated Jean-Paul Willaine in 2013 while editing the seventh edition of the *Formes élémentaires*, takes us to the center of the current living process in which "The humanization of religion, on the one hand, the sacralization of society and the human being, on the other hand… unfolds" [209].

Mary Douglas herself has wonderfully told us—and only those who have seen and heard her speak and discuss can fully understand the depth and simplicity of her written thought—that of *Purity and Danger*

> [The] central argument… [is that of] classifications… They do something, they are necessary in organization. The pollution theory that I have seen develop over the last thirty years shows that where lines of abominability are drawn heavy stakes are at issue. The classification of the universe is part and parcel of social organization… If chapter 11 of *Leviticus* was a case for pollution theory the classifying of the animals should correspond to some important classifying for the internal organization of society. [210]

Social organization in the forms of human settlement in the era of globalization becomes, moreover, the environment in which the pandemic breaks out, causing various degrees of system entropy: entropy that can determine the spread of contamination and affect the principle of authority that regulates—with varying degrees of social acceptance—the social measures of limitation and prevention of the pandemic.

It is the diversification of the authority of power that determines the degrees of acceptance of the measures of preservation of purity and protection from contamination:

> Where the social system is well articulated, I look for articulate power vested in the point of authority; where the social system is ill articulated, I look for inarticulate power vested in those who are source of disorder. I am suggesting that the contrast between *form* and surrounding *non form* accounts for the distribution of symbolic and psychic powers: external symbolism upholds the explicit social structure and internal, unformed psychic power threaten it from the non-structure. [211]

Today we reflect every day, between the fear of contagion and the hope of prevention and salvation, on how important both the degree of authority in the political systems of defense from contamination, and the importance of the legitimization of that command power that is inherent in those systems and that can be accepted to varying degrees and measures.

Central then, in an organized social system, is to counteract the lack of legitimization and the low degrees of obligation: whether legal, moral, or religious.

And then we cannot forget the fact that Mauss had presciently stated that the holders of power in segmented societies were the "intellectual elite" [212] of such societies: personified in the sorcerers ("les magiciens"), they held power. Today we would say: "the power of political-administrative governance".

But it is precisely in the tension between the legitimization of power and its degree of effective articulation that the acceptance and pursuit of measures to contain contamination and the degree of risk acceptance are measured: it is this degree of acceptance that regulates social practice—between the individual and the collective—of the defense of the entire community from contamination.

If "the social system is well articulated, I look for articulate power vested in the point of authority" [213] said Mary Douglas, just now quoted...

And it is exactly on the degree of risk acceptance in defense from contamination that the great English anthropologist has left us a great legacy, in her last years of a lifetime's work:

> Social structure is a moral system; social accountability creates the main lines of cost-benefit payoffs and produces the different ways of categorizing the physical world. As with animals, human attention is focused by the concern of survival. But for humans, survival involves the human kinds of communicating, and this involves establishing the conceptual categories for public discourse. A cognitive psychology that ignores the process would

seem to trivialize its own project. It would certainly disqualify itself for considering risk acceptability. [214]

The most important "Maussian" research in this regard, moreover, not only addresses all aspects of this "total social fact", but pushes us forward in the analysis.

With the advancement of the pandemic and its not rapid domination, personal psychic potential appears disarmed in the face of the onset of death and even more so in the face of the need to never accept the pandemic risk, as it happens. But this is the result of the mass unawareness of the historicity of human processes. In recent decades, the "murder" or "destruction of history" has been perpetrated, as Adriano Prosperi recently defined this kind of disease of the spirit [215], and thus the sense of the transience of being in the world has been lost.

It was, as I have already mentioned, a hegemonic operation neoliberal after the collapse of the USSR. It led to the construction of a "pragmatic acceptance" which has as its archetypal psychic point a kind of absolute present in which humanity has sunk.

It is what Krzysztof Pomian called the loss "of the order of time" [216]. The loss of relationships "... that individuals and groups maintain with the elementary structures of temporality in a given society... the 'regime of historicity'... according to places, times and societies... these categories of thought and action that are the past, the present and the future" [217].

The present would have been attributed, in the last decades of the twentieth century, a disproportionate place... a "monster present", full of a past that no longer seems to be able to be surpassed and always engulfing a future that has become more a source of anxiety than a principle of progress, hope or renewal [218].

Is there a precise, organic link between the social fact *à la Mauss* and the "total presentism"? Certainly yes.

The curator of the collective work that intends to understand the cultural significance of the pandemic in perhaps the most organic form so far appeared, referring precisely to the French master, is so convinced that he begins his reflection that opens the collective work with this statement: "Humanity is plunged into total presentism" [219].

And then: "Against all illusions of progress and domination of nature, we return to the wise awareness of our common vulnerability" [220].

Here then is the proper reference, in the sense of "appropriate", to the "total social fact": the pandemic affects economic supply and demand and social reproduction; the pervasive economic aspect of a universe that is falsely presumed to be only mercantile is brought back to its proper dimension in being in the world—and therefore no longer in the dominant position it has had in the neoliberal counter-revolution of the last forty years.

It is brought back to the plurality of historical agents of human sharing in the historical reproduction of the species: sharing that in any regime of social relations of production, in the pandemic, is possible only by challenging the virus, protecting the human, that is, defending oneself from contamination.

Hence the reference to the "total fact of Mauss" and hence the reference to the rites of preservation of purity and hence the ontological questions that reflecting on them raises.

Essential, therefore, is the reference to time. The virtual reality of the mass media symbolization of the pandemic in the "eternal present" that, all over the world, every day "represents" Covid, forces us to reflect on "presentism".

That is, the symbolic "eternal" pervasiveness of Covid in the flow of the subject's vital experience.

The theme of time is essential in the experience of life. An experience that in the face of death by contamination presents itself as an interruption of the substance of being, that is, it becomes a manifestation of that *Zeitlichkeit* of the *Dasein* (the Heideggerian "temporality of existence") that cannot subsist without a "future-presenting".

Time in pandemic existence becomes, as Giacomo Marramao asserts in an important reflection that completes a decades-long research, "an experience of living constantly pushed back in a circle towards the past: so that the 'being-future' allows existence to repeat the past in the 'how' (*Wie*)of its having been lived and the 'no longer' becomes 'the authentic future'" [221].

Contamination and possible death become the manifestation of life itself in pandemic time, where the flow of existence may not lead to the future.

Contamination and possible death become the manifestation of life in a time that seems to be only present.

The present time becomes the only possibility of existence and thus reiterates a symbolic universe that we have seen described in "apocalyptic" anthropologies, that is, in that post-Crocean and distinctive school of Italian intellectual experience that was the anthropology of Ernesto De Martino, dedicated to the study of the experience of the "end of the world".

The "end of the world" becomes apocalypse because the future does not exist and the possibility of existence becomes only being in flight from the "total pandemic fact", as happened in more archaic experiences and not for this less similar to those not only of Boas, but of all the experience of studies on magic and rites of Anglo-Saxon anthropology, from the Pole to the "South Seas".

In reality, the apocalyptic experience (today "via pandemic") is mediated by a profound alteration of the dimension not only of time, but also of vital space due to the virtual mass media reality in which we are immersed that "presents" the pandemic and the possible contamination in every "present time" social media, which continuously "disorients" us in a deadly present.

It seems to never end, due to the daily reiteration in communicative globality, in pervasive globalizing actuality, recalling De Martino's annotations on "psychopathological apocalypses":

> The margin that separates the products of today's apocalyptic [the 1950s] from the psychopathological document thins - and in extreme cases disappears - as the artificial and programmatic disorientation of the world, left without effective recovery, ends up merging with the radical disorientation of the crisis and with its processions of insolvent convulsions of recovery and reintegration. The valorizing recovery of the psychopathological risk is thus transforming into a technique to second such risk, and this technique of the catabasis without anabasis is always on the verge of losing the acrobatic balance it tries to maintain on the edge of the abyss. The image of a world devoid of human operative memories, the idol of a nature prior to any communal domestication of man in society, always risk notifying a blind and anguished experience that makes prisoners and leaves without voice or gesture... [222]

And he continued by not coincidentally citing Camus's *Le mythe de Sisyphe* ...

In the pandemic humanity

> Rediscovers the fear of the cosmos and the telluric forces that govern it. It is grappling with the question of "pure life" in its biopolitical dimension. *Against all illusions of progress and domination of nature, we return to the wise awareness of our common vulnerability...* [my emphasis]there is now a complexity of borders, the pandemic has its own borders which are not the usual borders of man. The first borders of the epidemic are the body and the skin. Bodies thus constitute networks. We then speak of "cluster", this epidemiological concept where the social unit is formed by a network of associations. [223]

Frédéric Keck, director of the "Laboratoire d'anthropologie sociale - Ehess" and the AXA Research Fund, developing this analysis, arrives at the essential problem: he believes that the "elements" constituting this global process reside in the diffusive and genetic center of the relationship between man and nature through the relationship between man and animal. Only anthropology and not just medical science can intimately understand and therefore cure the pandemic, thus laying the foundations for its overcoming. The reasoning is too important (and unusual) to miss the opportunity to propose it here in its heuristic entirety:

> Borders, the relationship to bodies and fears through anthropological tools [are decisive]... In the course of the 1990s, with avian flu, we began to understand that, in the medical field, local dangers could have a global impact...

And so Keck continues:

> Each country is capable of anticipating incalculable events according to its cultural, social and political tradition. Japan, for example, has a culture of the event whose point of reference is the earthquake. In France, the flu and the strike have been thought of together, within French socialism, for example in Péguy and Jaurès, as catastrophes likely to collapse economic activity... Since 2003 and the SARS crisis, Asian countries have made massive investments in the field of microbiological research, but also in public hospitals in order to best anticipate the next atypical respiratory disease. Alongside this, they have set up batteries of tests as well as a practice of population surveillance through information technologies... Asian countries, to prepare for pandemics that come from animals, do not make a clear cut between men and other species. In the West, we have been using this reference for two centuries: the famous distinction between nature and culture. On the other hand, the perception of the catastrophe is different.

> In the West, we perceive the catastrophe as the end, the collapse; in Asian countries, the catastrophe is seen as a cyclical event that regularly returns. [224]

These are themes that, starting from the French case of eugenic research against the life of domestic animals, I have also placed at the center of my recent work.

This reflection places us directly in front of the theme of symbolic universes and therefore to the theory of the person in their relationship with the world: this is the unveiling that the pandemic places us in front of, between time and being and fear of being in time. Reflection on the Self becomes fundamental. Perhaps, then, it is to the "last" Marcel Mauss that we must return: to the thinker who, after decades of silence, returned to "speak" in the famous conference at the Royal Anthropological Institute of Great Britain and Ireland, in London in 1938, when the Second World War was on the doorstep and Nazism had fully unveiled one of the most horrible pandemics possible and unthinkable until then [225].

A Mauss who reflects on the most terrible of pandemics: the exterminating war, the advancing and announced Shoah that questions Durkheimian evolutionism for a broader and always very current awareness, as Camille Tarot taught us [226].

An awareness aimed at verifying a reflection that no longer proceeds par réfutation, comme les philosophes, que par relecture, [but] comme les historiens. He is exemplarily scientific by this double conviction, that science is always a collective work and that it never produces, as Bachelard would say, but an "approximate knowledge". He, therefore, intended to show that a complement of historical and ethnographic investigation is needed to remove the problem of the individual from the modern Western ethnocentrism that made the individual the property of the West by relying on the evolutionist simplifications that postulate a degree zero of culture and consciousness, at the risk of naturalizing the great colonial break between civilized and savages, which he has always questioned since his inaugural lesson in 1901. If there were primitives, they are neither in America nor even in Australia, where they can no longer be observed. What we see everywhere, today, are societies where there are languages, classifications, representations, and symbolizations, difficult to describe, to understand, to decipher, cultures already engaged in the practical work of producing complexity and identity around roles, statuses, names, and rituals.

CHAPTER 11

After the City in Capitalism as Religion

"Capitalism as religion" has become universal and has fueled its ideologies through the mechanisms of hegemonic power, that is, late financialized capitalism.

In the war of movement of financial capitalism, it is in the governance of cities that an important global power game is played to reproduce the dying late capitalism, a devastating agony [227].

Many scholars and merchants of capital exercise in reflection, but they distort reality and distort it.

Exemplary is the case of the *mainstream* discussion on cities.

Urban rent is never talked about in it. It is the underlying mechanism on which the restructuring of the territory with stable human settlements of late financialized capitalism in debt is based... and that's why it is never talked about.

Therefore, it is necessary to talk about it in this book.

Reflection on urban land rent is today at the center of the discussion of a minority of scientific observers: non-neoclassical economists and territorial geographers who focus as much on the production as on the reproduction of social life.

Their contribution is particularly important because the discussion on globalization has obscured the themes of the historical-concrete genesis of the new late-capitalist city that is emerging before our eyes and has shifted attention more to the themes of *government* of the city than to

G. Sapelli, *States, Markets and Wars in Global History*,
https://doi.org/10.1007/978-3-031-26716-1_11

those of its economic-social significance. It can only be as symbolic as it is material.

The reason for this is evident. The globalization of the economy de-hierarchizes, in the global rings of power, the role of national states (but does not eliminate them) and places cities, understood as social circles of aggregation, more or less dense, of gift relations, of exchange values, of use values: as much of human aggregates as of sedimentations of capital stocks, which are valued or await to be so. Everywhere, real estate work is intense, dressed in scientific-creative, museographic clothes, of *villes des loisirs* or of new *landscapes* artistic, biodynamic, neo-forestry, etc. Now we talk more and more frequently about local marketing that have become cradles of professions and therefore of social classes, which make their voice heard with the activity of *lobby* and with the *advertising*.

Moreover: improvised scholars have introduced the category of Habermasian public discussion to hypothesize that the creation of cities is possible with an argumentative logic—which they define *governance* instead of *government*, revealing their cultural fragility—rather than with that inevitable mix, perennial, between the latter and the role of the situational power of the predominant invisible actors who often secretly define the same agenda of the discussion… which is public only for those, Prezzolini would say, "who drink it".

The merit of such discussions, in any case, is to put on the agenda the theme of the profound transformation of the urban dimension and to allow us to reconnect it to themes that are essential to understand what is the mechanism of capitalist accumulation that is taking shape in new forms before our eyes.

Continents, indeed, where the metropolitan dimension is prevalent, with all the consequences of the case that I will try to highlight, assuming and not granted that I am able to do so. The common fact, in any case, is the increasingly relevant role of government authorities in shaping the face of new cities or metropolises (from now on I will use the term indifferently, after the warning just given). But it is a role different from that of the past.

It used to be expressed with the hierarchical tool of the master plan, that is, with the intervention of the public hand to which private *desiderata* had to bend, except for the processes of *bargaining* preceding. Now prevails in every latitude and longitude, on a global scale, a contracted design, which co-defines with the privatistic actors the physiognomy of urban transformations. It is the realization of polyarchy on a widespread scale, that is, the unveiling that alongside, and even more strongly than territorial representation, in the making of the decision, the situational power of fact operates forcefully.

The problem of power thus becomes central, even if the rhetoric on "regulation" of French matrix has often had the role of euphemistically obliterating it. What cannot be obliterated is the role of cities in both creating demand for goods and services, which they are powerfully capable of activating even after the deindustrialization of some of them, especially in Europe, and as potential activators of the supply of productive and symbolic goods and services, as is evident in particularly important studies of urban anthropology, which are developing with increasing intensity.

Consumption unfolds according to logics that only develop if the services offered by the public hand also improve their offer, for example, and this radically reclassifies the relationship between public and private starting from the urban dimension.

The market thus finds support in the network of services that the city government is able to offer, and this is a formidable incentive to reclassify the relationship between directive and decision-making functions in the urban aggregate. This is the underlying reason that explains the growing interest in cities as networks of knowledge and potential aggregative poles of excellence in work performance, with all the ensuing jargon about creative talents. The valorization of capital is no longer based on the logics of the city as merely productive, but on those of the city of services, both in Europe and in continents where cities still have an industrial role: think, for example, of Agra, Beijing, Mumbai, etc.

These transformations require reflection on the very concept of land rent.

The classics defined urban land rent as the fruit of the possession of a scarce or irreproducible good. In this case, the soil with a destination aimed at residential or productive or service construction: an eternally scarce good and therefore a producer, precisely, of a profit not subject to the typical risk of the enterprise. Today we live as much in the years of not absolute, but differential urban rent, that is, not generated by the change of destination of the soil (from agricultural to building), as in those of the formation of a profit that is produced thanks to the particular position of the owned soil in relation to the territory in which it is located, or for its particular characteristics that make it even more scarce and irreproducible.

The salient feature of this differential rent, however, is that of its proliferation like an oil stain or radially or archipelago, extensively, not intensively: with diffuse cities, diluted in space, with urbanized countryside and the city colonized by the countryside, as Kemal Karpat [228] had predicted in his pioneering studies on Istanbul in the early 1960s. A human settlement that has upset all the "Le Corbusian" assumptions of linear and similar cities, to be based, instead, on the chaos of individual transport and mass energy waste, with dense and variable hive conurbations, such as had never been seen before in world history. From a dichotomous world, urban–rural, center-periphery, we move to a fractal world with variable and unstable geometry… with very high sustainability costs, just when the latter has become the leitmotif of the unsuspecting who have taken the chair. But while all this could imply, cartographically, a city increasingly "encapsulated" in localism, technological and commercial and intellectual relationship terminals despatialize and deterritorialize the fractal settlement and connect it with the universe of the lowering of transaction costs of time and space, achievable thanks to ICT and the possibility of moving masses of people thanks to that same transformation of transaction costs (*low cost*, etc.) [229].

Complementarity and synergy are the transnational relational paradigms of the fractal city. The universalization of the "loss of beauty" that the oil-stain development has caused worldwide is significant. Perhaps it is not possible to maintain beauty in a fractal city. I am reminded (I found a newspaper clipping in an old book from my second youth) of what Antonio Cederna said on the occasion of his election as a Roman deputy in 1989:

> The city continues to expand without rules or measure, chaotically towards the south, increasingly tightening its grip on the Appian Way: new crossings are implemented, new suburbs are densifying, the city spreads without interruption, like an infection. The detachment between the city and the hills disappears, everything becomes an uninterrupted series of shabby, dirty suburbs: a new immense growth spreads to the south, with all its deleterious effects on the city, confirmation of the anarchic oil-stain expansion, disappearance of all green areas under a single concrete pour, congestion and threat of destruction of the historic center, defeat of any rational planning. [230]

This is what has happened, but not only in Rome: all over the world. The world, especially the non-European one, as anyone who entrusts their heart to a surge of knowledge that crosses the Atlantic, up to the Pacific, knows...

The phenomenon of the expulsion of regular residents from historic centers around the globe has been known for some time and is due to the exponential increase in housing area prices. Only in Italy, moreover, between 1998 and 2005 the average increase in property values was 69%, compared to an income increase of 16%.

The European and North American city, except for those extraordinary exceptions that are still the cities of the automobile and steel industry in the USA, has radically changed. It is no longer the space for the reproduction of an industrial workforce whose political representatives co-managed the functions of urbanization in a complex balance between conflict and participation. The French conflicts in the *banlieues* were the most exemplary epiphenomena of what I mean: the new immaterial, autonomous, widespread, small and medium production around the family that carries out entrepreneurial activities in new forms compared to the past is still institutionally invisible and in some ways ungovernable precisely where—the medieval and then bourgeois city—the very idea of government of the *polis* was born. On, in, among, this invisible informality is incised, with arrogance, another form of rent: the financial one, globalized par excellence and by definition, which has nothing *embedded*, but everything transnational, and yet must find a foothold for the same logic of its valorization, which otherwise does not become possible. Urban rent, land rent, and financial rent merge into a magma of fractals. But that fusion is very powerful because without finance urban rent does not materialize. This is the other great transformation before our eyes. The same territorial marketing loses its recreational density and competition *des loisirs* to become hypostatization of a model of city government assimilated—tragically—to that of capitalist companies. Cities become bearers of a real economic policy directed transnationally by the most aggressive real estate and financial companies that have buildable areas and debt recovery plans that have proved disastrous. A real Simmelian aggregation of secret societies is taking shape, which aim, in the new cities, to allocate financial, political, real estate interests that everywhere have a very fine plot of homophilic, familistic, consanguineous relations. Transnational globalization is the quintessential formative essence of such secret societies. The perfect presupposed market is nothing but the reification of collusive hemophilia inside, at the margin, outside the law.

Hence the new link that exists between injustice and the city and that must become the new ethically oriented field of study in the future.

In this light, we must rethink the genetic factors of land rent that underlie the two nineteenth-century models of Ricardo and von Thünen. While for Ricardo the amount of rent in agriculture depended on the different fertility of the land regardless of the geographical position occupied by them, for von Thünen the element of differentiation was the distance from the market as the distance determined the amount of product transport costs that entrepreneurs (agricultural and only agricultural at his time) had to bear to obtain a *return from cultivation.*

It is important to remember that for von Thünen, the price of different products was formed on the market under competition and was independent of the activity of the individual producer. Von Thünen's "ring theory" would be very useful today to interpret the levels of urban geolocation that gave rise to metropolises, constituted, precisely, with the gentrification of the same: concentric circles that, while segregating populations by income classes and situational power, spatially reproduce the social hierarchy of that "dual society" masterfully described by Peter Temin [231].

Von Thünen envisioned rent variants by hypothesizing the interference of traffic axes, which, transforming the concentric bands into "curves of equal transport cost" (isodapane), change the game of distance and produce a differentiation of land use zones in bands adhering to the axes [232].

In fact, if rent is linked to locational advantages in which information and the level of demand play a decisive role, then it can become an equally decisive element for the realization of the physiognomy of the city and the territory, whatever its new form, like the one previously evoked.

But this can only happen if effective forms of rent control are put in place. It is necessary to limit the scarcity of land for urban use and the social cost of such production must be borne by those who benefit from it. Moreover, the rent must be redistributed with the creation of infrastructures that make it possible to equip non-advantageously located places with building capacity. Finally, tax collection must return to being, after decades of *supply-side economy*, a central tool of distributive justice [233].

In this way, the economies of agglomeration and the increasing returns of urban scale would continue to constitute the fundamental reasons why *cities exist*, but would see processes produced within their own midst such that not only the logics of the relationship between *rent and profit* would be in force, but also a dynamic that identifies in urbanization a potential to generate non-segregating innovation.

In this way, the spring of urban development would not only reside in the differential level of profit expected by entrepreneurs compared to that expected by real estate operators.

The other element of the engine of the economy and the city could be represented by innovation (and, therefore, by Schumpeterian profit) understood as a variation of technologies in markets and products, and, in the specific urban, in the activities present in the city: the owner of the urban land would be able to appropriate, thanks to the "agglomeration" of the advantages of the "urban atmosphere" generating innovations, the Schumpeterian profits.

In this way, as innovative scholars who have left an indelible mark in studies such as Allen Scott [234] and Neil Smith [235] have well said, urban land rent would no longer be understood only as an obstacle to capitalist diffusion and its expanded reproduction. After all, the "fractal" city is proof of this.

Rent becomes, now, one of the tools of a new original accumulation that allows the creation of the immense citadels of capitalist consumption and therefore its cyclical reproduction: shopping centers, dormitory cities extended to the universalization of metropolitan disintegration, with the flight from historic centers, fuel such phenomena by also providing them with a sort of cultural legitimization…

Moreover, the "gentrification" of urban areas leads to a new requalification of historical centers. And this while the valorization of the land is strongly inserted in the process of financialization of the global economy: it is a pure land investment, which can be treated as a derivative, as a process of selling shares of construction companies before any productive and building activity has begun. It is the joint-stock company that reappears in its pure form for the risky valorization, from *securitization*, of the same differential urban land rent. These new strategies for realizing rent are before our eyes: they are the cathedrals of new buildings that, today in times of global economic depression, the interruption of the interbank liquidity circuit has reduced to motionless skeletons waiting for a new injection of capital that will take a very long time, but which for now, with its interruption, reminds us that every model of capital valorization, especially those that occur through rent, is pervasively in place. But it is subject to that instability—the dangerous innovation, remember!—that the forgotten Hyman Minsky [236] had described to us forty years ago with unsurpassed—and unheard—foresight. This report also talks about the relationship between rent and profit whose symbols live with us, today, as new "citizens" of globalization in the midst and after the pandemic crisis. The first thing to analyze would be the genealogy of urban planning ideology, that is, the sense of the formidable reduction of the city to a simple artifact, because this ideology still makes us incapable of really understanding what is happening today and produces extraordinary damage. But this presupposes a very heretical research program, based on the reversal of what is taken for granted today. For example, as long as we continue to think that the city is a machine—as many still think today—it will be impossible to achieve any result, even after having established the role of cartographic mediation, according to the connection: the map is a machine, therefore the city, which is a map, is also a machine. Thus we get not very far [237].

CHAPTER 12

The Mystical Body of Europe and Central Banks

To get far, perhaps we need to return to thinking about the economy with the breath we once had: the infinite breath of intellectual issues, before political or economic ones.

The opportunity may come from reflecting on Europe of the unique mechanism of financial technocracy that opened with the edition of the book by Kenneth Dyson and Iva Mars, *Architects of the Euro: Intellectuals in the Making of European Monetary Union* [238]. The ongoing debate on the euro and more generally on the European Union needs, in fact, to raise the level of reflective quality, resuming the threads of both economic theory and the history of economic thought, with a decided return, also, to a constitutional law that does not dress in a congratulatory rhetoric, but in a reflection, instead, on the diversity and non-complementarity of the legal systems arising from the most recent European event [239], resuming the threads of economic theory and together with historiographic reflection. This last reflection, in this case, needs a synthesis between the history of economic thought (a discipline less and less taught and studied in universities around the world) and prosopographic research [240]. A research, therefore, aimed at reconstructing the multiple personalities (for this reason prosopography is a cognitive exercise quite different from biography), who acted for several decades, in different forms and ways and with different cultures, in the first emerging European institutions, then in the consolidated European structures, and finally in the very

G. Sapelli, *States, Markets and Wars in Global History*,
https://doi.org/10.1007/978-3-031-26716-1_12

imagination of these latter, when one wants to rethink the *status nascendi* of the Union in the euro.

The theme is very important because the most acute problem of the European and global twentieth century was the realization of a socio-technical construct never hypothesized before: that of a continent without States, adopting as a tool of such construction the currency. I use the term "construction" not by chance because that realization of the European Union took place gradually and increasingly with a structuralist and functionalist logic: an attempt that had never been undertaken before in world history. Only the imperial design of Charles V can be compared to the enterprise of European construction. The way to build the Empire by a descendant of the Habsburgs was—as recently stated by perhaps the greatest historiographic interpreter of the Empire—the agnatic way and biological succession combined with a diplomacy of "descent" possible only in the states of the old regime. In them, as Max Weber teaches us, traditional power is very strong and is embodied in a sort of prophet monarch who interprets charisma from a theological perspective on which Kantorowicz has written unforgettable pages. "The two bodies of the King", according to the great German scholar (a natural body, subject to death, and a mystical, unnatural, and uncreated body, which cannot die), are a functional explanation of the possibility of transmitting power by acquiring a legitimacy that is not "inscribed in law, but is instead formulated by the sacredness with which the whole process of succession of power after the 'death of the King' is invested: in fact, power is not 'ceded' directly to the dynastic successor, as the power of the latter will be legitimate only at the act of coronation - one of the main symbols of political dramaturgy: to ensure the continuity of power, in fact, the mystical body of the King never dies" [241].

The mystical heart of the sovereign emperor of Europe today is based on the symbols of the construction of a continental unity that has a sovereign quite different from what historiography or comparative sociology delivers to us about political power. The mystical body of Europe today is that of its founders transfigured into a rhetoric that is renewed through an immense corpus of mythological narratives. Founders however quite different from the "architects", from the "Architects of the Euro" [242].

Robbins in his Geneva lectures before the Second World War hoped for a kind of non-socialist European federalism, while Altiero Spinelli, on the other hand, during the years of political confinement, drafted the manifesto for a European socialist federation. Schuman and Monnet in 1950, sharing the federalist objective, proposed a fully capitalist implementation of it in stages.

And this was the project with which European construction began. But this design was and is the mystical body: invisible to most and never discussed, under penalty of exile from the *inner circle* of power.

The project envisaged the creation of community bodies in specific sectors. They would have been added one after the other until they covered the entire area of represented interests, in a long process of decanting the systems of weights and balances between interest and pressure groups that were exerted on the building technocracies.

It is fundamental to briefly retrace Monnet's design, because he will be the true architect of the euro, with Triffin. Monnet had accumulated as an entrepreneur and as a *grand commis d'État* a fundamental experience of "transnational regulator" between the European world and the Anglo-Saxon world, when, as Gaetano Quagliariello very eloquently says,

> In 1915, he became the personal representative in London of the Minister of Commerce Étienne Clémentel, who conceived the idea of ending the prevailing disorder in the Allies' supply system by creating an inter-allied body with vast powers and composed of three directors: an Englishman, a Frenchman, and an Italian. At the end of 1916, the *Wheat Executive* was born, in which Monnet was appointed permanent representative for France, and which would serve as the model for all other allied executive councils created for the purchase of products necessary for the war economy. [243]

Monnet proposed the initiation of the European integration process in forms that were considered politically and economically advantageous by the reference political parties of Western Europe. From the fifties until the mid-seventies, he carried out constant action in support of the European integration process, based on a method called "functionalism". To understand the origin of the method and how his vision of international relations evolved, as well as the formation of his networks of relationships and knowledge, it is necessary to go back to his work experiences in various international organizations during and between the two world wars, as I said earlier.

Over decades of work, Monnet creates networks of *interlocking* relationships that will provide him with direct contacts with the political leaders of almost all Western countries. For Monnet, there will be no peace in Europe until two objectives are achieved: the re-establishment of democratic regimes in all countries; the liberal capitalist political and economic organization of a "European entity". This latter condition is essential to avoid repeating the mistakes made in the post-First World War period, when states were rebuilt primarily on the basis of national sovereignty and pursued policies of prestige and economic protectionism; on the other hand, only the constitution of a European market and the liberation of economic resources no longer invested by the needs of strictly national defenses will lead to the satisfaction of the new demands for well-being coming from the European peoples.

Monnet shares the diagnosis of the most radical Europeanists: he is convinced that the maintenance of nation-states has led to the two world conflagrations. He also shares their political horizon: in the not too distant future, national sovereignties will merge into a single European sovereignty and, to move in that direction, the sovereignties of nations will have to be progressively dismantled. However, unlike the federalists, he starts from a realistic analysis and a pragmatic method, which lead him to oppose any form of ideologization of the European question. The realistic observation is that public opinion is neither can be a brake or a driver of the organization of Europe, as there is no type of patriotic sentiment at the continental level. The organization of Europe has never been nor is a priority on the agenda of the governments of European democracies. Therefore, unlike the emphasis placed on public opinion by many federalists, he believes it is more important to work on governments "from within" or through party leaders; to focus on the establishment, on the high bureaucrats of the state and its agencies, as well as on industrial and trade union lobbies. Monnet supports the idea of starting the construction of Europe by gradually bringing out the common interests that exist. Concretely, this means developing integration in some limited sectors—particularly in key economic sectors—through European authorities capable of changing the rules of the game and gradually evolving the behavior of the protagonists. Through this progressive merging of interests, a de facto solidarity will be created in some economic sectors, which can later be extended to other sectors and therefore to the whole economy, demonstrating to the European populations the benefits of integration and bringing to light the common interest in collaboration.

Monnet is particularly concerned about Europe's economic, financial and military dependence on the United States [244]. Hence the birth of the still current divergences in the conception of power balances between European technocracy and pro-European parties and the USA, as clearly demonstrated by reflecting on the permanent conflict regarding NATO: first between the French and North Americans with de Gaulle and Gaullism and then, in our days, between the USA and reunified Germany, especially when power conflicts have—as today—the role of Western powers towards China, an aggressive power that provokes that split of the North American power system that today brings the system of Western international alliances to the brink of collapse [245].

Faced with the unavailability of the British government towards the European institution, as well illustrated by the role played by Roy Jenkins in the techno-eurocracy, it was decided, always following in the footsteps of Monnet, to focus on a Franco-German-based Europe. And it has remained so until today, always overcoming the inevitable power conflicts between the two nations that have bloodied Europe and the world for centuries. In the years following the end of the war, the position of the Western powers towards Germany changes profoundly due to the outbreak of the Cold War. Western governments, in fact, agree on the need to defend the Federal Republic of Germany (FRG) both to give strategic depth to the defense of the western part of the continent, and to prevent a possible conquest by the USSR from allowing the Soviets to use the human and industrial potential of the FRG against the West. At the end of the 1940s, in the face of escalating tension between the blocs, the problem of defending Western Europe becomes increasingly urgent and the French position—which proposed the dismemberment and international surveillance of Germany—appears increasingly weak. For this reason, from the beginning of 1950 the United States strongly presses to push the Europeans to cooperate and encourages Franco-German reconciliation.

It is from here that the design to unify what until then could not be unified, namely the "currency", when the collapse of the USSR disrupts the balance of power causing German unification.

The foundations to proceed towards a single currency were laid in a decisive historical moment. I am referring to the situation created after the Hague summit of 1969, when a new and different Eurocratic historical phase began. Volumes of liquidity attributable to private subjects, moving from one currency to another, created, influencing their exchange rates, difficulties in managing the economies of the four major European countries, France, Germany, Italy, UK. At the Hague summit, a proposal formulated by the Vice-President of the European Commission, the French Raymond Barre, was approved. It was incorporated into the plan named after the Luxembourg Christian Democratic leader Pierre Werner. The goal was to achieve a fixed exchange rate regime in three stages, until around 1990 the acceptance of fixed exchange rates, in practice a single currency. In 1986 and 1992, two related Treaties were signed: the SEA, Single European Act, and the TEU (Maastricht). The original project of the TEU underwent significant changes during the negotiations. Many of the principles and hopes nurtured over such long decades still form the subject of widespread beliefs. The first of these (a decisive part of the "mystical body of the King") is the legend that there is an "Economic and Monetary Union", the EMU. The "architects" have limited themselves to creating, instead of a political union, a "single market": a large economic space in which the principles of free private initiative (freedom of enterprise) and the widest opening of national markets apply as dominant.

Today most of the economic relations of the globe are governed by disciplines inspired by the same principles of free private initiative, therefore of freedom of enterprise in an open market. A "single" market has been built at almost a global level, but no one would define it as an "Economic Union".

The monetary issue was, then as now, embedded in the actual reality of the conflict that arose with the United Kingdom: its unwillingness to give up the pound promoted the "opting out" agreement. Granted to the United Kingdom, the clause could not be denied to Denmark and was effectively granted, in the absence of formal derogation, to Sweden, the first country to join the EU after the signing of the Treaty.

Just as the United Kingdom had declared that it would not give up the pound, so Germany specified that it would join the Union and the single currency only if it was similar to the mark. The goal of currency stability entailed, in the assessments of Otto Pöhl, president of the Bundesbank, shared by Jacques Delors, that limits were set—through regulations and therefore without compulsory powers except for the fact of non-legal arrangements!—to the indebtedness of each member state in percentages, relative to GDP, of 3% in annual indebtedness, 60% in total debt. The Italian and British delegations took an active part in the final debate. What is often underestimated is the fact that before agreeing on the characteristics of the currency, measures had been agreed upon that would have conditioned the entire architecture of the system. I refer to the fact that all the "intellectuals" builders, although coming from different schools of thought (the *Ordo-liberalismus* Teutonic to Walter Eucken and the French regulation school) [246], agreed on the fact that the States would have participated in the Union preserving their sovereign character and that they would have ceded not sovereignty, but the exercise of it, in vast areas, which would have been predetermined. Thus, after all, Monnet's functionalism dictated: to subtract sovereignty from the peoples without them noticing, never choosing between confederalism and federalism. The consequences of this covert functionalism were and are devastating: the ordo-liberalist assumptions became rules of a state that did not exist and in fact the Union did not have and does not have a Constitution, with disintegrating consequences on the legal level, transforming the rule of law into a jurisprudential state (the Court of Justice) constantly in conflict with national constitutions and therefore the parliament replaced by the judgments of the judges.

The prophecy of Max Weber was fulfilled and is continually fulfilled. From this point of view, even the explicit reference that art. 2 of the TEU makes to the "rule of law" does not matter too much, since, in light of this process the "rule of law" spoken of in the language of Union law has become something completely different from what it has always been in the past. It is, if anything, an informal rule of law [247], which claims to qualify as such simply because it wants to be inspired by those "values" materials, and that is to those political and institutional contents (separation of powers, independence of the judiciary, principle of legality, etc.) that historically have accompanied the affirmation of the rule of law, but which, understood in a material sense, of the logic of the rule of law are the deepest denial.

Whoever understands the rule of law in these terms—and that is in material terms, as a "value" to be paired and balanced with other values—forgets that the rule of law is, first of all, *a complex of technical-legal devices*, which supports a margin of adaptation, but which does not lend itself to a reorganization or a partial adoption of it.

And then we should admit that despite all the transfers of functions that have taken place from 1956 to today in favor of the Union and its law, and despite all attempts to construct the system of Treaties as the functional surrogate of a real constitutional order, it remains true what

C. Schmitt taught us almost a century ago about federal systems: that is, that "Sovereignty is not a competence: and not even a competence of competence" [248]. It is then understood why, from the beginning, the relationships between legal systems have been supported by coordination paths between national and European judges, both on general issues and in the smallest cases. Because, in the original logic of the European project, it was the judges, rather than the legislators, who were to carry out that operation of dismantling and reconstructing the classic legal categories (and therefore of de-formalizing the law) which alone could have achieved the final objective of the European project. Which was then the creation of a *lex mercatoria* transnational, which started from the uniform discipline of exchanges to then become a comprehensive discipline of the societies it crossed, and which, through this path, could extend its dominion over national systems, progressively reshaping their contents according to an economic-commercial logic. A law, in short, for which the formal national law would have been essentially a hindrance or, to use a more current language, an "obstacle" to the affirmation of the "single market" and competition understood as a dominant value, compared to which every other would have had to yield.

The competences of the Union would have been only those specifically contemplated by the Maastricht Treaty. The resources of the Union would have been, in addition to the revenues from external duties and a few other incomes, those transferred to the Union by the States (defined as "own"). The Union's budget would have had to balance every year. It followed that the Union could not go into debt. In matters of its competence, the Union would have issued regulations and directives, with direct binding effect in the Member States.

The post-Weberian steel cage of the single currency was an unnatural and artificial event. It forced into transnational unity a set of nations that had not even unified with the creation of a territorial state much more territorially limited than any European state and belatedly unified. All the southernist thought from Fortunato to Dorso to Gramsci up to Compagna and Amendola, ending with Rossi Doria, documents this my assumption. Europe was a great missed opportunity for Italy because only from Europe could come a harmonious insertion of Italy into a federal superstate in which the "being in the world" the plurality of nations that for centuries had coexisted and coexist under the roof of the unified Italian state. Think about the history of the United States: I have always wondered how they could have remained such after their great and terrible civil war, on which Marx and Engels have written, to this day, the most illuminating pages. And yet it was a war where perhaps more civilians than military were exterminated. The secret of the non-division of the Union from the Confederation, or vice versa, lies in the loyalty to the federal principles dictated by the Founding Fathers. With the relative economic and political instruments of the case: the Federal Reserve, with its statute antithetical to that of the ECB, and the very delicate and unstable balance of powers between the president and Congress. In Europe nothing of all this. Here instead is the re-emergence after two world wars of the Franco-German conflict and the secular flight of the United Kingdom from Europe. After all, Germany has never finished avenging the unspeakable humiliations that France inflicted on it with Versailles and the French have never finished avenging the defeat suffered at Sedan about fifty years earlier. Stalinist communism first and its collapse later did nothing but first suspend that mutual hatred and then rekindle it with the reappearance in the heart of Europe of eighty million Germans. Of course, we cannot forget Tacitus and how that masterpiece of cultural anthropology begins *Germania*. The problem is that it came to my mind, now that I follow the rapid travels of Mrs. Merkel—no more than four hours, for goodness sake, to Lisbon, Athens, Paris, Rome. Except for France, everywhere she finds vassals. Naturally, for our luck, the world now has an archetypal point that can make us escape from the nightmares of rereading the *Germania* of Tacitus. That point is the United States, which can want anything except a German Europe. The United States wants what the Italians want: a European Europe, that is, federal, that is, polyarchic and therefore endowed with non-democratic situational powers that compete with democratic territorial powers and therefore with a parliament that decides instead of a commission that decides. But this means the end of the factory of lies. It means the end of the absence of legitimacy and legitimization. But this means a new economy, hoping that one day instead of Tacitus, we can read Goethe's *West-Eastern Divan*.

With global trade falling and Europe declining, the problems in the coming years will be terrible.

The knots of the European Union have now come to a head. This is evidenced by the data of twenty years of non-growth in Italy, twenty years in which Italy has grown by 1.9%—while Germany grew by 30%, the United Kingdom by 33%, France by 29%, even Greece by 13.5%.

The political, not economic, philosophy that governs Europe today is based on the work *Die Grundlagen der Nationalökonomie* (*The Foundations of National Economy*) by Walter Eucken, which is the manifesto of ordo-liberalism, a school of thought that saw in Hitler's economic policy a degeneration of Keynesian thought, because the Führer had supported his government with public spending. The book has the merit of saying important things about it, as well as saying well about the "French regulation" school, the other dominant theory in the complex of ideas that have led to today's Europe. When Germany lost the war and was liberated from Nazism, these thinkers carved into their Constitution the principle that there must be no form of modulation and integration of the free market. They thus configured a principle contrary to liberal thought, which would never have inserted such a restrictive formula into a Constitution. Hence the disintegration from secular deflation, to say it with the great Hansen [249], in fact, that seems to never end. The British government enters a deep crisis, which well expresses what is slowly undermining the socio-political foundations of Europe and from which perhaps the United Kingdom has not had time to save itself. Secular deflation goes hand in hand with the disintegration of European political subcultures.

Jacques Delors, who from French trade unionism had risen to the leadership for many years of Europe with a single currency, was the most important representative in the European institutions of the so-called second left, which does not refer to Marxism while making it an object of analysis, and of the regulation school. Moreover, the "theoretical heart" of this current of thought is the criticism of the neoclassicals who consider institutions as rigidities, obstacles to economic growth, while, on the other hand, the "regulationists" interpret them as conditions often facilitating development. In some way, they form the real "invisible hand" that gives the market a certain coherence and certain purposes. Moreover, Boyer stated, "the most essential economic institutions do not always have an exclusively economic logic or origin. If we adopted this perspective, it would be a principle of efficiency that would govern the selection of institutions" [250].

Delors, on the indication of Mitterrand, of whose governments he was a minister, on July 18, 1984, was appointed president of the European Commission by the Member States, in agreement with the German Chancellor Helmut Kohl.

Reflecting on the events of the creation of the Weberian "steel cage" of Europe, one is surprised by how the germinal ideas of Triffin [251], another fundamental translator of nationality and economic policies, from his native Belgium, to the USA and the EU, were then carried out by a man completely different from the brilliant economist that Triffin was. It fell to a former French trade unionist to verify the design of the single currency, which we now know almost everything about. Regarding the construction of the European monetary system, Triffin, in fact, plays a leading technical role, introducing the reference to a unit of account that favors the use of the most stable monetary instrument and not the strongest in the text of the agreement that will become the European Union of Payments (UEP): the first attempt in the immediate post-war period of a *European currency board*. This instrument has since then not been defined exclusively in relation to gold and constitutes de facto an embryo of a European currency. Triffin, it should be remembered, also plays a fundamental role as a negotiator. He particularly exercises his influence among the Belgians and the British, coming up with technical solutions that guarantee the interests of the Commonwealth and protect the pound from the potentially negative effects of integrating pound balances into the UEP mechanism, *conditio sine qua non* for the United Kingdom to accept active participation in this new payment system. At the end of the negotiations that lead to the implementation of the UEP in the summer of 1950, he is appointed alternate member and then head of the American delegation on the board of the institution. He actively participates in solving the German deficit problem that emerges in the winter of 1950 and is overcome with the opening of an exceptional credit: this not only allows the UEP to survive, but also allows Germany to lay the foundations of its economic model that will serve as a motor for Europe in the fifties.

As President of the European Commission from 1985, Delors leaves his mark on the history of European construction thanks to his exceptional ability, all political, to amalgamate economic policies and national power logics. For this reason, his figure is counted among those who have contributed to making Europe an institutional reality, even if dangerously without a political constitution [252].

In 2010, in what was perhaps his last interview on European issues, Delors argued for the need for a "partial mutualization of the debt of individual States" as a means to "restore meaning to" community cooperation. "I have always said that the success of Europe, on an economic level, is inscribed in a triangle", he concludes. "Competition that stimulates, cooperation that strengthens, and solidarity that unites" [253].

Statements full of warnings and subtle despair.

But if we want to understand how it was possible to build the steel cage that will lead—if not dismantled—a magnificent continent—as Europe was before Maastricht—to ruin, we must penetrate further into a mystical body of the European Economic Union.

This other mystical body is the theory and practice of the so-called independence of the central bank.

In this regard, one cannot start the reflection without citing the final page of one of the last works [254] by a Master like Alberto Predieri. This work will then be followed by that golden booklet, written in the last year of his life and which prophetically enclosed all the problems in which we are now immersed, namely the too forgotten *Euro, democratic poliarchies and monetary markets* [255]:

> The reorganization of the administration for independent authorities that regulate markets and govern the market (as much as it can and should be governed in a non-command economy that is closely linked to the market) in the logic of subsets and the subset recognized as essential to the system, within the scope of the state as well as the European market, is equally a new arrangement. They are grown, tested, placed, balanced, *checks and balances*, which surpass the institutions of the state, even osmotic, the representation of interests, the parties, the central bank, the nodes, the companies. Institutions that are partly or conform to state institutions. In part, they remain different but correct, compensated, balanced, in the movement of society, in the osmosis of the state, in the *politeia*, which overflows from the state, horizontally as well as vertically, with the organization and the apex community law and structures a different architecture of spaces and constructions, of fullness and emptiness, of prefixed disorder.

Because the problem of the independence of central banks is exquisitely a problem *à la Lindblom* [256], that is, of polyarchies and their operating systems.

By polyarchy, the North American author means the intertwining of economic interests that, by their organized form (the company and the association representing interests), exert a power of influence or control (which I define, following the reflection of Alessandro Pizzorno, "situational power of fact") [257] and the political institutions of both liberal democratic states (parliaments and bureaucracies) and variously authoritarian states (single parties and their bureaucracies). This gives rise to a conflict or a balance of power between what I define as functional representation (functional autonomies, economic representation associations, intermediate bodies) and territorial representation (that governed by the Ruffinian principle of majority, i.e., parliaments, municipal councils, and all the various forms of political representation). Market and State, exchange of goods and command over people, incentives and authority, are the pairs of fundamental principles on which—according to Lindblom—the social and economic organizations of contemporary society are based. Starting from an analysis of what is implicit in these principles, Lindblom studied the functioning of various types of political systems and how the market and the state can have contradictory effects both in terms of economic efficiency and in terms of democracy and freedom. Lindblom showed how large private economic organizations represented and still represent an unresolved problem for the functioning of democracy and thus analyzed, in an original and realistic way, the essential features of the relationship between politics and economics.

The polyarchic relationship becomes overdetermined in the specific European continental context by the overlap of powers and rights in an institutional construct, before being political, dictated by overlaps of law and technocratic alterations relevant to the fluctuation of competences and powers, previously mentioned, due to the neo-Weberian cage of community and functionalist steel *à la Jean Monnet*.

European institutions more than ever demonstrate a sort of constant polyarchic rule: the public (political) and private (economic) relationship becomes a trinomial public–private-technocratic (EU institutions and Central Bank). In this way, it is shown how the hypostatization of the public–private dichotomy is always very simplistic because it hides the complicating presence of technical powers, that is, public, but not politically legitimized.

It is in this context that the substantive issue of the independence of central banks should be understood, which goes to the heart of the legal tradition of the two worlds of *common law* and *civil law*.

They have historically confronted each other globally.

But to fully understand the problem I address in these pages, an immediate reference to this opposition would be misleading. Not only because of the osmosis and overlap between legal systems that has materialized in Europe and the world with the advent of globalization, on one hand,

and the creation of the EU—and here any irony must be suspended to proceed serenely—on the other.

Osmosis and overlap and coexistence with a strong Anglo-Saxon legal domination concerning the economic system and in particular its subsystems, starting from the company and the rules of its *governance*, from the *audit committees et similia* [258].

And this remains beyond Brexit and this is precisely the ironic and tragic together, in the classical sense of the term and not in the journalistic one.

But my point of view is more historically determined looking at political thought and the construction of political systems and civil liberties.

The tradition of the independence of central banks has very little to do with the history of the United Kingdom: the Bank of England, founded in 1694 (it was the first central bank in the world), received what is defined as "independence" three centuries later, namely in 1998, when the *Bank of England Act* granted the Bank of England independence with respect to the monetary policy to be adopted, particularly in relation to interest rates. If inflation deviates by more than 1% from what is planned, the governor must write a letter to the Chancellor of the Exchequer, explaining the reasons and stating what measures he intends to take.

But our theme is not understood unless it is inserted in the climate of the global economy of the 1980s, when faced with a fall in the rate of profit, companies responded with an increase in private debt. Thus, at the beginning of the 1980s, there was a real explosion of credit, both consumer credit for families and credit to states. Banks, after having indebted third world countries in the 1970s with eurodollars, to the point of bringing them to the brink of bankruptcy, now had unlimited outlets to "attach" to developed countries, which let themselves be "attached" by opening their arms and, more prosaically, by ending all regulations. The financial deregulation that began then was a decision aimed at offering outlets to capitals that no longer found prospects for profit that justified productive investments. To make possible such valorization of an increasingly large financial capital in the face of a reduction of the original manufacturing capital, all the barriers established after the 1929 crisis were torn down. The list of all the deregulation measures decided by governments would be too long, but some can be mentioned: in the United States, the decision of the federal bank, in 1979, to raise interest rates, which were quickly multiplied by three, then by four, plunged third world countries that had loans in dollars towards bankruptcy. Also in 1979, there was the complete abolition of exchange control in Great Britain. Throughout the first half of the 1980s, in the United States and in Great Britain, there was the progressive suppression of all control measures and regulation of the prices of banking services, i.e., interest rates. Previously exclusively decided by central banks, the interest rates of new financial products were created by the financiers of Wall Street and the City themselves. And at the same time, barriers to the movement of capital were removed. States adopted one after the other measures that allowed holders of foreign currencies to freely speculate on their markets. At the same time, they eliminated the barriers between the various sectors of finance or the various markets that were previously separated (insurance, commodities, currencies, etc.).

One of the last vestiges of financial regulation was torn down on November 12, 1999, under the Clinton administration: the *Glass-Steagall Act*, which was already less and less respected in fact, was repealed by the North American Senate [259].

This process of formidable power had little importance for the Federal Reserve in the USA. The ***deregulation*** in the USA did not bring with it the independence of the central bank. It already existed.

And this is because the independence of central banks is not a principle that is realized by following the economic traditions of social and state systems in osmosis with the markets and the market, but is a matter purely of constitutional traditions and signals a difference also in the systems of *common law* that do not have—in the comparison between the USA and the United Kingdom—similar constitutional traditions, but—as is known, and as is often not remembered—very distinct.

Just as different are the systems of personal freedom and therefore constitutional between the United Kingdom and all of Europe [260], beyond the existing national differentiations on the continental platform… on the Schmittian "Earth" [261].

The independence of central banks was, all over the world, a consequence of the transformation of the global economy that brought with it, everywhere except in the USA, also a profound modification of the de facto, material constitutional systems [262].

To delve into this topic without making interpretative errors with respect to what are the orientations of the supporters of the independence of central banks, we cannot fail to refer to a text that will remain foundational: the *keynote address* by Yves Mersch, member of the Executive Committee of the ECB Board, delivered at the opening of the *Symposium on Building the Financial System of the 21st Century: An Agenda in Europe and United States* [263], held in Frankfurt on March 30, 2017, in which it is clearly stated:

> From a legal perspective, the Treaty on the Functioning of the European Union established the European System of Central Banks (ESCB), consisting of the ECB and the national central banks (NCBs) of all EU Member States, and assigned to the ESCB the primary objective of maintaining price stability. To pursue that objective, the Treaty assigned to the Eurosystem, which is composed of the ECB and the NCBs of Member States that have adopted the euro, the core task of defining and implementing monetary policy, together with a number of core central banking tasks in the areas of foreign exchange operations, foreign reserves management, the smooth operation of payment systems, authorizing the issuance of euro banknotes, and the collection of the statistical information necessary to undertake these tasks. With respect to the prudential supervision of credit institutions and the stability of the financial system, the ESCB *is mandated* [my emphasis] to contribute to the smooth conduct of policies pursued by the competent authorities. In addition, Article 127(6) of the Treaty *permits* [*idem*] the Council to confer specific tasks upon the ECB concerning the prudential supervision of credit institutions and other financial institutions with the exception of insurance undertakings. That provision was activated recently through secondary legislation establishing the Single Supervisory Mechanism (SSM), which confers tasks on the ECB relating to the prudential supervision of credit institutions.

And again, more precisely:

> Some scholars *and one national Court* [264] [my emphasis] have been even stricter in their interpretation, arguing that the independence of central banks is an exception to the principle of democratic legitimacy. This exception allows an independent institution outside the normal process of democratic and political accountability to be entrusted with authority for monetary policy only under the condition that it has a clearly defined mandate allowing the public to hold it accountable for the performance of the technical tasks assigned to it by the legislator. The clearer and narrower the mandate of a central bank is, the easier it is for the citizens to monitor its performance. In the case of the ECB's monetary policy, the Treaty sets

> out, in very clear terms, that the primary objective of the ECB is to maintain price stability. Also, the permissible rate of inflation is quantified by the ECB through the Harmonised Index of Consumer Prices (HICP), which is easy to understand and is updated at frequent intervals.

It is said, therefore, that the bank must be *accountable* in the pursuit of its *technical tasks* to the public. But what are the tools of this control of the "public" that is not entrusted to any particular body or institution? Who actually takes charge of it? And with what tools? In other words, it is said that transparency is needed for the central bank to be *accountable* but how is this *accountability* enforced? And with what effects? Mersch's seems really like a play on words.

What is the bank's margin of discretion in setting the HICP? It is clear that if one can refer to the determination of "desirable" inflation, one can act on both the *goals* and the *instruments* of monetary policy. It is precisely through the decision of the BVG that an attempt has been made to make the ECB's actions *accountable* with respect to the objectives of the Treaty.

On the Court's judgment, it is important, then, to refer to what Davide Sardo wrote on *Pandora* [265]:

> The Court of Justice finds itself cornered: if, on the one hand, it provided an extensive interpretation, the German constitutional court could declare Germany's participation in the program constitutionally illegitimate, effectively decreeing its end; if, on the other hand, it provided a restrictive interpretation, the program could risk losing its effectiveness. This is further complicated by the fact that the German constitutional court has already specified, in the referral order, what the limits are beyond which the OMT program would be considered as adopted *ultra vires* (i.e., beyond its own competences) by the ECB: these limits are at first glance such as to completely inhibit the effect that the mere announcement of such a program has so far had on the markets... it is worth asking whether the unfriendly dialogue currently taking place between the German constitutional court and the Court of Justice has characteristics that should sound an alarm bell with regard to the correct balance between the functions of the different institutions. It is possible, in short, to draw moves from this complex judicial affair, to look from a further point of view at the more general democratic issue that now rightly occupies an increasingly important part of the debate on European institutions. In this case, in particular, it is striking how some of the main European judicial bodies, in their relationship with each other and with other institutional actors,

> appear to adopt an openly negotiative attitude, which goes well beyond the protection of legal cultures and judgment standards, but seems rather to pertain to the defense of specific political interests…

Looking at the bigger picture, the ECB itself and, in many ways, the European Commission, are non-political occupants (or, at least, not properly so) of a space that is political by nature: the decisions made in this context do not cease to be political simply because they are made by formally neutral, technical or third-party bodies. If the invasion of the field does not, therefore, produce any difference with regard to the politicization of the process, the effect (deteriorating) is, however, imposing from the point of view of the legitimization of this process, both in a formal and substantial sense. In the presence of political decisions taken by bodies more or less independent of electoral dynamics, the link between discretion and responsibility weakens, and the structures connecting popular will and institutional representation are endangered.

It is worth remembering here, to reinforce Sardo's interpretation, that the initiative of the German court in Karlsruhe was prompted by the co-founder of the right-wing AfD party Bernd Lucke, by the representative of the Bavarian conservatives of the CSU Peter Gauweiler, and by law professor Markus Kerber, whose goal is to prohibit the Bundesbank from participating in *quantitative easing*.

Markus Kerber is the professor at the Technical University of Berlin who has hindered the MES, the state rescue fund that establishes *a financial organization with such and so many powers* as to effectively create a new European Monetary Fund in competition with the International Monetary Fund. Kerber was also the inspirer of the sequence of 37,000 appeals to the Constitutional Court of Karlsruhe that would later force the supreme German body to impose *significant limitations* on the MES. The latter, in fact, will not be able to operate without explicitly asking for the authorization of the German Parliament. In this way, in Germany, an *accountability* of the ECB has been judicially constructed in front of the German Parliament alone and, secondly, in front of the BVG. This creates an anomalous situation, because in the other nations adhering to the Treaty this *accountability* is lacking. Moreover, the absolute and supreme inviolability of the documents and minutes of the body falls, which cannot derogate from the principle of transparency.

The themes of the question thus precisely clarified and illuminated are also the tearing themes that the independence of central banks poses.

In a state osmotic to the market with situational powers of fact and between osmosis and such powers constituting the polyarchy, independent authorities and *in primis* central banks—for the power to define the degree and strength of the aforementioned osmosis—operate as credit institutions in the last instance in the context of a functionalistic subsystemic praxis, that is, that decision-making mechanism subtracted from any political control that constitutes the warp of the de facto legal order of European technocracy. Decisive is the concept and practice of the "mandate", that is, of the delegation: a decisive function in the construction of the ribs of the capitalist socio-economic system.

The functional delegation is not legal, in this case, and is never definitively written, as contracts are never definitively and completely written [266].

Delegation and mandate are not contracts, but functions that are implemented thanks to a procedure that needs to be identified in a dark forest no longer illuminated by the clarity of the principle of majority and the determining and superordinate power of the legislature, as it was in the law and in the constitutional praxis of Napoleonic derivation in Europe.

The question is what is today the power that—in the much wider articulation than the original Montesquieu division between armies, on the one hand, and "can", on the other—makes the function of giving the delegation and attributing the mandate executive.

And what gives this power? Charisma? The state of exception? Tradition? The territorial representation that legitimizes? The threat and use of force?

The path chosen in Europe is the functionalist one *à la Jean Monnet*, that is, the transfer of powers from individual States to supranational institutions, European in this case.

But where does power reside and what is its source?

Institutions are technocratic because they lack political legitimization of support according to the principle of majority, and parliaments and national institutions retain the power that comes from political representation to deliberate on matters not assigned to technocratic institutions as technical routines, as we have studied in the theory of the firm [267]. But nothing can be entirely subsumed by the routines of technocracy and this explains the continuous re-emergence of powers not subtracted: they do not hinder technocratic measures where they are not required to ratify the mandate or delegation, but arise whenever new transformations of associated life imperatively pose the problem of legitimization that technocratically cannot be established.

It is no coincidence that the confederalist theory supporting an association between States that do not renounce sovereignty continually resurfaces. There is indeed, in addition to the so-called sovereignism of right-wing and far-right nationalism, the constant claim of weak integration, typical of nations with active traditions of strong States that in Europe coincide with ancient or present great colonial powers. The United Kingdom and France are the champions of weak integration and aimed at controlling strategic sectors of the economy (and one cannot help but think of Margaret Thatcher and Charles de Gaulle, not to mention Winston Churchill).

They do not talk about procedures of democratic legitimization: they are not necessary because the Confederation is silent and always gives the floor to the States that, "de-saussurianly" sovereign, coordinate the language remaining faithful to their language (the Nation). And in this way they achieve degrees of efficiency unknown to federalist tribes: decisions must be taken unanimously and not by majority. The consent of the citizens is active only in national form and each people preserves its community of destiny by shielding itself from Hobbesian oscillations that more easily manifest where traditions are challenged.

What constitutes, what founds the independence of central banks? Now we can ask ourselves this with a broader awareness. The question can be better developed by turning to the conclusions of Mersch's essay, which is of a definitive clarity:

> *The rationale* [my emphasis] of the principle of central bank independence, as set out in the Treaty and interpreted by the CJEU, is to protect the ECB from political influence primarily when defining and implementing the Eurosystem's monetary policy. *The additional mandates and functions conferred* [my emphasis] on the ECB after the financial crisis with regard to micro and macroprudential supervision and crisis management are not covered by the very high level of independence provided to the ECB under Article 130 of the Treaty. Nor does it apply to the contributory role of the ECB with regard to financial stability under Article 127(5) of the Treaty, as the ECB is not the policymaker in this field. [268]

Rationality, mandate or delegation, conferring of functions.

The transfer on a scale of the organization of osmotic powers of a vital and fundamental sub-systemic power.

The power of central banks has been underestimated.

There is not only a problem of legitimacy and legitimization. That is, the subtraction of power without having a supporting morality that allows me to do it and the fact that the delegate, like the delegator, also exercises the function without a supporting morality.

My thesis is that the process of conferring powers was only possible due to the threat of the use of force exerted by the situational power in fact, which was considered stronger when it was decided to transform a European Union without currency into the EU with a single currency, namely at the time of the collapse of the USSR and German unification.

This historical process had its own internal nature typical of the power mechanism with few causal references to the economic situation. And this must be said to avoid too easy mechanisms. It took place while that great neoliberal ideological offensive was developing, which laid the foundations of the theoretical justification for the independence of central banks and constituted the deep background of an upheaval that would fully reveal itself during the crisis of the USSR, being amplified in unprecedented and extraordinary forms for intensity: capitalism seemed invincible and, with unregulated finance deployed, bearer of limitless development.

Today we are facing a profound transformation of the composition of capital on a global scale, in which capital expenditures for the creation of powerful large-scale manufacturing industries have been increasingly replaced, percentage-wise, by new and different capital expenditures to build the new service industry with lower fixed capital intensity and lower transaction costs.

This was primarily the effect of the advent of the latest cycle of innovations *à la Kondratiev* [269] based on *information technology*. A different organic composition of capital has thus led on a global scale to a thirty-year fall in interest rates. This has greatly benefited the high-risk financial component of modern capitalism, as seen with the risk excess crisis that struck the global world after the *deregulation* of Clinton and Blair. This *deregulation* has helped to cushion—as is well known—the cyclical crisis of overproduction due to low rates of international consumption, which nevertheless struck like a hammer on the globalized world.

Finance has allowed this crisis due to unrealized profit to "buy time", by securitizing debts and delaying the fall of the *corporations*, which not by chance have transformed themselves, expanding financial returns alongside industrial ones.

On the other hand, the monetary expansion policy advocated by the Federal Reserve has convinced international capitalists not to withdraw such large shares of capital from investment spending to the point of causing a perhaps irreversible collapse of the global capitalist system.

High-risk finance and expansionary monetary policy have allowed the US, and the world, to overcome the lowest point of the crisis and now allow Europe, plagued by ordo-liberal austerity policy [270], to breathe, thanks to the advent, in the eurozone, of new financial capital expenditures that allow promoting an illusion, precisely financial, of new growth.

But the problem remains that of the increasing social disintegration: the growing inequality with low consumption slows the increase in interest rates, as does low capital expenditure: everything intersects and overlaps.

European-Teutonic austerity does the rest, that is, the constraints of budget balance—where they exist institutionally (only in Europe and for structural reasons that are well known)—are a further incentive to the decrease in interest rates, because they prevent the advent of that capital investment that could break the vicious circle, namely public spending for investments.

But it is precisely this investment that has been and is wanted to be prevented in Europe in the first place, pursuing a policy of social exclusion and attack on the achievements of post-war welfare with a violence never before seen in capitalist history.

The deflation of Euro-Teutonic origin is nothing more than the monetary seal of this transformation—with immense consequences—of the structure of the cycle of enlarged capitalist accumulation and its European institutions.

European rhetoric calls low inflation what is deflation and hypostatizes the independent variable of budget balance as an essential measure to guarantee economic growth. Anyone who knows the history of economic thought—we are increasingly few—knows well that the hard core of this hypostatization lies in the French monetarist school of the thirties with Jacques Rueff at its head, the great supporter of the return to gold.

The strong franc and military power were to be the main axes of a France that was to dominate Europe and even challenge the United

States. A great champion of this policy, as is well known, was General de Gaulle with his *force de frappe*.

The Hegelian cunning of history has meant that this paradigm, which no one wanted to listen to, and which the first steps of European politics threw into oblivion, with avalanches of public interventions and public debts, instead constituted the structure of Europe and all its states until German unification, starting from an agricultural policy that had an almost Soviet tone.

It was then that the monetary flight (let's keep the pound...) of the English on their island, the economic ignorance of the Italians, the French imperial grandiloquence, brought out from the feluccas that idea *à la Rueff* [271] that ennobled the German dream not only of unifying, but also of unifying by unifying Europe around itself, with a mark that had been, instead of the franc, so strong as to be able to disguise itself as the euro and continue to generate for Germany, which now had eighty million inhabitants, a trade surplus that made all the other European countries tremble.

The French dream became the nightmare that the Germans imposed and impose on all of Europe. Trade surplus, strong currency, increasing productivity higher than wage increase, reduction of public spending: this is the German song that all Europeans had to and have to sing. And they also have to be happy.

On the experiential bases of that policy, the collapse of the USSR generated, as is known, that Franco-German agreement, in which Italy always participated in a vassal position, which gave life not only to the single currency, but also to a system of fixed exchange rates to a single currency governed by a European Central Bank modeled on the *silhouette* of the Bundesbank.

This was the final mirror game allowed by ordo-liberalism: yes to the independence of the European Central Bank on the North American model, but its statute had to be a copy of that of the Bundesbank, not of the Federal Reserve, and the only objective to be pursued—thanks to such independence—would have been price stability, and therefore European deflation congenial to the *export-led* model of the German economy and the European-Teutonic sphere.

That result already foreshadowed the insurmountable European contradiction: it is impossible to keep together a system of fixed exchange rates to a single currency that prevents competitive devaluations, typical of flexible exchange systems, if not by resorting to internal devaluations, in the presence of nation-states with different total productivity rates, as is precisely the case in Europe, with consequent high structural unemployment, increasing impoverishment and accentuated inequalities in a strongly deflationary context.

How did all this happen?

It was another *power's follie* [272]: Europe itself contains diverse socio-economic formations, as I demonstrated in a 1994 study [273], where it was predicted that this system could not function without immense social costs and dramatic vertical drops in the production of goods in fixed capital stock.

This has been made even more evident by German cultural hegemony, which became manifest in the Maastricht agreements and those that followed.

In the centuries-old competition with France, the Germans had to ensure the supremacy of the national economic system. This was only possible with the general application, in the very marrow of European bureaucracy and technocracy, of the principles of *Ordo-liberalismus*, as they are consecrated in the theoretically very weak text of Walter Eucken [274], but propagandistically very successful for its simplicity, to the point of transforming into the incredible dyad of the social market economy, even more poorly theorized by Wilhelm Röpke [275] in his unfortunately not forgotten texts. The assumption of the *Ordo-liberalismus* is not only that of Robinsonian market freedom, but above all the hypostatization that a state without debt and with a low deficit is possible perpetually, in a world without capitalist cyclicality and with equal levels of territorial and national productivity.

If this does not happen, the fate of such human settlement communities is that of perennial subordination [276].

Subordination of all the weak nation-states chained by technocratic-oligarchic functionalism in a relationship of servant-master to the state or states with a commercial surplus, guaranteed both by higher national productivity and by the importation of low-cost goods.

In the current vernacular, all this is referred to as the relationship between creditor and debtor states, where the fetishism of commodities presents the interstate relationship as a double-entry affair.

This is the situation in Europe today, with Germany at the center and France in a subordinate position.

The most interesting discovery, however, is that the Freiburg School, in its quest to construct a legal barrier, which would oppose a steel order to the possible re-emergence of Nazism, found it in a series of norms—because it is the norms that make the orders—a constitutionally perfect path for its purposes in being inspired by North American constitutionalism: a law that could no longer be changed and that contained within itself the hypostatization of the free market and economic liberalism as the only suitable tool to create it, the market.

Anything but a liberal constitution, if what is believed to be "liberalism" can be implemented, in the economic sphere, only and always as "liberalism", which contradicts any liberal spirituality, according to the famous distinction of Benedetto Croce [277].

These were elementary distinctions in the sign of cultural civilization: today they are forgotten and outraged from the chairs to the pulpits.

This discourse is, in a completely different way, essential for my reasoning, well developed by Étienne Farvaque [278]:

> The foundation is what animates North American federalist thought: the need to control the executive power and at the same time the fear of losing freedom due to demagogic agitations leading to the dictatorship of the majority. [280]

The executive remains marked by the seal of history, a violent history in this case, and the goal of modern constituents is indeed to tame this power, to put it at the service of the people's interests. The whole difficulty then comes from the fear that the executive could divert the Constitution to serve its own interests.

Two options then open up.

The first option agrees to control the executive power by the legislative power, allowing the latter to monitor the acts of the former. In this perspective, the legislative: (1) represents the people; (2) defines the law in accordance with the mandate that has been given to it (whether this is imperative or representative matters little here), and (3) has the law executed by the executive power, which achieves the parliamentary objective under control. In this conception of the separation of powers, it goes without saying that the executive power does not have the freedom to modify the law.

It will be readily agreed that this vision of the constitutional order is not very conducive to the delegation of powers. We then understand that the principle of independence of central banks has had some difficulty in making its way in Europe, where this first conception predominates. The

British case is representative: the Bank of England (created in 1694, it is among the first central banks founded) only obtained its instrumental independence late (in 1997), but still not formal. Monetary policy, as part of the executive power, therefore, remains subject to the legislative power until a very recent date (and, formally, the subjection remains, despite the recent loosening of the governmental constraint).

On the contrary, the second constituent option fully admits the particular power of the executive power, but strives to define the mechanisms capable of dominating it. According to this conception, it is necessary to create the instruments of power that will stop power. This task will be accomplished, during the American Revolution, by the Convention of 1787, which brought together the drafters of the future American Constitution. This event provides us with an archetype of rational decision about the adoption of a Constitution, at the same time as a new type of founding text, what we will call the Federalist [281].

And it is precisely in article 78 of the *Federalist*. This sets up the profound justification for independence: it is necessary because it is the essential remedy against instability. And this is because the independence of the central bank is very similar to that of judges: elected by the people, they are so because they are examples of virtue. In this way, democracy is not corrupted, but defended and assured the same conditions of existence thanks to stability and permanence.

Essential in this sense is to shield the management of money from the vicissitudes of politics: hence the slow affirmation in 1913 of the Federal Reserve which is configured as an essential tool for the defense of money, not its stability, but the government of money from crises.

Here emerges a concept well expressed by Blinder [282], once vice president of the Fed, according to whom the Fed had obtained political legitimacy through what I call a "transmission" of legitimacy from those who—having obtained their legitimacy directly from the voters—appointed the members of the Central Bank's board. In this sense, Blinder affirmed, public accountability was nothing more than a moral corollary of the Central Bank. A theme, this, that is already evoked in the widely cited text by Mersch and that raises heavy questions similar to those consonant with the so-called corporate social responsibility, rather than a legal discourse. In a democratic society, the freedom of action of the Central Bank carries with it an obligation to transparency: independence and responsibility are configured as symbiotic elements never in conflict. For Blinder, it is responsibility that legitimizes independence in the context of a well-defined political structure.

The principle of independence, therefore, does not pervert democracy: rather it guarantees its permanence.

The ECB, conversely, does not have at its base a complete political theory that establishes a theoretical legitimization that is not enclosed in the precepts of the dominant doctrine of neoclassical economics which drip from our bookshelves and our libraries and our social networks. This long and embarrassing quote from Jean-Claude Trichet, in 2000, when these disarming words of the governor of the French Central Bank and later president of the ECB, mercilessly taken up in the important contribution by Étienne Farvaque, is worth all:

> It is a hypothesis that remains to be rigorously demonstrated. But I cannot forget that, in our country, the institutions of our political democracy have examined with extreme attention the question of the independence of the Central Bank and the final objective of price stability. On four occasions, in June 1992, in September 1992, in August 1993 and in December 1993, a multipartisan consensus amended our Constitution, voted the Maastricht Treaty and modified the law of the Bank of France to give independence to the Central Bank and assign it the final objective of price stability. Like all independent central banks in the world, like the European Central Bank and the Eurosystem itself, the independent Bank of France is the daughter of a powerful transpartisan consensus and its greatest permanent challenge is to prove worthy of the honor and trust that have been given to it. [283]

The ignorance of the political tradition in which the independence of monetary authorities is inscribed is disturbing.

The fact, therefore, that the highest-ranking leaders of the ECB are appointed by the highest political instance of the EU (the Council of Heads of State and Government) should be a tool for "transition" of legitimacy. The appointments to the top of the European central banks and the ECB itself are, therefore, fully political. But legitimizing independence in terms of the rationality of political decisions should then be definitively and explicitly the safest and most certain way to configure a path towards legitimacy and legitimization of what are not economic theories on which consensus does not exist.

There exists only a cultural hegemony, contested and questioned by the same sphere of legitimacy that surrounds the Fed, which does not, precisely, aim institutionally only at price stability, but instead at the multiple direction of stability together with employment and GDP growth. These are political objectives par excellence, which have as their supreme guarantor of their perpetuity the Supreme Court of Justice of the United States [284].

In this context, the acuteness of Mauro Calise's judgment about our *quaestio* inserted in the more general context of both the party machine and the American Constitution is striking:

> In the American experience, the intertwining between parties and state is therefore important not only because it responds to a process of mass mobilization and the criteria of democratic responsibility that are affirmed there. No less important is the fact that this intertwining occurs within precise areas of state intervention, and that the parties prove incapable of subjecting large economic concentrations to any form of government control. The American party system, while seeming to impose democratic control on the state, also very clearly circumscribes its breadth. With the result of leaving out of party government precisely those economic powers that are at the center of the development of modern industrial nations. [285]

This is an important contribution to start thinking again about the State also as a "committee of bourgeois affairs", that is, realistically studying the situational power in fact beyond any outdated Marxist mechanism, as has commendably begun to be done in a series of researches that should interest, for example, the ECB without fear of being subjected to any kind of reprisals in case such researches prove true [286].

And here we come to the heart of our question: how the opinion of the theoretical—if not parliamentary or constitutional—independence of non-American central banks could reasonably have been formed. They—we have observed—belong to a completely different social and legal world, and it is to this world that we must turn our attention.

Strong from what we have so far affirmed, we must now turn our attention to the ECB. We are supported by a fundamental article by Eric Dehay published many years ago but on which the attention it deserved was not focused [287].

The heart of the argument is based on the falsification of those arguments in favor of the independence of central banks that derive precisely the need to achieve this goal by supporting the thesis of the always existing relationship between such independence and the ability to curb the inflationary process that derives from the electoral process and therefore from the circulation of political classes. Independence would neutralize the ancient principle already described by Gaetano Mosca [288] (which none of the current economic solons has ever read) of the temporal inconsistency of electoral policies, thus justifying the theory of the necessity of the independence of central banks.

This assumption implies that the same central banks would only have the task of controlling inflation in a slavish imitation of the statute of the German Central Bank, which still operates under the nightmare of the recurrence of Weimar inflation, on which our Costantino Bresciani Turoni [289] wrote unforgettable pages that prove that it was a typical event of Teutonic exceptionalism.

The arguments in favor of independence mainly concern the relationship that may exist between it and the control of inflation. The problem of temporal inconsistency of discretionary policies justifies an independence that isolates monetary policy from electoral cycles. This justification is countered by the idea that a central bank conducting monetary policy without being accountable to a legitimized political representation constitutes an exception to the democratic principle that is not acceptable [290].

The reasons for these assumptions are well known: at every election the circulation of political classes seeks consensus by distributing miniature sesterces of unmarcescible: a process studied for many years, long before today's graduate economists who are making a name for themselves—for example—on German newspapers in Italian! [291].

All in all, it lies in the fact that the theories of ordo-liberalism [292] tragically met with those of the North American constitutional to justify the independence of the Bundesbank in a tragic overlap of intentions and foundations, as mixed and incongruous as ever, but justified and exalted by the context of the European civil war then in progress.

It imposed to strengthen Germany and with it every bulwark against political-social instability: hence the emergence of ordo-liberalism as the most congruent doctrine to justify political stability and social order.

The only real theoretical incongruity lies in the fact that ordo-liberalism presupposed and presupposes from the German Central Bank only price control, that is, the non-return to any inflation, after the unforgettable Weimar experience.

While we all recognize as non-falsifiable the assumption that order and therefore stability derive from a series of causes much broader than the stability of the currency, as the North American experience teaches.

CHAPTER 13

The Return to Moral Economy

The anxieties that weigh on the whole world are today, not by chance, summed up by the question of what form our social relationships will take when we overcome the ongoing pandemic crisis. And the conviction is increasingly emerging that the way out will be the result of a sort of great creative transformation of products, technological projects, and even lifestyles, even if the latter will certainly be the slowest to change, to transform. It is no coincidence that the sector in which these challenges are most concentrated is that of telecommunications and in general of the so-called network and the goods and services that we can exchange and create on and through it. It is the sector in which technology and change, lifestyle habits and cultures, continually intertwine. Of course, even here the sky is full of clouds. It is a sector as energy-consuming as ever and in which large plants are very difficult to manage; it is also a sector in which the battle rages between different conceptions of what the meaning of so-called public goods and freedom of information is, essential for achieving a broader freedom (a typical public good) in the responsibility of expression. This is precisely what the network sector needs to fully develop its potential with respect to opportunities for inclusion in culture and information. There are few large companies in the world today that can connect the entire planet with formidable technological information assets (think, e.g., of Google). But they, at the same time, can circulate on the network, in every corner of the planet, messages,

G. Sapelli, *States, Markets and Wars in Global History*,
https://doi.org/10.1007/978-3-031-26716-1_13

expressions of interest, and tastes and cultures very different from each other and that often challenge every current morality. The temptation to avoid these challenges too often immediately triggers and is already realized in almost all nations of the world: from dictatorial China, which blocks entire internet networks and bans access to an infinity of sites, to various States of the freest North America, where federal laws are very strict invoking public morality and a sense of decency.

However, these resistances seem to slow down in the short term the emergence of a sector of great potential such as information exchange and social networking, but at the same time they are destined to clash with an irresistible tendency to open the network itself to any topic and content that everyone wants to circulate thanks to it. What these processes announce is rather the transition from a society of rights to a society of duties not only by the company that transmits the content, but also and above all by the consumer or end user of the content itself. The box turns upside down: the forbidden fruits are always reachable, but it is up to the person at the other end of the line to decide whether or not they want to draw from them, in a call to personal responsibility that is increasingly broad and determined, which can no longer be avoided. I cannot create a guard post with an armed sentinel for every access to the network: I would have millions of sentinels and too many things would escape them.

The only resource to govern the network is the self-government of the end user, with due assurances regarding minors, who must be recognized the right to be protected from error. But for an adult, this right is no longer possible to invoke. Contracts between companies and users in this way are reversed. From being entirely public, they become increasingly private, but without their privatization excluding the pursuit of a public purpose, which in this case, as in the abolition of the crime of vilification, is a higher degree of responsible freedom. Where the emphasis is placed on the concept of responsibility: I sign an access contract primarily with myself and it is my subjectivity that regulates the effectiveness of the contract itself, according to a higher degree of freedom without which not only will we not get out of the current crisis, but we will not even build future economic and civil development.

It emerges from all this that the principle of personal responsibility becomes a fixed point of the new reconfiguration of entire social structures. It is not the market that can reconfigure them: it is the person and their behavior determined by their moral autonomy.

Let's think about what has happened in recent years in the field of relations between capital and labor. Let's start with a concrete historical example. Over the last thirty years, the South Korean government has continually announced exceptional measures to curb the power of trade unions. After the great general strike of 1989, which forever shattered the image of South Korea as the homeland of low wages, this will is an absolute novelty in the global landscape. But at the same time, it is an exception. In Korea, representing the workers and their will to fight against the consequences of the global economic crisis that only now are beginning to truly concern them, are the unions, large organizations that, imitating their Japanese counterparts before the Second World War, have developed with enormous speed. Elsewhere the landscape is different. Workers are indeed fragmented as never before in terms of types of work, company size, working age, and even family status (singles, e.g., are increasingly numerous and therefore more willing to risk struggle and strike, but also isolation). But they are also fragmented in their forms of protest against the crisis. But they protest because human labor is refractory to disintegration in the face of the crisis: the human person can only be physically destroyed. It can certainly be changed in its capacity and competence. But to change profession, mentality, workplace, it takes time, extreme willingness to change, it requires financial, psychological, material and immaterial resources that are not always in the horizon of life, the deep and true life, of workers. For this reason, they are today affected by an unheard-of suffering, whether they are employed or not. If they are, they fear for tomorrow, for themselves and their families; if they are unemployed, they are destroyed by the uncertainty of the future and the loss of status. Of course, this tragedy was already in the air [293]. We should have prepared. Now seen from the perspective of the crisis, the various laws on temporary work, part-time, which prevent starting a family, even realizing the most powerful force of being, that is love, those laws, which did not physically destroy the working person, but already tore and still tear them morally apart, were the first clouds announcing the storm of pain on workers. Accepted and negotiated by unions around the world, workers, with those laws, today also reject many of the union practices and invent new ones instead. The most creative are, all over the world, the grassroots unions of the precarious, the young, without a family behind them, with an open vision of the risk society that makes them not completely reject precariousness. But it is one thing to live it in times of economic growth and another to live it when there is a crisis.

Then the glass of flexibility is half empty and not half full and the cheerful variety is overlaid with dark and dangerous anxiety for mental health, before the level of material life. The USA also in this case prove to be the most pluralistic and best country in the world where there is everything: new, more combative and grassroots unions are formed, immigrants and illegal immigrants are organized with the AFL CIO. A phenomenon that seems unheard of in Europe. The union, in the USA, as in the Scandinavian countries and in Australia, while negotiating also worries about welfare, not state, but self-managed from below. Because this is the new horizon: the defense of work will no longer only pass through negotiation between the social parties (and here the unions continue to be indispensable), but also through the creation of new community forms of welfare that will also take on forms of new non-capitalist economic units. An example? The self-managed Argentine factories that indicate the right way to resist the crisis: to do it yourself united in the struggle and in the construction of new active subjectivities on the markets [294]. Yet, in the face of this ferment, the indifference of political representatives reigns all over the world. But if this indifference continues, a widespread, unprecedented conflict will erupt, which will overwhelm many of our certainties and above all many of our ignominies.

Hence, a horizon that is much darker with clouds than what the theorists of the risk society presented to us. Here, destiny returns to the hands of the subject. Offended, scarred, and wounded, he is not annihilated. He remains the only point on which and thanks to which to generate communally a form of overcoming the regressive transformation of the economy and politics that is currently underway.

There can be a virtuous overcoming towards a politics and an economy generated by the rebirth of Christian humanism only if we persistently implement that part of the Encyclical *Caritas in Veritate* dedicated to the care with which we must look at different forms of business ownership and non-economic organization of human social aggregations [295].

The awarding, in 2007, surprisingly as ever, of the Nobel Prize for economics to the late friend Elinor Ostrom [296] was an event that perhaps contained a sign of the times.

Are we in the midst of a path mutation of which, in our misery, we do not discern the contours, but which already operates powerfully? It is the basis for refounding the debate on the meaning of profit and property. Nowadays, moreover, where it still develops minority but beneficially, that debate increasingly includes the one on "natural rights to property":

that is, on the unwritten right that is embodied in history through the life experience of communities that once were defined as "primitive". They have been gradually surrounded, more than integrated, by the capitalist market and by societies like the ones we live in. In those societies, which also coexist in the general capitalist mode of production, community forms of land, or essential goods ownership, such as fishing basins, running waters, have been created for centuries and centuries, without any written right. And they have also been preserved for millennia thanks to this unwritten right. The written right is typical—today, of course—only of societies born from the right of merchants, first, and from the right of parliaments or judges, then. Andean communities, aboriginal communities, communities of the Slavic world, communities of Brazilian landless, Chinese and Asian village communities, etc., have, instead, become today elements of contradiction in the expansion of the area of private law. In large parts of the world, it was silent and allowed the reproducibility of the de facto legal systems typical of this collective possession. It is a theme that touches on that of the *common goods*, or goods that are defined as "public" not for the state ownership form, but because such form not directed to individual profit is essentially cooperative, property of small or large social groups and allows their reproducibility and use for all those who want to access them, following rules that ensure, then, their infinite reproducibility. And the communities of unwritten property to which I referred have allowed the millennial reproducibility of forms of human sustenance and environmental sustainability that would otherwise have been destroyed. They live today beneficially and coexist virtuously with markets of any form and nature, reproducing in society the community with an uninterrupted fertility, despite all the difficulties. Such goods and such forms of cooperation have come to the fore thanks to Elinor Ostrom, breaking a long silence with a theoretical reflection of enormous importance. Highly civilized societies that have coexisted and coexist for centuries with the societies mentioned earlier have fortunately characterized themselves, providing an important example for all, for state or meta-state episodes of recognition of collective pre-capitalist rights and legalization of the same, in a sort of posthumous recognition or transformation into collective property rights through written law and not through the custom of the de facto legal system. Thanks to Ostrom, a great field of reflection and study was opened, which still today, and today more than ever, has an unexpected relevance for our capitalist economy, when we ask ourselves whether we should consider *common goods* even goods not yet commodified or to be subtracted from the same commodification already occurred, as happens with water and protected areas of the environment. Even in the world in which we live today, immersed in the economic crisis, there unexpectedly arises the need for a reflection on the different forms of possible property and on the different ways of managing them. In fact, we must ask ourselves: until when will a market based on private goods allow the reproduction of essential goods for associated life, such as the purity of the air, the reformulation of the same labor standards, a land property that guarantees essential goods, such as housing, for all the people of the earth? [297] Until when will it guarantee the same production of goods and services under the sole shelter of the capitalistic form of property? Until when will it allow the person to reproduce himself, that is, his moral autonomy?

What is certain is that the market without morality destroys society: the community rebuilds it and makes it grow. We have the need, starting from this assumption, to formulate an answer to these questions.

In this global scenario that brings moral choices to the fore, a reflection on the relationships between moral action and economic action, on which I have been reflecting for a long time, cannot fail to re-emerge: from the mid-eighties of the century just passed, as documented by the introduction I wrote to a collective work edited by Hopt and Teubner, a work that I consider, for my training, of fundamental importance and that had the role of stimulating in Italy the reflection on what at that time was identified as "the responsibility of senior management" [298].

That commitment was and will be inserted in the increasingly widespread growth of the themes of the moral responsibility of the company [299], which not only naturally concerned the undersigned, but, in the Durkheimian increasing social differentiation of scientific disciplines, also social researchers *tout court*, up to producing a real corporation of analysts of what today is called *corporate social responsibility*. But this corporation seems to me to have failed its purpose. The moral action of the company is incompatible with the *owner capitalism* and the short-termism that derives from it: the *oil spill* in Louisiana is there to prove it. The Louisiana disaster has raised, in fact, a tragic dilemma: is the current system of stock market valuation of large companies with profits and dividends in constant growth and with quarterly ratings and therefore in the very short-term sustainable? No, it is not sustainable, because it induces not to fully and completely respect the rules of technological safety and therefore to face the high costs that drilling at enormous depths (of the seabed, not the sea!) make necessary. Now we are certain, from the data that continuously come from a series of indisputable sources, that BP was aware of the risks that the actual cost and time cut entailed and that other large companies enabled to carry out those works were also: this is the case of the technicians of the very competent Schlumberger (an extraction services company among the best in the world and therefore very expensive...), who abandoned the platform shortly before the fatal and terrible explosion that now risks destroying a huge ecosystem. What we old Cassandras of energy have been repeating for years has come true: but no one thought of such a terrible confirmation of our theses. The current level of profits of the *corporations* and the market conditions that only value the very short term is incompatible with safety when research is carried out under very high risk conditions. And this is a decisive consideration for changing the paradigm: the shift from the predominance of finance to that of industrial profit is becoming increasingly imperative in a world that for future centuries will not be able to do without fossil hydrocarbons. Handle with extreme care, then! But continue, however, in research, because today we have all the scientific and technical conditions to challenge depths and climatic conditions once unthinkable: just act with supreme discernment putting first both the need for extraction, and that of the relentless pursuit of the principle of prudence.

The responsibility of the company is therefore dead. But a resurrection is possible, provided the paradigm completely changes. It can be realized in the hope of a decisive transition to a more courageous testimony of the necessity of the philosophical dimension in the study of the relationships between the supporting morals and the most significant modern social aggregation of the economic action itself: the company.

On an international scale, these relationships have been addressed, instead, with an analytical and managerial intellectual twist, finding resistance only from the German and French tradition—under the guise of the thought of Luhmann and Habermas, on the one hand, and the phenomenology of Ricoeur, on the other—and from the Anglo-Saxon one in the sole sector of the philosophy of law—as documented by the works of Lyons and Green. That twist has paved the way for the triumph of an economistic reductionism of which we are only now beginning to perceive the social, moral, and institutional damage.

Not only are ethical ratings talked about: we move from "theory" to economic action, precisely. Agencies and companies are created for actions that, while assigning ratings to companies, then sell to the same companies the ethical-organizational implementation (as if the organization was not made up of people before systems and if ethics could be reduced to "packaged" consulting) and finally sell, also, in the financial markets, the "ethical" funds. They are very fashionable in the new affluent class, but they are also very successful among those who are animated by good intentions, falling into the deception of the merchants in the temple. There is also a desire to attribute to companies the stamps of an "ethical" certification that diligent consultants not only "measure", but also "maintain" and which should constitute for the companies themselves a sort of entry barrier to obtain contracts, concessions, participate in consortia and so on.

The confusion that is made between reputation and morality, on the one hand, and between reputation and ethics, on the other, is deep and is as dangerous as that between reputation and image. Reputation is what citizens as well as markets think of a company and must be affirmed in a continuous fidelity to ethical principles, but it must also inevitably measure itself against the changes in the great ideal currents that disrupt human aggregates. For example, let's ask the following question: nowadays, do you enjoy a good reputation if, as an investment fund, you invest in nuclear companies? The answer is simple: the reputation of my investment fund is not affected if this is done in France, but it certainly is if the same act is committed in Italy. The image of a company is different, which borders on the wise advertising operation and which can be built in a much shorter time than reputation, and much more quickly than reputation can melt like snow in the sun.

The discourse is different again if we reflect on the moralities that are found in companies and on the propensities and ethical choices that can arise from them. Here, we are not talking about reputation, nor about any kind of image. These are personal ontological choices, even when acting in an associated form as always happens in a company, which must be made out of deep and profound conviction. From this deep and profound conviction, fruits can be had on the levels of reputation and image, but in the long term and with the impossibility of measuring their impacts on the economic performance of the companies themselves.

The company is a very special social construct with an economic foundation in which the fight against evil must continue to engage the human.

To do this, a subjective moral commitment and a collective moral commitment are necessary: ethical, precisely.

But the institutions responsible for this are also extremely important: the Anglo-Saxon rules of good *governance*, first and foremost, and then those that can arise from the practices of personnel management when the latter places the person and their universal value at the center of all policies that can be pursued thanks to a very broad technique, as rich in tools as it is poor in theoretical reflections.

This is all the more true today, when, from a conception of business management as the golden commitment of a management class aimed at asserting the continuous mediation between economy and the listening and respect of *stakeholders*, we have passed, as I have already said—but it is worth repeating—into a proprietary context that has wrapped up the managers themselves. They should no longer be the golden mediators of growth, but rather, the servants of the only prevailing actors in the company: the shareholders [300]. The agency theory has made decisive theoretical steps in this direction and only recently has a reflection on the rational allocation—that is, economically more profitable—of property rights [301] appeared on the horizon, which will open the way, I am sure, to a new season, both theoretical and practical. In it, the moral justification of property itself and the forms of participation that are unfolding before us by business leaders will be placed at the center of attention. The social differentiation resulting from the lack of moral justification for such forms of participation, which have paved the way for a thousand opportunistic practices, is becoming increasingly strong, worldwide. It is paradoxical that the beginning of this drift was located in the most virtuous and civilized capitalism in the world: the Anglo-Saxon one. But if it is so in terms of the rules of and for the markets, the same can no longer be said—as it once was—for what concerns the sphere of the moral legitimacy of inequality. Quantity has indeed transformed into quality. And this widening of social divergence threatens to destroy the intersubjective ties that make societies cohesive. It is all of capitalism that in this way puts its legitimacy to a hard test. This cannot continue: this divergence is destined to tear society so deeply that the latter will have a reaction. Let's hope it's not uncomposed and vicious. The Bible tells us that the wrath of the meek can be terrible…

What I have said so far reveals the dominant secret reason for a new season of research: to lay the foundations for a conception of business ethics and in business that is relevant to the reflection on distributive justice and commutative justice. That is, as is known, in the first case, a justice that proposes to be in the shared over-determination of the social division of goods and resources of any nature based on the merits that each one acquires by contributing to their production and reproduction. In the second case, and here too Aristotelian, a justice that tends to balance advantages and disadvantages in all social exchange relationships, whether voluntary or involuntary. In both cases, justice develops norms that realize—or rather, should realize—equality between merits and advantages or advantages and disadvantages of each. It is the *à la Rawls* horizon of "justice as fairness" [302] that is invoked here, with a very attentive and preferential look at communitarian themes, as will be seen. It—the *fairness*—is often translated as "impartiality" or "equity", but in its Anglo-Saxon etymological root it refers to a structural value of the theory rather than a subjectivity or an orientation to the action of the parties involved.

And it is this theoretical structure that is now of interest. The reason is consequential to this approach and it gives it a particular theoretical light.

Indeed, the injury to distributive and commutative justice is an outrage because it violates the rights of others, with fraud, violence in all its forms, and therefore humiliation, contempt, inflicting suffering on the human. Hence a necessary action of reparation both in the case of injury to distributive justice and in the case of an offense to commutative justice. Hence, the essential role of ethics in guiding action directed at the construction of organizational rules.

I believe that this will be the new horizon to which, in the future, the moral bases of support for the market and its organizational populations, capitalist and non-capitalist companies, will have to look [303]. For this reason, if we do not want to be dragged into an abyss from which we could no longer rise, we need to rethink our social action in a revolutionary way.

As always in world history, French critical thinking comes to our rescue.

Necessarily subversive (our) reflection assumes that the economic machine can cease to have as its essential function to ensure the reproduction of the social system. However, political power, which has, by essence, no interest in change, is the only one capable of undertaking it. However, unless the rise of new aspirations compels it, politics will only ever manage social contradictions. We can think that, the contradictions becoming insoluble, the political powers will be overwhelmed. It indeed seems that ecological and energy constraints will make in the long term *impossible* a growth intimately associated… with the inequality of power: *mentalities will then evolve according to the necessities of new production and material organization relationships* [304].

Nothing is more in line with the spirit of the times than this reflection written more than forty years ago by two top intellectuals to start a non-trivial reflection on the themes of the so-called circular economy.

The spirit of the time is exactly what was already gathering at the end of the 1970s and which from the top of the Parisian mountain was seen to overlap like tumultuous clouds. Today they turn into threatening cumuli and first of all, it is necessary to orient oneself in the storm. Rereading the classics is always the best solution.

Indeed, a refoundation of the concepts of the "circular economy" cannot begin without referring to the thought of Gilbert Simondon and his writings on "technique" [305].

Because this is what it is about today: giving a signifier a meaning and moving from the *concept* to the theory.

Under what conditions can technique be a promoter of true progress for humanity? This was Simondon's question. Moreover, social life cannot be understood without its technical dimension, just as the developments of technique (positive or negative) are not independent of psychosociological factors. The thought of the great and almost still unknown French scholar helps to understand how, from education to advertising and culture in general, it is possible to think about the technical dimension of society without reducing it to a source of alienation. A psychosociological approach gives men the possibility of not being slaves to technical development, but, thanks to a renewed relationship with beings, with *the other*, to feel at ease in the current world.

Dealing with the different aspects of man's relationship with technique and with the world, Gilbert Simondon highlights the authentic sense of technique: that of being able, for man, to be the true mediation with nature, the *metaxu* between man and the world. This was the task that André Leroi-Gourhan had set himself, many years ago, especially in his *The Gesture and the Word* [306], in which he tackled the complex and delicate theme of humanization and its ties with technique and language, traversing the territories of paleontology, ethnology, aesthetics, and sociology, precisely describing the progressive "liberation" of the human species through material behavior in space and time.

It was the concept of "operating", in fact, that most interested Leroi-Gourhan: the treatment of matter and the action exerted on the environment by man. Actions that are cultures and that are closely linked to the communication that the human being develops and the forms it creates. From gesture, through an evolution of humanity's technical abilities, we move to the word, conceived as a technical tool itself, which in turn leads to higher forms of sociality [307]. Hence, the foundation of an anthropological epistemology [308] which we absolutely need today to give the rhetoric of the "circular economy" a foundation that unites the "gesture" of production with the "gesture" of consumption, the "gesture" of care with the "gesture" of reproduction, both of society and nature. Only by starting from the transformation of production can the transformation of the social forms of economic activity overcome those limits clearly indicated by Attali about half a century ago.

For this reason, bringing the economic discourse back to its classic relational anthropological foundations is essential, today more than ever.

From this point of view, it is essential to consider that André Leroi-Gourhan's social anthropology always emphasizes that the individual-society relationship varies according to the evolution of the technical–economic structures of a given historical moment. Throughout his work, the term "liberation" also returns, not by chance, forcefully, as a *leitmotif* it is the liberation "of time" that is created with the division of labor in associated life that constitutes the factor that determines, through associated human action, the factor of change.

Stabilization in space, the end of nomadism, and the possibility of increasing in situ resources by increasing the number of individuals create an environmental situation that coincides with the liberation "of" time. From this stabilization, primordial, but no less foundational, begins the accelerated progress of techniques in a social system made up of dense territorial units, intercommunicating, thanks to a network of peaceful or warlike exchanges in which the various phases of anthropological change transform communities into differentiated societies.

Those societies on which Durkheim [309] wrote universal and today very current pages. It is the techno-economic base that is the driving force of cultural production, giving it "meaning".

Not by chance, the one who opened a decisive path for a new interpretation of the theses on the circular economy, following a path that Jacques Attali had already traveled from a completely different point of view [310], is Bernard Stiegler, especially in *Technique and Time* [311].

Stiegler's thought can today offer us a refounding starting point for moral action in economics [312], action of small groups rather than states, action aimed at strengthening the ties between man and nature and between humanity and justice, tempering a capitalism that increasingly manifests itself as a social disruptor and therefore a disruptor of humanity itself. The increase in inequality is but the most evident manifestation of this transformation that should induce us to change our models of economic and social analysis, adapting them to the level of globalization in which every economic system, understood in the Marshallian sense [313], that is, of functional aggregation, no longer has national boundaries, but transnational ones, as Branko Milanovic explains well to us:

> Believing that the rich always have an interest in defending the rule of law or property rights in their own country made sense when transnational movements of capital were difficult or even impossible, but this no longer makes sense today. Similarly, equality of opportunity cannot be a goal limited to the scale of the nation-state: it must be pursued at the global level. [314]

Signs of this disintegrative process of the national dimension (to which, this is the point, nothing replaces as solid and relational as local communities once were) [315] we see everywhere due to the increase in international flows of capital and data (i.e., knowledge, information, and intellectual property) with a de-territorialization of production processes. This leads to a lower circulation of intermediate goods with a tendency to fall in the rate of profit and with a structural marginalization of activities that from productive and economic become mere hobbies.

However, the very important observation remains that the same technologies produce other trades and jobs: according to the U.S. Bureau of Labor Statistics, we will go from 911,000 jobs to 1,342,700 in the next twenty years.

Philip Howard [316], of the School of Internet Studies at the University of Oxford, warns how much the giants of the digital industry control the so-called platforms that have become the fundamental infrastructure of public life. They are a means of communication for our political culture, as much as the post office, the monopolies of newspaper headlines, televisions, and radio stations that had a structural socio-political function in past decades, very different from the current one. And

Michael Lind argued that "it makes no sense to discuss automation, and how to manage its impact on work and employment, without also talking about a global economic policy" [317].

In my latest book *Beyond Capitalism. Machines, Work, and Property* [318], I stated that the occupations that will grow will be those dedicated to personal care, understood in the broadest possible sense, to reduce the general flow of anxiety of those who live up to a hundred years. But it is not enough to create only nurses, we need to train readers, jugglers, psychologists and psychiatrists, architects and promoters of cooperative values the occupations of the future seem to be creative therapists, mechanical supervisors installers and repairers, emergency activity executives, social workers in the field of mental health, audiologists, on the contrary, insurers, mathematical technicians, tailors, notaries and accountants, call center operators will be rarer. In short, all jobs based on interpersonal and emotional relationships and on the skills and technologies of complex maintenance of artificial and intelligent systems will remain, even increase, while all occupations that have strong impersonal mechanical components of any technological complexity (even if they are surgeons, for example, who will be fewer in number than choreographers) will decline until they disappear.

The Fordist or Taylorist, but one should say Keynesian, organization of work, born to respond to the urgency of the '29 crisis, has been in crisis for at least thirty years. Although until today capitalism has managed to make such organization of work appear as the norm, and that it can continue to be the norm, with the exponential development of job automation that will also touch those intellectual professions that Anglophone sociology designates as *white collar* (from lawyers to doctors), such organization can no longer be normative. Traditional intellectual professions have been proceduralized to the point of becoming a sort of intellectual routine, easily replaced, for this very reason, by the automation of algorithms. From this starting point, it is no longer possible to further postpone the restructuring of the macro- and micro-economic organization, and hence, the urgency to rethink the organization of the entire circulation of the production of goods by means of goods and the entire circulation of capital. But to do this, it is necessary to start from the reconstruction of *knowledge* and *know-how*.

It is no longer enough to buy time with financial strategies or job subsidies. Tactics cannot substitute strategy. Proletarianization, intellectual before economic, is underway on a much larger scale than what happened in the first industrial revolution. This new proletarianization is the loss of ***knowledge*** of man in relation to the technical object he faces: this is Stiegler's thesis. When we use smartphones, computers, and many appliances, we totally ignore their operation: in this sense we are absolutely proletarianized in relation to them and it is in this ignorance of the production of an object, and therefore of its operation, the new, Marxian, "fetishism of the commodity".

The possibility of reducing to an algorithm even "intellectual" jobs is a symptom of the fact that one is less and less in the position of ***knowing***, and therefore of having the prerogative to be able to change the rules of the game, to "fork", that is to find alternative solutions to a problem that goes beyond standardized procedures.

On the threshold of the 2008 crisis, Alan Greenspan, then governor of the Fed, admitted that he was absolutely unable to predict the crisis or understand its reasons—he too, despite the bonuses, was proletarianized, in an era where economic and financial flows pass more through algorithms than through human choices.

We are in a society of ignorance, and therefore, it is absolutely necessary to open a virtuous spiral, so that future generations are able to interact with "knowledge and know-how", "know-how" suitable for the complex artificial systems that surround us. It is on the future that we must invest to reactivate and increase the "abilities" or "capabilities", to use the notion of Amartya Sen [319], to whom we are inspired, when he observes that in Bangladesh or Harlem the inhabitants have greater resilience in the face of adversity than Westerners precisely because they have not been proletarianized of their knowledge: the knowledge of everyday life, artisanal and spiritual knowledge.

Entropy and the deconstruction of trust between social bodies have thus pervaded society, thanks to the exacerbated division of labor on which capitalism has been built in recent centuries.

Indeed, proletarianization does not only concern the realm of work. It also affects the "knowledge of everyday life": the knowledge of parents, the ability to educate in short: people enjoy many services, follow procedures or ways of use, but they no longer know how to do anything. The tragedy is that it is precisely these skills, which the inhabitants of Bangladesh or Harlem have not lost, that constitute the infrastructure of social cohesion: what Fernand Braudel defined as "material life" [320].

Today, instead of learning, we tend to unlearn more and more. We are an information society that has nothing to do with knowledge: we are very informed, but we do not "know". In this way, as Stiegler argues, entropy increases in its triple meaning: thermodynamic, biological, and informational. But the entropy of information is embodied in the current paradigm of post-truth and, therefore, destroys trust in institutions and others. Society is first and foremost a system of trust [321]. So whoever deconstructs trust also deconstructs the relationships between social bodies. Without trust, societies do not function: where there is entropy, there can be no trust.

The technologies that are developing, based on algorithms and calculability to automate production and work, tend to become more and more what is called in systems theory "closed systems" and therefore structurally entropic.

For this reason, a dialogue between all social parties, that is, between all interest associations and intermediate bodies, companies and solidarity systems, is indispensable.

According to the perspective of entropy [322], the classic notions of value, such as use value and exchange value, do nothing but increase entropy itself: use value is nothing more than the wear and tear of the good, and therefore, it increases entropy, since entropy is nothing but the dissipation of energy. And the exchange value, that is, the possibility of a good to change location infinitely (to be exchanged), does nothing but increase entropy: very empirically, consuming energy to move the good in question always generates new entropy. If we define "practical value" as what does not increase and possibly reduces entropy, we discover that true wealth is something that is not mathematically or algebraically calculable: it is relational value, *immaterial asset* like trust, Rousseauian piety, mercy, benevolence [323]. The "practical value" embodies a knowledge that takes care, or rather, responds to a problem and, as such, can only be local, even singular, whose anti-entropic value is local and not necessarily global.

Because what may have value in Scandinavia, does not necessarily have it among the nomadic tribes of the Sahara.

The locality of the "practical value" is not reduced to the simple local scarcity of raw materials or products, although it may be a component that determines its practical value, which always implies an increase in "knowledge" and therefore the possibility of "bifurcating". And you cannot monetize those dimensions of extra-economic exchange that occur through the evaluation of a service on a platform like Uber, Amazon, or Deliveroo: these logics are always internal to the algorithms that structurally produce entropy and no real value, no ability to "bifurcate".

But this does not mean that we must, like the Luddites, reject technique and new technologies: on the contrary!

It is necessary to establish a community that has the "knowledge" that allows it to "fork", produce alternatives, interacting consciously with the complex artificial systems that constitute its own social environment. In the face of the exponential development of technologies, it is necessary to foresee that working hours (not employment) will have to be integrated and alternated with hours of training, updating, research to best express the subjective potential during working hours. The real challenge is the territorialization of institutions without losing the scalar dimension offered by digital technology and the global market: the technology *blockchain* can structure the local interactions of the economy, but also try to lay the foundations of a device capable of "accounting" the "practical value" at all its micro, meso, and macro levels.

The technical dimension, as well as the developments of the technique (positive or negative), is not independent from psychosociological factors.

The reflections presented in this book aim to help understand how, from education to advertising and culture in general, it is possible to think about the technical dimension of society without reducing it to a source of alienation. A true psychosociological approach to economic life gives men the opportunity not to be slaves of technical development, but, thanks to a renewed relationship with technical beings, to feel at ease in the current world. Dealing with the different aspects of man's relationship with technique and the world, Gilbert Simondon highlighted the authentic sense of technique: that of being, for man, the true mediation with nature, the *metaxu* between man and the world.

From this point of view, Bernard Stiegler's text on "taking care" [324] is a fundamental book. Reinterpreting the concept of *phàrmakon* taken from *Plato's Pharmacy* by Derrida [325], Stiegler identifies in information and digital technologies the "poison" with which contemporary financial capitalism (now totally crushed on the consumerist imperative of growth and short-term profit) tends to enslave, if not destroy, the psychic structure of individuals and communities, producing, through the colonization-deformation of our neural circuits, new forms of individual and social stupidity, as well as pulsional regression; and, just like in his previous work, Stiegler proposed, in his too short earthly life, to use the same technology in a homeopathic key as a "remedy" to get out of the "symbolic misery" of our time and reproduce through a ***positive pharmacology*** the "spirit value", or "re-enchant" a world now dried up by "nihilism" and unable to plan the future. With a massive recourse, in fact, to the Simondonian notions of psychic and collective individuation [326], Stiegler hopes for the pharmacological reconstruction of those "circuits of transindividuation" that feed individual and social intelligence, as they express the entirely human faculty of ***inter-legere***, of linking together generations of "ascendants" and "descendants", through a positive use of grammatization—even that conveyed by the network.

Everywhere arises a resilience to the dominance of a de-localized capitalism, disintermediated from the human substance of being, and such resilience invites to shift the axis of economic policy from the prevalence of the consumer to the producer freed from the imperative of the short term: the only strong instance of life on which to refound an economy for man in the revitalization of his knowledge and his know-how.

Only in this way will a new bond between humanity and nature be built. This must become the new grammar of the so-called sustainability: the relationship. And the relationship does not "sustain" itself: it is ***generated*** from the vital worlds of subjects, not created by the unsustainable artificiality of reified processes. The relationship is foundational and regenerative of the being who wants to ***know*** and ***know how to do.***

Therefore, we must create "vital" economic structures.

Consider the ongoing debate in agriculture. The school of Jocelyne Porcher [327] has rightly placed at the center of the farm of the future animal welfare for a new agriculture based on the continuity of natural processes in a technological universe and therefore not "Luddite" and of "degrowth". A new centrality of agricultural enterprises at the base of an agriculture that includes not a production of meat in the laboratory [328]. There are significant differences between those who raise their own animals, the breeders, and those who produce meat synthetically. The former are "bound", they are "in relation" with their animals thanks to an emotional relationship pursuing capitalist profit, not denying it. In the case of production, however, the emotional factor is removed to focus solely on the realization of profit. Many animal rights or dietetic movements based on abstention from animal derivatives such as veganism often rest on a fatal misunderstanding, crossing synthetic meat production with what breeders do, the only ones in fact to know the animals well, to be close to their real needs, the only ones capable of really living side by side with their animals. Jocelyne Porcher strongly opposes the idea that the costs of industrial farming are increasingly lower than those of small breeders. The costs of meat are not only those we bear at the time of purchase. That is only the most obvious part of the cost, in fact the indirect costs of industrial production fall on the entire community and are very large [329].

In our radically artificialized and industrialized world only animals, which remind us what nature is, can help us recover our humanity. The ability of men to coexist peacefully with nature depends on their ability to live decently and in peace with animals and the relationship of work and interdependence that binds humans and animals since the Neolithic must be safeguarded. The ability of men to coexist peacefully largely depends on the ability to live with animals respecting them and ensuring them a good life.

Now we must ask ourselves the fatal question: where is capitalism going? Certainly not towards its collapse. So, is it going towards the continuity of a staunch defense of the consumer with hyper-regulations that maximize the role of the State as Natalino Irti [330] and Henri Pirenne [331] have taught us? The State that "creates the market" with the sword dictating its rules? This is what Franco Debenedetti has stated, for example, with his usual clarity [332]: "European economic policy was built on the confluence of British liberal thought and German ordo-liberalism: the State dictates the rules, including those of competition, the rest is up to the market".

Today the sword, in fact, is that of the new Leviathan of independent authorities [333]. A sword so powerful that it has recently given rise in the USA, the homeland of this sword, to a new school of thought aimed at reevaluating the role of Brandeis in defining an antitrust architecture that is sustainable and not econometric, that is, which includes in the "reasons", in the variables that guide the "technocracies of the markets" that decide the degree of regulation, not only algebraic indicators, but also considerations dictated by the philosophy of a revived concept of "common good" (employment, defense of intellectual property, support of local endogenous development) [334].

The conclusion of this innovative reasoning will inevitably lead us to argue that the consumer should no longer be dominant, but at least considered on par with the producer and therefore with the social forces of companies, employees and capitalists, and entrepreneurs.

A concept radically different from the *mainstream* neoclassical and ordo-liberal. Consequently, it is a matter of abandoning the neoclassical hypostatizations that construct the ideal types of optimal rationality and today rediscover Simon [335] and his bounded rationality. Hence, the consideration of the market populated not by individuals, but by organizations, by historical constructs such as companies and therefore by people who found not only the surplus value, but, with their culture and countless *assets* immaterial, those same companies, historical and social constructs [336].

Will we return to reading Schumpeter's *Business Cycles* [337] and Sylos Labini's *Oligopoly and Technological Progress* [338]?

It is impossible to say, but what is certain is that the transformation of unregulated and financialized capitalism has been too intense in its social disintegration not to produce a reaction not only political, as has already happened, but also intellectual, before that of economic policy.

Even the birth and increasingly impetuous development of the so-called circular economy is nothing more than the rise of this intellectual reaction.

This is the underlying thesis that inspires this essay.

In fact, from multiple sources of thought arises a philosophy of the person, for which the economy must contribute to the perfectibility of man. In this light, even the *good governance of the economy* changes paradigm. The "goodness" of economic governance, Felice Balbo [339] and Giorgio Ceriani Sebregondi [340] taught us, depends on the fact that those who obey it can at the same time honor it. It is a "sense of obligation". Which gives life to a concept of economy that Amartya Sen [341] will then take up. A concept of a "just" economy because it gives life to *entitlement*, that is, it organizes society in a way to offer more spheres of opportunity to the person.

The "circular economy", finally, is a concept to be "handled with care", like the one that also forms its backdrop: the concept of community.

Why? Because, for many, the community is the immediate relationality between subjects and between subjects and society.

But in this way, role divisions are abolished, forgetting that even where society has established itself and seems to have destroyed the community, it always re-emerges with association. Hence the irreversibility, throughout the world, of the principle of association, which reappears, in different forms, certainly, even in modernity. Modernity that, instead, many think should be entirely determined by individualistic monism and society based on roles: which would have destroyed the community, which should have thus defined itself as typical only of segmented society.

In this way, the contract should become the exclusive transitive form, in contemporaneity, excluding all others. A theoretical foundation, the one I propose, instead, quite different from the one that hypostatizes, in a sort of Spencerian evolutionism, a destiny marked by an uninterrupted path towards a sort of anthropological obligation before than legal, based on exchange and its value in any action, for all actions should be only economically oriented: inescapable transactions between individuals, rather than relations between people. As they always are. But if this is true, the "circular economy" can only arise from association, that is, from ethics. And ethics is nothing more than a moral sphere shared by more people, associated people: it is a transitive morality, not intransitive [342]. And so the circular economy requires the determining force of associating: organizing, organization. It requires the rationality of Simon [343]: the one that overcomes its limitation with associating, with organizing.

The community does not historically oppose the contract—just as the market does not oppose society according to zero-sum historical scansions, as some erroneously predicted, describing the birth of the *welfare state*, for example, as a sort of inevitable defense of society from the market. Émile Durkheim, as always, had already understood everything: it was the social division of labor that allowed this co-evolutionary coexistence between contract and community: community in society to ensure that the market did not destroy society, reducing everything to material exchange, thus disintegrating social being.

This is the decisive conceptual nexus of my reflection.

This nexus is based on the conviction that only by understanding the transformation of both post-industrial—financial—capitalism and the cultural transformation of the ideological *landscapes* that have resulted from it and to which it—that transformation—has accompanied, in the transition from modernity to the post-modernity of the desacralization of the world [344], the future of not only capitalism, but of humanity itself, is at stake, as the 2020 pandemic has taught us [345].

The same phenomena of the transformation of transnational labor markets dominated by the liberalist reaction that has imposed in Europe and the world the transition of migratory flows from state control to market dominance and consequently has favored—when not created—the uncontested affirmation of criminal networks in the trade of the human person, which is today increasingly reduced to the neo-slavery exchange of migrant traffickers who dominate uncontested under the justification of the free market [346].

Cities and metropolises around the world have been the areas of encystment and superimposition of such networks of intra and transnational segregation. All of this, as I have already demonstrated, in the transformation *rentier-capital-liberalist* of the "cities of the world", which have become the exemplary epicenter of the financialization and gentrification of late capitalism established on the territories:

> The majority of the large cities, national capitals or not, are mainly occupied with the construction, service and informal sectors. The main part of the extra-European immigrants find some sort of employment in the industrial or services jobs left vacant by the resident populations who are no longer socially and economically interested in them. Thus cultural and religious heterogeneity increases, and the tertiary vocation… (is) confirmed around the few central areas of industrialization that continuously intensify and restrict their capital investments. Historically speaking, as Bairoch (P. Bairoch, *Sizes of cities, living conditions and economic development*, Éditions de l'EMHSS, 1977) tells us, urban dimension and social forms of growth go together. Thus, the circle of the type of modernization that leads to social fragmentation, close with the ethnic segregation and the consistent threat of new imbalances and social conflicts. [347]

As I had demonstrated in *Southern Europe since 1945. Portugal, Spain, Italy, Greece, and Turkey. Modernization and Tradition* [348]—and as I see reiterated in a very important text on the themes of migrations in global capitalism [349]—the reference to migratory chains (Collier uses the term *diaspora*), that is to the increasingly powerful attraction in the times of migrations that follow for the lowering of costs and the creation of a *habitus* of ever more congruent reception, not only renews the anthropological cultures of migrants but also allows to renew those "local" economic practices, which have been mentioned following Stiegler, of origin of the "chains". They are very often and in many ways comparable to the forms of allocation of non-capitalist property rights and especially to *common goods*, thus overcoming the contradictions inherent in the untempered deployment of the capitalist form of property allocation.

This allows, when it happens, the development of social relations not overdetermined by pure economic transaction and determined, instead, by the phenomenologically intended affective relationship [350]: the "personal relationship" unfolds beneficially, which also has extraordinary economic consequences, *primarily* the coexistence between culturally divided life communities, but which can in this way not start integration, but the journey together, the path of coexistence thanks to "care".

The only way out of the crisis of secular deflation that awaits us is not the construction of heavy state-worshiping control systems, but the frugal and light work of cultural transformation that leads market actors to self-regulation. The "circular economy" must find—in the *being* in the market—its role of self-regulation and orientation compass.

Fairness, simple rules and *compliance* not statist but entrusted to social actors.

This is the real innovation we need: a positive anthropology. But this implies a return to humanistic tradition. And this is because, as Leo Spitzer teaches us, "The humanist believes in the power that the human mind has to investigate itself" [351].

Today, there is much discussion about innovation, but without the ability to investigate itself, innovation is a dry leaf carried away by the wind. Everything must, today, be new, brand new, everything must hinge on the gamble of innovation. The equation that sustains the ardor of innovators is, however, surreptitious. It has to do with truth: in fact, every attribution of meaning to life must be tied to a justification, epistemological and moral.

Well, for the innovator *tout court* the justification is the equation that is taken as given and as indisputable, between truth and innovation. A truth of an actualistic stamp, because it does not, as a rule, have a gnoseological, cognitive foundation: it is an act, it is a positioning in the world of change, and it is the change that is true, whatever its contents.

It is immediately seen, if one is not blind to the reification in progress in the world of goods and symbols deconstructed by knowledge and historical acquisitions, that this hypostatization of the truth-innovation nexus is absolutely illusory: it is nothing more than the continuation of innovation. The lack is in the excess of instrumental reason; it is in the excess of managerialism.

"Innovationism" goes with "managerialism" [352], with the theoretical presumption of bodily and spiritual control. Innovating, thus always inventing a new fashion, which is believed to be able and should always be carried out. When managerialism has reiterated its ideology of which the agents who epidemiologically spread it are the carriers, the hypostatized individuals do not—naturally—have creative wills, but only amorally familistic utilities. Therefore, one cannot even think of trusting them.

The managerialist enlightener is convinced that control over the individual is not only bodily—Taylorism *docet*—but also spiritual—business psychoanalysis *docet*—and therefore, that it can be infinite and indefinite.

If it is indefinite it controls change, the magic word and concept of managerialism. For such ideological reification, it is assumed that one can always achieve control of volitions. Moreover, the motivational technique of every kind and nature reverses the Pavlovian principle from experimental to behavioral and it is believed to be possible to guarantee cohesion and performance of large or small organizations thanks to the breviaries of directive action. The psychic is "induced" by every index of subjectivity. We are points of interference of determinable relationships.

The condition of life is placed outside the individual. The result is an accumulation of suffering such as society has never produced until now. How to coexist with it is the essential problem of today's social sciences. That's why they don't make it a subject of study. There is no doubt that a first sick answer lies in the fact that large and small organizations amalgamate suffering with the spontaneous socialization that no power can completely annihilate; they produce security, support, and informal cohesion because of the extraordinary resistance that the person emanates from his being and from his becoming every day in the transformation of the Self. And this is the only true way to produce therapeutic practices in organizations.

It is no coincidence, then, that in organizations and in the different subjects who live in them—one does not work without life—the will to rediscover tradition continually returns, in these times.

Why?

The answer to the question is found in a phrase by Leopardi, who does not speak of tradition, but of the relationship between subjectivity and truth. This relationship is the essence of tradition and this relationship is the opposite of the deified overflow of innovationism:

> It is not enough to understand a true proposition, one must feel its truth. There is a sense of truth, like passions, feelings, beauties, etc.: of the true, like the beautiful. He who understands it, but does not feel it, understands what that truth means, but does not understand that it is truth, because he does not experience the sense, that is, the persuasion. [353]

It is understood how we act: with the heart and never just with the mind. This, after all, is the behavior of humans compared to other living species on the globe. Man is the only one of these species that poses the problem of moving from being to ought to be. And he feels this need regardless of his position in society: by social classes or professional intentions or similar differentiations that characterize our modern living. A sensitivity that is grafted onto a rationality that only nihilistic reification has made us forget, but which always returns when we think that knowing is not understanding and educating is not educating oneself.

Is truth certainty? No: truth emanates from questioning and doubting and can be reached by always reflecting on the plurality of worlds, a plurality that constitutes our life. It is dense with the results of reason: such results constitute the powerful structures of economic growth, the continuous progress of scientific disciplines, the opening of the spaces of the knowable in increasingly new and widespread forms. Is all this truth? It is undoubtedly the result of reason, of instrumental reason that accumulates achievements in an uninterrupted succession and which is such because it is directed towards a goal, towards the achievement of an objective that arises from cognitive planning or from the unpredictable course of reasoning individually or in a group. In this way, our availability of means of transportation increases, the possibility of getting hands on the treatments that defend the body from aging and weakening thickens, as do all the technical devices that surround our disposition in the reality that surrounds us.

But is all this truth? It is certainly the result of reason that creates more and more artificiality and possibilities of survival for the human species.

But do these results respond to the imperative that emanates from the Leopardian phrase: do we feel all this in us and for us? Does it belong to us? Is it the world in which we place ourselves as objects, or is it the world that we participate in building as subjects because it is the fruit of our meaningful action? A meaning that goes beyond the result and comes to us as a human and virtuous conquest, humanistic. Why? Because it helps us in that very important and dangerous passage of being that goes towards the ought to be and which is the true substance of being human and subjects of history. Feeling the truth implies, therefore, understanding it as a fragment of an obligation to emancipate oneself from nothingness in a continuous reflection on the value of our acts and their meaning. This is what constitutes the meaning of life: its dedication to another than us which is beauty, which is faith, which is the search for the good of men one by one understood and not as ideological ornament that produces monsters and generalizing lies. This must always be thought, at every topical moment of our life. This is tradition.

The truth of tradition is the first of a path of individuation which is the true essence—as Jung teaches us—of personality. It is a path that never ends and that always lasts, that has no beginning except in mythogenesis and entelechy and that therefore is before us and that will not die with us. Before eternity there is the legacy of our works that continue our very life.

Truth is a source of life if it is wisdom, if it is wise to pose in front of the questions of conscience and therefore of the world, for it all emanates from the latter and all defines it. This is being in the world with anti-nihilistic phenomenological amazement that gives back sense and dignity to being and, with being, to our life, to the person who can be in each one of us all [354].

CHAPTER 14

To Conclude (in the Global Pandemic and in the Russian Aggression Against Ukraine)

The pandemic crisis of 2020 has made the issue of work, along with the digital theme, central to the reproduction of society in a homeostatic form with the defense of health and never in a separate form: this is the trend that will prevail if we want to survive and that makes incompetence and conflicts of interest appear as manifest residues of a dying world.

But "les morts saisi les vives": and this is true, today, in an emblematic form.

Our way of building polyarchy up to now—without good *governance*—with the separation of private interests from public ones—with the prevalence of particular interest over the general one—must transform, under penalty of the destruction of society, without alternatives.

Globally understood innovation, from technology to morality, is the only way to salvation.

Socialisme ou barbarie is no longer Castoriadis' lemma regarding the renewal of revolutionary thought, but the theoretical and practical leap ("Hic Rhodus, hic salta") necessary for the very reproduction of capitalist society.

It will arise, if we find the strength to bend over study and metaphysical moral and philosophical meditation, the very concept of community, as understood by German sociological thought between the late nineteenth and early twentieth centuries: *Gemeinschaft* in the *Gesellschaft* because the

G. Sapelli, *States, Markets and Wars in Global History*,
https://doi.org/10.1007/978-3-031-26716-1_14

community can always rebuild itself in society, as that great economist Alfred Marshall also taught us.

And it must arise, it already arises spontaneously, from associated human work a sort of new territoriality with the discovery that delocalization is not inevitable.

Today, even those who believed in the market (or still believe in it), in the optimal allocative virtue of the market, discover that delocalization has negative externalities on multiple aspects of social life: from work to the environment, to the quality of products and production and distribution processes. Without this rethinking, the circular economy as a new production model and not just waste recycling has no chance of coming true, as well as the fight against climate change.

In this way, the so-called national interest will be reclassified and will find a wise, non-aggressive, but constructive foundation.

And there are already emblematic creative entrepreneurial achievements in this regard all over the world.

Rebuilding and building, for example, manufacturing in the territories of both the South and the North of the world, will be part of a continuous work of maintenance and reproduction of territorially established social systems on the planet, both in a stable form, and in a migratory form and in search of rooting.

Forms of constitutional interstatuality and not functionalistic and jurisprudential—as is, instead, the European Union—will have to find a more suitable environment than today, to arise. And this will happen with the enhancement of those forms of allocation of property rights more suitable for this transformation such as the *not for profit* and the *common goods*.

The neoliberal regulation of the economy—which overflows into permanent (secular) deflation—can only be abandoned.

The theme that will arise will be that of a new definition of the roles of polyarchic communities, with the exit of public law from the condition of intellectual and regulatory minority to which it is today confined and which will necessarily have to be abandoned.

And with it will be abandoned the eruption of "Independent Authorities" (as Alberto Predieri [355] defined the dawn of the sad time in which we live today) with the affirmation, in step with what has been the slow, until now inexorable, euthanasia of the constitutions of the "Rule of Law" accompanied by the emergence of "Interstate Treaties" managed by monocratic regulators *extra lege* and veiled, hidden, by inept and merely spectacular parliaments.

All this will fortunately have to be abandoned and replaced by new forms of statehood and social justice.

Never as in these days do the words of a masterpiece, that of Ernst Wolfgang Böckenförde [356] come to mind: "The secular liberal state lives on assumptions that it cannot guarantee".

The parable of liberal democracy could not but evolve according to the trajectory that triggered the global civil war of the twentieth century and which is now over, that trajectory, to decompose in its state forms: the trajectory of social democracy that was supposed to develop and not abolish liberalism in a Hegelian synthesis never realized, buried by the capitalist dictatorships of the State: Soviet, Maoist and—today in China—post-Maoist, not to mention the historical abortions of Cuba and Venezuela. The European Empire without law and constitution is a variant of this disintegration.

The result was the breaking of every bond between liberalism and socialism, even in its welfare anticipations, both Bismarckian and labor in terms of historical origin.

Financialized capitalism has transformed all the assumptions of the same constitutional political form in the States with a Napoleonic code, under the impulse of capitalist centralization, as is the case with the European Union. It, in fact, to realize itself has abolished every form of constitutional law adequate to this centralization: neither federal nor confederal, but functionalistic, and has replaced the law with power relations exercised through European bureaucracy. It is a new dominant technocracy (and here the reference is to the work of Alessandro Mangia) [357].

In *common law* civilizations, on the other hand, the transformation caused both by financialization and by institutional centralization has occurred without interstate technocratic structures, through the creation of powerful managerial cohorts of what I have defined as the *owner capitalism*, that is a capitalism that is no longer managerial and therefore controlled by shareholders, but instead by the aforementioned cohort constituted in a class no longer salaried, as once by shareholders, but itself the owner of capitalism, through *stock options* (owning the shares of the shareholders that it should represent).

You will tell me: what does all this have to do with the coronavirus? It is instead essential to understand what is happening in global capitalism divided, of course, still by national states that are in fact only an obstacle to both European and financial centralization just evoked.

What has happened is what especially French culture has been studying for years with different and dramatic points of view. From the aristocratic distance of Amin Maalouf [358] to the political intelligence of Jérôme Sainte-Marie [359] to the statistical drama of Christophe Guilly [360] up to Pierre Vermeren [361] (*The Downgrading France*). In Italy, there is nothing similar, except for the heroic attempts of Raffaele Alberto Ventura (*The War of All* and *Theory of the Discomforted Class*) and the bright and foresighted book by Gabrio Casati [362] which I had the honor to introduce for the publisher Angelo Guerini (*Luigini against Peasants*). What do these studies demonstrate (to which we could add a handful of texts that come from the Anglo-Saxon world and all arise from the path opened by Thomas Frank with his essays on the "reversal of representation" voting orientations among the poor and rich and traditionally understood right and left)?

From all this intellectual turmoil, it is clear that the social elevator has not only stopped, but that this end of the upward mobilization of the subordinate classes has indeed increased inequalities and shifted income from labor to capital in a form never before seen on a planetary scale, but also the end of any cognitive communication between the upper classes and the last and penultimate classes of society. If we consider that among the major transformations of the last thirty years the most relevant are the decrease in the average size of companies, the great transformation of collective factory and office work into individual and small group work and therefore the enormous discrepancy between a few large companies and myriad artisan and family businesses whose economic and social ontology is still almost unknown, it is well understood how the upper classes that sit in political or functional government through technocratic means know nothing and want to know nothing about this human economic-social universe. They, therefore, cannot be able to undertake any social economic cure through governmental means.

The political classes that are at the top of the nationally understood deliberative-administrative government machines, or intranational or international according to the functional divisions between post-Wilsonian universalistic organizations like the UN or the FAO, or post-Bretton Woods economic ones like the International Monetary Fund, the World Bank, etc., without counting the already mentioned functional institutions like the ECB and the other European technocracies children of international treaties, know nothing about what happens and underpins the life of these new social organizations still not studied and that should be the recipients of the *issues* of emergencies to emerge from crises, epidemic, and/or social. In most nations, political classes no longer circulate according to the forms illustrated to us by the classics Gaetano Mosca and Vilfredo Pareto, but based on the peristaltic movements of economic and cultural pressures that are exerted on small and very small groups of *caciques* entrepreneurial-political often armed against each other even if subjected to electoral tests under the aegis of the same list symbol.

This is the worm that disintegrates both democracy and liberalism according to Böckenförde's prophecy.

And it is evident, therefore, that this peristalticity is all the more damaging the more the economic and social forms through which human settlements live interact more and more on the international level, as is made evident by the epidemic spread. But, at the same time, it is always on the level of international competition between nations, whatever the form of cooperation that has been established (from the European Union to the UN), that life and economic competition unfold, which is yes between companies but also and always between nations in the game of world power. It is in this game of power that social and economic life develops. Nations, in fact, let us remember, have remained state-actively in the world much more than the globalist rhetoric of every kind or form recites. And therefore the weaker the nations are in economic, military, and cultural competition, whatever you want to say, the more their forces can be damaged by what is always a competition as much of companies as of States that move in support of national economic interests. The latest interesting confirmation of what I affirm is in the pioneering work of Richard Davies on "survival economies", today the most widespread in the world, even in capitalist centers [363].

The experience of world governments today, in these pandemic and post-pandemic times, is an impressive confirmation of these theses. Everything converges, in fact, in the inability of political classes to react to events that require quick, cohesive, and at the same time realistic decisions, that is, based on a knowledge of the economic and social universe in which they want to act. In this case, to alleviate the consequences of a black swan event like a viral epidemic. This is necessary because the consequences of the previously mentioned competition do not even stop in the face of epidemics. And the consequences will be all the more severe the weaker the income, the *status*, the moral and not just physical life of human settlements and therefore the agglomerations of companies, classes, and communities: all forms, in short, of social life [364]. All this while the often ideologically denied competition between nations takes place with extreme cruelty, not even stopping in the face of disease, but exploiting and amplifying weaknesses.

Proof of this? Reread the modern and postmodern gazettes and discover that Germany appears to be the source of a coronavirus outbreak far more powerful than thought. Yet nothing was said for days. Italy, on the other hand, is seen in the global symbolic *landscape* as the plague spreader of the terrestrial world. And what about China? What do we know about what really happens and has happened in the Middle Kingdom?

Nothing, yet everything seems to continue as before. While in China, everything is changing.

China appears to many national and international observers as a nation that emerges victorious from the pandemic crisis. The data that was released on the global gross domestic product seemed to confirm this belief in 2020. While all the other nations that are a reference for understanding how the world will go—starting from the USA to continue with Russia, Germany, France, and the United Kingdom and India, ending with Italy—recorded strong falls in GDP, China grew by 1%. So it seemed.

The issue is of great interest. Many international observers rejoiced reading that Chinese GDP increased by 1%, not reading anything of what can be and could be read in the world on this topic. I always think, for example, of David Pilling who in the *Financial Times* has long described the rapid decline of what he calls "Chinese debt imperialism" in Africa or the articles of IFRI (the French institute of foreign policy that rivals in studies with the American institute on national security).

Not to mention the texts in English, French, and German on the real political and economic conditions in China. From this point of view, international attention was not focused on the exceptional fact that during the meeting of the People's Council Xi Jinping had only given a very short occasional speech and the central report—also short and less than an hour—was given by what was and is Xi's historical rival, namely Prime Minister Li Keqiang. Li is in fact the undisputed leader of one of the fundamental chains of command of Chinese power: the Chinese Communist Youth Federation which has always constituted—since the Long March—a current that has also fought against Mao and against absolute power in the CCP and for collegial leadership, and which not by chance strengthened under the rule of the current of Deng Xiaoping—the father of modern China. That modern China that began to be built only after Mao's death and only after the radical elimination of the so-called Gang of Four. The Shanghai group and Bo Xilai—whom Xi literally physically exterminated under the veil of the fight against corruption—were defeated by Xi but not Li, who has been resisting attempts at elimination for years. The question opened by Li and the FGCC reveals what is happening in these times in Chinese power shaken like a tree by the storm of the pandemic and by the failure of Xi and his concentration of power [365]. Even in the army, the contrasts are increasing. After the aggressive turn theorized by a multitude of both military and civilian theorists, today we are witnessing a silent battle unleashed by the army. It has garrisoned the nation during the pandemic. And, strengthened by this, it rises again against the economic and bureaucratic dominance of the Navy and the Air Force, to thus return to the power it held when foreign policy was defensive and anti-Russian and anti-Indian and therefore involved land wars unlike the Silk Road, all based on the dominance of the seas, as evidenced by the violations of maritime law in the South China Seas and in the Indian Ocean.

That 1% of GDP was a 1% "drag", in a nation that previously rose to 6% of GDP. Assuming that Chinese data is truthful and not false as was always the case with the USSR. It too was a nation like China with state terrorist monopolistic capitalism. The difference with China is that in China there are still about four hundred million small and large capitalist families that are alive and well, which were even called to be part of the CCP by Deng Xiaoping in his policy of liberation "of the cat as long as it eats the mouse".

The problem is and was that the absolute neo-Maoist power of Xi Jinping is hardly compatible with so many "kulaks".

Stalin was able to kill forty million of them in the 1930s. Killing hundreds of millions is impossible and this explains the attempt to suffocate them, as was unsuccessfully attempted before the pandemic, which was providential for Xi. He had tried to impose that law which would have marked the end for the Chinese bourgeoisie that found in Hong Kong the jugular vein of communication with the circulatory system of global capitalist finance that nourishes China with it.

The old Deng Xiaoping guard does not want this, nor does it want a war with the USA, which Xi's policy makes, sooner or later, inevitable. So inevitable that it has provoked the closing of ranks of the North American elites who from Biden to Trump have found themselves—divided on everything—united in preparing for an anti-Chinese roll back.

It can only be based on new massive investments in aviation and the navy compared to ground troops. And this explains the US coldness towards NATO and the conflicts this produces within European nations. Germany continues to propose its leadership not only European but worldwide by allying itself more and more closely with China. And this while the Atlantic Mediterranean lake is on fire and the permanent war in Libya is looming.

Proxy war between Turkey, which adheres to NATO, and Russia, which NATO and the USA oppose.

All this while the world is becoming unregulated and de-statized.

But if the world goes to pieces, it is possible that from its unraveling a re-composition of the threads of history will arise and that the USA and Russia will return to that competitive dualism which is the last hope before the end of the world.

In any case, 2020 will be remembered as the year of the deceleration of globalization and the evident crisis of a world that fails to regain stability and to grow economically due to the absence of leadership.

Deceleration, in fact, and not a sudden break in the interconnections of the international economy. Deceleration because it has been more than thirty years that the WTO has not been able to reach a multilateral trade agreement. The Seattle conferences of 1999 and Cancun of 2003 ended without any agreement. 2003 is the decisive year and the failure of that year reveals the structural limits of the globalization of the real economy: the agreement does not materialize because the twenty-two nations of the "South of the World" opposed the subsidies to agriculture distributed by the USA and the EU to their farmers and only in 2004, in the Geneva talks, the nations of the North of the world, the "industrialized" one, commit to reducing subsidies to farmers, while, as a counterpart, developing countries commit to reducing tariff barriers to manufactured goods from the North of the World. It is clear from history that the only globalization that has been realized on the planet is financial globalization: the symbolic currency created by central banks and the digital one originated by universal banks on derivative bets is the only commodity that moves around the world without barriers and at transaction costs tending to zero.

It is this discrepancy between super-financial globalization and semi-manufacturing globalization that creates global crises and adds up with the secular deflation induced by the European economic policy based on liberalism with low intensity of public investments and high restriction of internal markets and capitalist profit hit by deflation.

China has added to this scenario an unexpected asymmetry that seemed unstoppable until now with its entry into the WTO.

The coronavirus, if we look at this terrible danger to human health in this unusual context, may contain a virtue and this virtue is humility: the humility to recognize that the unstoppable growth of financial globalization and China—which is intimately linked to it—can both suffer a setback.

In the last twenty years, we have read too much of the *Manifesto* of Marx and Engels that magnified the progressive fortunes of the capitalist bourgeoisie and forgotten the great Giambattista Vico with his theory of historical cycles.

China, as I have already mentioned, in the fifteenth century reached Africa with its immense army, as demonstrated by François-Xavier Fauvelle in his archaeological masterpiece on "medieval" Africa [366]. It arrived there thanks to the expeditions of Admiral Zheng He, imperial eunuch of the Ming dynasty, between 1435 and 1443. China's retreat from Africa is still a historiographical mystery that has fascinated great scholars like Needham, Granet, Wittfogel without any result: why this happened remains an enigma.

But then as now the geopolitical consequences will be spectacular. An acceleration of the reflux of financial globalization and a consolidation of manufacturing trade with the current bilateral rules as has been done for more than thirty years will then be inevitable. The agreement between Mercosur and the very different one with Canada—from this point of view—were very important agreements, but also very discussed and not by chance they still have to find their full application in Europe: they did not announce global agreements with China and the rest of the world according to the inspiring dictation of the WTO, still today checkmated both by the politics of the USA of the last twenty years and by the global competition between France and the USA. They are both industrial and manufacturing powers and therefore are divided internally, before externally, between protectionist (farmers) and free trade (industrial) fronts, thus preventing in this way for reasons of domestic politics any supranational agreement.

The postponement of the "Agriculture Week" in 2020, a fair that took place every year in Paris, was a terrible event and should have predicted with little chance of error that the sector most affected by the coronavirus would have been the agricultural one. And these are reasons not only economic but *primarily* cultural. Agricultural products from which food is derived are not only food, but as such are also symbolic constructs that decide our lifestyles. There is no need to refer to Indian castes to remember how strongly what we eat and how we eat marks our taboos, our habits, and our social relationships. Symbols determine social life, just as economic rules do. In fact, I have always maintained that it is cultural rules; it is culture in the anthropological sense that determines the economy and economic relations. For this reason, I believe that this crisis of cultural universes that the coronavirus is causing will inevitably also have effects on European economic rules. And this will happen because they are based—in my opinion—more on dogmatic hypostatizations bordering on magic (the prohibition of debt and the belief that getting into debt is a fault and that public investments should not be made and that states are social constructs similar to families and businesses, which if they get into debt can only extinguish themselves, very differently from the state, as an imposing historiography shows us). But if nerves are kept steady and we do not fall even more into the domain of magicians and exorcists, those rules can only change. By political will, that is, for cultural reasons, certainly dictated by the emergency. From the emergency, the truth can emerge, from danger can come salvation, as Hölderlin said. It is said in newspapers around the world, in fact, that gradually even the peaks of European and national politics are beginning to question such economic policies.

Salvation is always present in history: you just have to recognize it and take it by the hand. The problem is, today more than ever, to understand that we need to unify in analysis and life experience the awareness that history is not over, neither in economics nor in political life, nor in humanity's struggle against diseases, and that inequalities and injustice only make this struggle even more difficult, disavowing any liberalist optimism: the market balance does not exist because the balance of and in history does not exist.

Indeed, as Richard Levins and Richard Lewontin announced unheeded, rather than announcing the inexorable decline of infectious diseases, we should realize that every major change in society, population, land exploitation, climate, nutrition, or migrations, is at the same time a health event with its always potentially threatening epidemiological framework and a result of property relations that determine the exploitation not only of human labor, but also of natural heritage, with the consequences not only climatic that we have today before us [367], hence, the importance of also studying biological sciences and the pharmaceutical industry itself in the capitalist production process. In this way, we escape both biological determinism and reductionism, understanding that medical science is part of a social science that must be subtracted from the pure development of capitalism and that the proprietary form of the production of medical and biological research is that of the allocation of property rights in a cooperative form and, even more properly according to the unsurpassed theory of Henry Hansmann [368], of the *not for profit* so that, as Elinor Ostrom taught us in her widely remembered works and set as a model of analysis and social action, scientific research is put at the service of humanity and not of capitalist profit.

And if we do not move from medical-scientist determinism and fear with a return to utopia, we will not survive pandemics.

After all, the relationship between associated man and nature has always been a relationship of feudal and then capitalist expropriation, as was discussed in the 1980s with Maurice Godelier, then busy collecting his essays in that masterpiece book that was and is *L'idéel et le matériel* [369].

Without utopia, we will not escape pandemics. The fact is, however, that while everything calls for a centralization of survival rules, according to sociological rather than medical logics, such logics alone cannot interpret the defense needs of living social systems.

And now comes to mind the ever-relevant teaching of Husserl on the failure of the "European sciences", incapable as we are, again, of escaping from a positivism of facts that killed and kills life and the life of knowledge.

But what has failed is, as a result of the end of those decaying "sciences", the myth of the internationalists, the proponents of the post-Wilsonian "Kantian peace" whose tragic path has been well described in a book as important as it is little studied as it deserved: that of Oona Hathaway and Scott Shapiro [370] which I have not coincidentally referred to from the beginning. The tragedy in which we are immersed is, as I stated at the beginning of this book, that of the increasing dissolution of the State throughout the world. In the bowels of this elitist process of "internationalist" governance from above and without selection operate "mixed technostructures" [371], that is, selected for weighted co-optation with triple-entry matrices between nation, political affiliation, and educational chains. These are immense saprophytic cohorts of government. In them and in their de facto power, in their de facto and not de jure orders, lies the core of the dissolution of the State on a global scale. The State, the nation-state, which is certainly dominion and institution, as it is represented by its borders, should always be essentially and always also a "community of destiny" of a people, which recognizes itself in that destiny, and therefore in the borders. If that "community" of destiny ceases to be realized, the State dies. The same was true for empires [372] which were nothing more than unions of States always in need—*à la Botero*—of "maintenance". If the State is also a community, as Otto Hintze taught us [373], well, treaties between States, on which the network of the internationalization of the world is based, decay and are not compulsory. As demonstrated by the ineffectiveness of the UN and the technocratic resources of the world economic governance institutes. From the International Monetary Fund to the various development and investment banks created by the "Brain of Jupiter" of the mixed technocratic supranational polyarchies, that network gradually tears, does not hold, collapses, unravels and with it the world that continues to be the world of States. We have been too attracted by local disintegration crises, also producing many researches. But researches that are the fruit of the weak thought of "blind kittens", blind to the meaning that those local crises assumed and assume, in the background of the destinies of humanity: it is from the local crises that we are blinded [374] thus failing to grasp, through these crises, the global crisis.

Only the realistic perspective of the "reason of State" can help us to recompose a theoretical framework that illuminates the present crisis of dissolution. After what I have already said at the beginning of this book about the perenniality of Botero's teaching, we must turn to the thought of Meinecke, which integrates well with that of Botero. And precisely, paradoxically, for his Machiavellianism. We must turn to Meinecke's *Die Idee der Staatsräson in der neueren Geschichte* of 1924, already announced by his masterpiece of 1908 *Weltbürgertum und Nationalstaat*, where the meditation on Fichte speaks to us still today. The possible reconnection between ethics and politics resides for Meinecke only in the always sought-after ethicization of "power" (*Macht*). Today throughout the world this does not happen while everything is resolved, inevitably, in the mere unfolding of "violence" (*Gewalt*), the ultimate reason for dissolving States, incapable of both diplomatic relations and acting with *soft power*. Indeed, the tension between ethics and politics can only be pursued in the sole human condition that can also bring truth to life in the exercise of politics: democracy, popular sovereignty. Sovereignty always denied by unelected powers [375]. If sovereignty is not pursued, what arises is the hypocritical unfolding of the ideology of human rights as a guide to the politics of international relations. The most unfolded form of international relations is that of Treaties. However, treaties between States that are dissolving, while local wars, by proxy, to defend "human rights" with wars deployed without any foundation of legitimacy, follow one another in general hypocrisy as clearly revealed in Iraq and Libya and Syria. And here is the modernity of the great German historian. In Meinecke's life, the theme of the need to prevent the rise of the demonic face of power was a tragedy that he lived in an increasingly anguished form, first with the collapse of the Wilhelmine Reich, then with the demonic power of Hitlerian capitalism. And Meinecke had already grasped the whole drama of our present time. Today, anomie—living without believing in anything—conforms to what remains of the people: it is the product of a state without a community, because without democratic legitimation, because of the technocratic power that emanates from above. This provokes the rise of what Meinecke called the "Machiavellianism of the masses", *Massenmachiavellismus*. Definition not by chance included in his last masterpiece: *Die deutsche Katastrophe*, written in 1946.

The Machiavellianism of the masses was and is nothing more than a re-edition of jingoism, already well studied by Hobson [376] at the beginning of the twentieth century.

The massification of politics, in fact, is very unlikely to occur on the basis of the ideologies of "human rights": such an *landscape* ideological is the set of symbolic universes of the minorities of newspaper readers and listeners of political talk shows, to which the masses do not have access; for them, a large amount of daily pornography and mass media violence is produced, which they then mimic in their real life, with very dangerous consequences for the reproduction of human settlements.

For the masses, as I said at the beginning of the book, quoting René Girard, the only political participation seems to be the identity or purely instrumental one, where power impulses overflow beyond any ethical boundary. The reflection on the "demonic", which was the heart of Meinecke's last anguished hours, contains many of the terrible unknowns of today [377]. But others continually arise, which could not be understood by a thought of great strength and which, however, in such strength found its limit because it bore the stigmata of the long European and world civil war. This war had just ended in one of its cycles, to return immediately after, with all the new anguish of the post-war period on the plane of geopolitical power relations. The defeat of the Nazi-fascist monster and Japanese militarism had opened a new cycle of wars and local conflicts and divisions, of faults, which fragmented the two North American and Soviet Empires, which were again opposed. The dissolution of the States and the class struggle pursued by finance and algorithms against dependent workers and the lower-middle classes had yet to come. And they came with the end of the European civil war due to the collapse of the USSR. The only confrontation between parliamentary capitalist polyarchies and the mass terrorist despotism of Chinese state monopolistic capitalism remained and remains. In the 1980s, the cycle of financial capitalism would have begun, illusorily strong from the leverage of debt and the financial speculative bubble. It was not only caused by the *new economy*, but also expanded by the Chinese demographic lever [378]. The year 2001, with China's entry into the WTO, marks the cycle in which we are still immersed and which is about to close with the realignment of the polyarchic capitalist-democratic powers in a new anti-Chinese cold war.

But at the same time, the State has dissolved and with it the large mass parties *rank and file*. Meanwhile, the old mole of social contradictions is not dead: it continually digs. Its traces have re-emerged with the fragmented revolts from new fractals, perennial in their renewal, and with the emergence from the no less deep burrows of a time of social divisions, inequalities, marginalities, and anomie.

Neither Meineckian thought nor the theory of the reason of state in the new Foucauldian version can understand, in their theoretical circle from the concrete to the abstract, the revolt that is spreading throughout the world. There is not only the Machiavellianism of the masses.

There is also a new rebelliousness destined to clash with the neo-Machiavellianism of the masses. A rebelliousness that extends, spreads, and then is reabsorbed by the anomie that marks our world. Many phenomena that are now spreading in the world, who no longer enjoys the Goethean gift of youth, have already seen them proliferate about forty years ago in Latin America [379]. I am referring to that transformation of class struggle that was profound, like that which occurred in the social fabric of the "dangerous classes", that is, the poorest social strata in the de-statized nations of South American societies, with the transition from poverty to marginality. A transition of which Loïc Wacquant was the first anticipatory scholar [380]. The decisive transformation, however, was described with generalizing logical circularity thanks to the anthropological immersion from the concrete to the abstract that is possible to co-live by reading the two great books by Janice Perlman. The first written after living from 1968 to 1969 in a *favela* in Rio de Janeiro [381]; the second after returning there in the years of the first decade of the second millennium and having met the same ethnographic "privileged interlocutors" and having found a deeply changed reality. Poverty had not only overlapped with marginality, but had made the latter dominant due to the advent of drugs and their traffickers and widespread violence and the destruction of social relations between middle-high classes and poor classes. Relations that once existed: no woman, however, on her return to Rio, went to the center to do domestic work and no young or old male went to the metropolis to do more or less legal work, but all based on that dignity of poverty that can only come from dependent or autonomous work, always on the border of legality, but never definitively exceeding it. The marginality caused by the increase in poverty and, at the same time, by the disintegration of the social fabrics of both the lower and the high and middle-high classes, had (Janice Perlman revealed) dissolved the capacity for resistance and struggle of those who were once poor popular classes and now revealed and transformed into "almost marginal" groups. The dissolution is not only state, therefore, but also social and this profoundly changes the cyclicity and the form of the protests themselves. The "revolt" becomes its dominant trait.

From the *favela* of Rio to the urbanized French and Bavarian countryside, to the outskirts of the great cities of the Greater Middle East, to the crumbling metropolises of sub-Saharan Africa, up to the great metropolises of financial capitalism—in Washington, in New York, in London, in Paris—and in the de-industrialized cities all over the world.

The dissolution of political parties and states goes hand in hand with this process of falling into marginality. When it does not occur due to internal force, it is the peaks of power of capitalism with finance deployed that provoke it, determining that disintegration of the state that the revolt cannot provoke, but only accompany or make unconscious use of, because that disintegration can fuel it but not provoke it. That process which became manifest in Italy with the so-called Tangentopoli of the first half of the nineties of the twentieth century can be considered a sort of large-scale dress rehearsal to accelerate these processes from above, as is happening today all over the world. A so-called fight against corruption that served to destroy the enemies of privatizations and to bring to power the "synthetic" leaders of the new *cliques* and the new *caucus* of polyarchic rule, which still had to find the trinket of territorial representation to seek constitutional legitimacy. But such a process could not fail to determine, inevitably, the destruction *in nuce* of the same parliamentarism based on "classic" parties. A peristaltic mucilage of *neo-caciques* cannot stably support, in fact, a parliamentary democracy. The situational power of polyarchy gradually replaces or overlaps with the territorial one [382].

Latin America is a continent that has been anticipating these profound international processes for about fifty years. They are determined in that very particular socio-economic formation before their appearance in other differentiated socio-economic formations, but on certain aspects increasingly similar: the transformation of poverty into marginality, the transformation of cities and metropolises from social and political agoras into spaces of social segregation and the elaboration of new lifestyles of the upper classes and of capitalist social domination. The birth of groups of extractive capitalisms supported by what remains of the nation-state determines this profound social transformation and makes models of marginality proliferate everywhere. These extractive capitalist groups, thanks to the "mixed technostructures", are encysted in the systems of unelected but delegated domination, where the difference in *status* is measured not only between the poor and middle classes, but also between the globalized ruling classes and those still attracted by the territories, in a constant and deep struggle of interests that corrodes the very peaks of capitalism.

The dissolution of the state brings with it on a global scale the emergence of the transformation of the judicial order into power. This transformation occurred first in Italy in the nineties of the twentieth century, due to the intimate institutional weakness of the Italic polyarchy in the face of extractive capitalism ("via privatization") financialized Anglo-Saxon and "Rhenish" [383]. The same process did not occur so quickly and through judicial means in institutionally stronger capitalist states, such as France and Germany. Italy anticipates the future of Southern Europe: its South Americanization. It is today accentuated by the conflict between the USA and China that fully unfolds in this Europe, as well as in the Balkan one. Since the Maastricht Treaty, moreover, the strength of the French and German states tries to assert itself extractively towards the EU states or what remains of them, upsetting any hypothesis of constitutionalizing the European continent, sunk in de facto and not de jure domination.

In Latin America, the judicial power as a political weapon has spread. There is no longer a need to assassinate Allende and exterminate entire generations as happened in Argentina. Of course: the USSR has collapsed, the world civil war has ended and the one with China has not yet begun. Now the *coups* are conducted by the power of the judges and the judicial fight against the dangerous enemies of extractive capitalism and financial capitalism. South America today sets an example [384]: it is no longer Italy that indicates the path of capitalist normalization.

But it is precisely the "capitalist normalization" that was questioned in 2022.

After the pandemic crisis, here is the crisis generated by Russia's imperialistic and imperial aggression against Ukraine.

It is in this telluric and apocalyptic context that the "Russian revelation" has been unleashed, that is, the emergence of the new imperialistic power that was gradually forming, after the ordo-liberal depredation produced by Yeltsin's financial capital in the years immediately following the fall of the USSR.

The reaction of those who took the flag of the Great Russian neo-nationalism into their hands is a decisive turning point in the global history of late capitalism. And it will be terrible.

The war of imperialistic and imperial aggression of Russia against Ukraine quickly reached its outcome that was already manifesting from the beginning, after the Syrian and Mesopotamian wars. Turkey in August 2022 recognized Crimea as a historical entity constituting the Ukrainian nation, undermining the entire Russian neo-imperial construction that had laid the ideological foundations of the war of aggression.

The issue is centuries old, as all those who do not base their opinions on today's knowledge desert, dominated by anti-knowledge hysteria, know. Catherine the Great made it a decisive point of her policy of creating that empire that was to wet its feet both in the warm seas of the Atlantic lake of the Mediterranean, as well as in the cold ones of the Indo-Pacific, thus giving life to the immensity of an empire that transformed the Mongol dominion of a time into a power as great as, however, still unable to contend with the United Kingdom for the dominion of India. Hence today's events, let's not forget. But the imperial Russia had to, however, in that way, from Crimea, extend its power both against Prussia and against the historical Mesopotamian States. Cavour taught the Italians what it was about and, read today with Tolstoy, enriches the mind and placates the furies of the fools. Italy is built as annexation to Piedmont on the problem of Crimea: it seems impossible if you only look at today's Italian panorama with its *landscape* ideological. Then begins, in the times of the European Risorgimento, in the nineteenth century, the war of the Great Middle East and, together, also that of the bloody Balkan struggle, history of Risorgimenti also that. And history of power on the part of Prussia and then Germany and France and finally also Italy, under the watchful eye of the United Kingdom.

One of these power wars never remembered would have already been unleashed at the end of the nineteenth century on overseas bases, as the too little studied Domenico Bonamico well understood, when American ships appeared at Moroccan ports to prevent Germany from becoming a maritime power through African imperialism. And then—when the Arctic would become a field of power—here are the USA in the field via strengthening of NATO to the north, as indeed happened from the nineties of the twentieth century. US presence, this time, for imperial annexation of European nations: it is powerfully shaping up, thus consigning the Italian shores to a perennial marginality of which there is no awareness, as demonstrated by the misunderstanding of what the energy crisis really is: not inflation, but a de-structuring, precisely, of power relations. De-structuring that aims again at Germany and its Chinese link, which must be broken by also weakening all European nations through economic sanctions to Russia and the EU at the same time.

The Arctic, the Mediterranean, and the Indo-Pacific were the triangle of imperial power designed as the destiny of the "Russian world" by Gorchakov, the brilliant *dominus* of nineteenth-century diplomacy, not only Russian, and the founder of Russian Eurasian greatness, of which Primakov and—today—the desperate Karakanov have been and are the deepest interpreters. Stalin's victory in the Second World War with the occupation of Berlin by the Red Army laid the foundations for the expansion of the Russian world as a great power as never before had so powerfully occurred. But the USA did not allow it, both at the time of the Moroccan crisis, the First World War and Versailles, and at the time of the occupation of Berlin, and they do not allow it today. The Greater Middle East and North Africa are their business. You can't sleep Italian-style if you rule the world, especially when such rule is increasingly in danger.

The empire can doze but it is not allowed to fall asleep. The retreat from Afghanistan made it clear: the fate is constant vigilance.

It seemed to the world that, after the Second World War and the victory of the Red Army in Berlin, the victory against Japan by the Anglosphere and the neutralization of European powers, with the German division and the French break from NATO, an Italian-French plan to prevent Germany from making too manifest imperialistic ambitions and becoming the maritime power that it then became and that the USA always crushed, could be possible. A land power cannot oppose such a plan. France could, the only continental maritime power, the only potential imperial force even if not in action. But it, due to its secular history and its Jacobin founding revolution, cannot dominate with hegemony: it can only disintegrate and possess nationalistically. But the Europe of Ventotene would need much more. A good that is no longer found: perhaps it is gone forever. Just like those heretical revolutionary socialists who wrote that never-read document are gone.

Today history repeats itself under Ukrainian and Turkish guises. The attempt to revitalize the anti-Islamist wing of the Turkish army and its *intelligentsia* failed, Gülen failed and the coup failed, leaving the USA with no choice but to seek an alliance with Turkey, flattering its neo-imperial designs. The Libyan and Syrian wars were designed to allow the realization of a new Turkish genocide, this time against the Kurds, even giving it international relevance with the annexation of Sweden and Finland to NATO, which had been prepared for years and years. Of course, let's remember, everything changed with the collapse of the USSR and the defeat of the designs of an Europeanization of Russia that would overcome its Eurasian destiny. The ruthless extraction of Russian resources by the unleashed financialized liberalism triggered the nationalist reaction that history had taught us to read in the events of the South Slavs and in the Balkan wars. Putin and Ukrainian nationalism are the faces of a coinage that has only generated war money, as Marx and Engels, with all the democratic thought of the nineteenth century, from Garibaldi to Herzen to Heine to Kossuth, would teach us to understand if only we still read them and always.

In the Greater Middle East, Putin had begun to effectively conquer power, unchallenged, as had happened in Georgia and Crimea in the first decade of the 2000s. The rise of the neo-Ottoman Empire in Syria and Libya now endangers the Russian bases in Crimea and Syria, nullifying their wars. Ukrainian Crimea can only favor the continuity of a war that is destined to never end and to remain a perennial Balkan-type ember. Until the exhaustion of the contenders and the worlds they represent. The real danger is that Russian imperialistic desperation—with the loss of Crimea and the stubborn will of the Anglosphere, followed by the EU, to favor it, that loss—transforms the words and writings of those who are convinced that in this way they want to destroy and dismember Russia. And that the only remedy can only be a nuclear war.

This is what needs to be taken into account. A much more serious issue than all the energy and food crises that scare us, distracting us from the problem and the impending drama. The "referendum" farce in Donbass was one of the Kremlin's responses to Kiev's military counteroffensives.

The outcome was that, without any democratic value, the territories wanted to be annexed to Russia. A tried and tested strategy, already applied in the Georgian republic of South Ossetia (where the referendum was suspended by a decree of May 30, 2022, by the de facto president Alan Gagloev). Thus began a continuous worsening of the situation.

Indeed, after the annexation, Russia would defend its own territory. Is this why Moscow has ordered partial mobilization?

Certainly, it means that total war begins. Pope Francis was right in saying that this accentuated a tangible danger of nuclear war.

Stopping the risk of escalation would only be possible with a jolt of realism, with Kiev renouncing Crimea and Donbass, but the prerequisites for this are not seen. We are faced with two opposing "resurgence" ideologies: Ukrainians rightly consider themselves Ukrainian; the Russians, on the other hand, consider them Russian. Moscow does not accept that Ukraine is separated from the novyj mir, from the Russian world.

Kiev's mistake has always been to exclude the hypothesis of a neutral Ukraine between the West and Russia. But the situation became complicated because not only did the US intend to humiliate Russia, but also China, the only possible mediator, while the United States never wanted the war to end. They needed and still need it to continue to have a strong influence in Europe and to put Germany in crisis. It is very sad to say, but their strategy marks a tremendous defeat of Christian and Western values. Everyone has failed: the US, Russia, which has revealed its worst side, that of imperialistic power, and Europe, because it has not been able to oppose American dominance.

Putin and the dominant ruling groups in Russia are marked by an "anguish" existential and political that has increased in proportion to their revanchist hardening because they feel surrounded, above all they no longer feel considered a great power. The climax was when Obama in 2014 defined Russia as a "regional power". Around Putin, there was a fear that Russia could be dismembered and occupied. The fundamental turning point was the "parenthesis" of Yeltsin. When Gennady Yanayev and the old Soviet nomenklatura tried to turn back the clock of the USSR and the West did not support Gorbachev. The neo-Soviet coup failed and Boris Yeltsin took power. But Yeltsin paved the way for Jeffrey Sachs and the men that Washington had sent to Moscow to privatize the former Soviet Union. High finance and the great American and German industry carried out a vast work of plundering the economy and resources. Part of the nomenklatura, including Putin, then Yeltsin's dolphin, opposed and put an end to the experiment and began a process that if not stopped would have dismembered Russia annihilating its economy. That's what the US wanted.

All this masked by a conception of international relations based on the abandonment of Realpolitik to assert, instead, the primacy of the "moral order" advocated by the US since 1928, with the Briand-Kellogg treaty. Thus inaugurating the North American project to replace international diplomacy with an order based on "human rights", to justify the ambition to extend the Monroe doctrine to the whole world, applied until then only to Latin America. Hence the increasing disorder of international relations: a disorder made of recursive but unstable, collapsing elements. The world had become "fractal" already with the signing of the Treaty of Versailles, which the US, then, did not ratify. In this way, they upset the West, because they created an order based on the national principle but without implicating themselves with it and its consequences. There begins the destruction of the system of international relations hitherto known and takes their place a new system, based on the conflict of power, the clear example of which was the Molotov-Ribbentrop pact: Stalin did not hesitate to sign it, ready to abandon it once Germany had advanced too far. An absolute ruthlessness no longer based on trust, the true keystone of the system of international relations, but on power. Today, moreover, the war between Russia and Ukraine exposes the weakness of the functionalist architecture of the European Union.

Jean Monnet and Alexandre Koyré, in the aftermath of Second World War, took on the lesson of Robert Triffin and his attempt to build a single currency system with countries at different levels of productivity. Koyré should be known not so much for having interpreted Hegel, but for having hypothesized that a world could be built on temporary power balances based on segmented technical solutions—the future European treaties—rather than on popular and legal constitutions. But an "empire" built on a treaty system had never been realized in the world.

Instead, only an attempt at a neo-imperial order has been realized, which was disastrous because it lacked constitutional foundations: this is what Europe is trying to do in the post-war period under American pressure. The USA understands that it is the least painful price to stop Stalin's advance in the old continent. It was Stalin, in fact, the real winner in 1945, because he was the first to arrive in Berlin, not others.

Can an institutional system like the European one, based on the euro and the stop to debt, survive this war that has hit it head on?

No, it cannot. The energy issue, which is nothing more than a deconstruction of power relations, shows that Europe is destined to succumb. In Washington, they understand this very well, and in fact with the war in Ukraine they now achieve two objectives: the destruction of German capitalism and the break between the German economy and Chinese imperialism.

Obviously, the destruction of power will drag the Italian economy of the North, from La Spezia to Rimini, which is closely linked to the German one, thus deconstructing Europe, today that the challenge is played elsewhere, in the Indo-Pacific against China, and there power resources must be invested.

But this only provokes another disaster: more ruins.

It is the possible advent of the next nuclear war. Because as Primakov and Karaganov said, when Russia finds itself in a tight spot, it will launch the bombs. There are no doubts. It will be easy for the first targets to be in Germany and immediately after in the country that challenged them after a long tradition of trust, that is Italy.

One of the possible ways out of the conflict is to transform military competition into economic competition thanks also to the joint diplomatic action of the "Latin countries" of Europe, Spain, France, and Portugal, which, together with Germany, find an agreement to counterbalance the USA, who want intermittent war, to destabilize the Balkans and Russia.

Italy is no longer part of the group of "Latin countries" because it is conditioned by local political representatives too subordinate to the Americans, a subordination that is expressed with "technocratic personalisms".

While Russia is increasingly prey to a very, very dangerous Great Russian ethnic mysticism. Our only hope is that Russian dissent strengthens and that there is a coup in Moscow. Otherwise, the danger of nuclear war will continue to grow [385].

In this context, the revolt does not stop and flares up everywhere. And everywhere that phenomenon manifests itself which in an old classic on social movements, too forgotten, was defined as "the great abortive revolution": "... The abortive revolution has, we now know, left unsolved a very great problem indeed... it is not a movement aimed at overthrowing our government - our 'old' regime - and putting another in its place" [386].

These are, in fact, revolts in a symbolic *landscape*, dominated all over the world by pervasive cultures that have in them mysterious and magical elements, as I mentioned at the beginning. They are certainly very different phenomena from each other and of which we often still know very little. Just think of China and much of Asia and Africa and the ***underground*** cultures of the capitalist accumulation center, with its separate and non-communicating worlds. The digital network, more than unifying, connects and spreads and transmits universes, images, and dreamlike places that bring together different cultures and traditions and different symbolic worlds. Everything is reassembling and again shattering in an infinite and uncontrollable movement by anyone. There are continuous seismic shocks that aggregate and at the same time disaggregate. The revolt feeds on those who we would once have identified as the heretical movements that shook the first centuries after the "Millennium".

I think of the historiographical legacy of Delio Cantimori and those who have succeeded him in the chairs of Church History in Italy. For all and above all Giovanni Miccoli and Arsenio Frugoni, with their reflections on Fra Dolcino and Arnaldo da Brescia magnificently collected and presented to our reflection by Giovanni Grado Merlo [387]. The words of Miccoli, commenting in a bibliographic note on an anonymous Ambrosian code—decisive for historiographical analysis—open us to the understanding of a world that today reappears before our eyes and through this meditation on the past we can perhaps better understand analogically the present:

> ... The picture - Miccoli affirmed - in which the Anonymous presents us the story of Dolcino preludes to the magical frame in which it will be seen later: "Magnitudo rei, que miraculose et inexcogitate pervenit", narrates

> the chronicler and the clashes, the sieges, the victories of the heretics and their defeats are placed under the reign of God and Satan: but only this is here of all the fantastic elements that will impose themselves later. [388]

A story, that of the heresiological tradition of pauperism, which, in my opinion, reappears today and should be studied with the tools not only of anthropology, but also of religious sociology and studies on magic. Secularization does not eliminate the sacred: it makes it appear in the psychic experience (not only in that of the marginalized) in other forms, forms different from those medieval and heretical [389], but no less pervasive.

Notes

1. R. Girard, *Things Hidden Since the Foundation of the World*, Grasset et Fasquelle, Paris 1978; Eng. trans. *Of Things Hidden Since the Foundation of the World*, Adelphi, Milan 1980.
2. Appadurai, *Modernity at Large: Cultural Dimensions of Globalization*, University of Minnesota Press, Minneapolis 1996; Eng. trans. *Dusty Modernity: Cultural Dimensions of Globalization*, Raffaello Cortina, Milan 2012.
3. P. Anderson, *The H-Word: The Peripeteia of Hegemony*, Verso Books, London-New York 2010.
4. J. Costa, *Oligarchy and Caciquism as the Current Form of Government in Spain: Urgency and Way to Change It*, Tesla, Madrid 1901.
5. It is the concept that Luciano Gallino formulated to make manifest the transformation of classes into fragmented clans that have not yet reached the concept of "for themselves" but are already "in themselves" active as aggregates carrying distinctive logics to social action: see L. Gallino, "A Sociology for the World Society", in *Sociology Notebooks*, 70–71, 2016, pp. 247–274.
6. The fundamental texts are by V. Ronchi, *The Metamorphosis of the Revolution. Social Liberalism in Salinas' Mexico (1988–1994)*, Mimesis, Milan 2015; *Narcomexico. Narcopolitics, Mexico, the*

G. Sapelli, *States, Markets and Wars in Global History*,
https://doi.org/10.1007/978-3-031-26716-1

Economy, Drug Trafficking, GoWare, Florence 2012; *Neoliberalism and Neopopulism in Latin America. The Cases of Mexico and Argentina in the Nineties*, Il Mulino, Bologna 2010.
7. M. Ostrogorski, *Democracy and Political Parties*, Fayard, Paris 1911; Eng. trans. *Democracy and Political Parties*, Rusconi, Milan 1991.
8. G. Quagliariello, *Politics Without Parties. Ostrogorski and the Organization of Politics Between the 19th and 20th Centuries*, Laterza, Rome-Bari 1993.
9. K. Polanyi, *The Great Transformation: The Political and Economic Origins of Our Time*, Beacon Press, New York 1944; Eng. trans. *The Great Transformation*, Einaudi, Turin 1974.
10. P. Dardot, C. Laval, *The New Reason of the World. Essay on Neoliberal Society*, La Decouverte, Paris 2009; Eng. trans. *The New Reason of the World. Critique of Neoliberal Rationality*, DeriveApprodi, Rome 2013.
11. W. Lippmann, *The New Imperatif*, Macmillan, London 1953.
12. W. Eucken, "Das Ordnung Politische Problem", in volume I of *Ordo. Yearbook for the Order of Economy and Society*, J.B.C. Mohr, Freiburg 1948.
13. Fundamentals by J.L. Rueff, *The Crisis of Capitalism*, La Revue bleue, Paris 1935; *The Social Order*, Librairie Sirey, Marseille 1945; *Epistle to the Planners*, Gallimard, Paris 1949 (Italian trans. *Epistle to the Planners*, Tipografia del Babuino, Rome 1950); *Monetary Regulation and the Institutional Problem of Money*, Fayard, Paris 1953; *The Age of Inflation*, Hachette, Paris 1963 (Italian trans. *The Era of Inflation*, Edizioni di Vita aperta, s.l. 1966); *Gods and Kings (Views on the Creative Power)*, Hachette, Paris 1967 (Italian trans. *The Gods and Kings. Views on the Creative Power*, Edizioni della Nuova Antologia, s.l. 1975); *The Monetary Sin of the West*, Plon, Paris 1972 (Italian trans. *The Monetary Error of the West*, Etas Kompass, Milan 1971).
14. On which the fantastic work of O.A. Hathaway and S.J. Shapiro, *The Internationalists*, Simon & Schuster, New York 2017; Italian trans. *The Internationalists*, Neri Pozza, Vicenza 2018.
15. On Leo Strauss it is essential to remember: S. Drury, *The Political Ideas of Leo Strauss*, St. Martin's Press, New York 1988; K.H. Green, *Jew and Philosopher: The Return to Maimonides in the Jewish Thought of Leo Strauss*, State University of New York

Press, Albany, NY 1993; L. Batnitzky, *Leo Strauss and Emmanuel Levinas: Philosophy and the Politics of Revelation*, Cambridge University Press, New York 2006.
16. By D.P. Calleo, the fundamentals are: *The Imperious Economy*, Harvard University Press, Cambridge (Mass.) 1982; *Follies of Power: America's Unipolar Fantasy*, Cambridge University Press, Cambridge 2009.
17. The obvious reference is to the book—fundamental to understanding our times—by O.A. Hathaway and S.J. Shapiro, which I have already cited.
18. P. Tucker, *Unelected Power: The Quest for Legitimacy in Central Banking and the Regulatory State*, Princeton University Press, Princeton 2017.
19. Mangia (ed.), *MES: Europe and the Impossible Treaty*, Morcelliana, Brescia 2020.
20. On this the great book by A. Pilati, *The Catastrophe of the Elites. Digital Power and the Crisis of Politics in the West*, Guerini e Associati, Milan 2019.
21. The inspiration of M. Kalecki is always unsurpassed, in *Theory of Economic Dynamics: An Essay on Cyclical and Long-Run Changes in Capitalist Economy*, Oxford University Press, Oxford-London 1954; Italian translation. *Theory of Economic Dynamics. Essay on Cyclical and Long-Term Variations in the Capitalist Economy*, Boringhieri, Turin 1957.
22. My loyalty to the teaching, full of doubts and warnings, but always truthful, of Claudio Napoleoni is evident. I remember—for all his works—the one most dense with foundations: C. Napoleoni, *Smith, Ricardo, Marx*, Boringhieri, Turin 1970.
23. J. Joana, A. Smith, *The European Commissioners: Technocrats, Diplomats or Politicians?*, Presses de Science Po, Paris 2002.
24. On this I allow myself to refer to my "From Dante to Luther. Italian-German parallelisms", in *Limes*, May 2020, pp. 119–124.
25. The reference to the unsurpassed text by P. Mansfield, *A History of Middle East*, Viking, New York 1991 is inevitable.
26. On which too little reference is made to the pioneering works of A. Elorza, such as *Integralism in Islam*, Alianza Editorial, Madrid 2002, and *The Circle of Global Jihad*, Alianza Editorial, Madrid 2020, which is destined to be a fundamental book on the subject.

27. A.W. Small, *The Cameralists. The Pioneers of German Social Policy*, The University of Chicago Press, Chicago 1909.
28. P. Schiera, *From the Art of Government to the Sciences of the State. Cameralism and German Absolutism*, Giuffrè, Milan 1968, and the same, "The administrative conception of the State in Germany (1550–1750)", in L. Firpo (ed.), *History of Economic, Political and Social Ideas*, UTET, Turin 1980.
29. G. Miglio, "The Origins of Administrative Science", in *The Science of Administration*, proceedings of the I Conference of studies of administrative science, Giuffrè, Milan 1957, pp. 9–62.
30. This is what O. Brunner still teaches us today in *New Paths of Constitutional and Social History*, Vandenhoeck & Ruprecht, Göttingen 1968 (then translated into *For a New Constitutional and Social History*, Giuffrè, Milan 1970).
31. L. Ornaghi, V.E. Parsi, *The Virtue of the Best. The Elites, Democracy, Italy*, Il Mulino, Bologna 1994.
32. R. Luxemburg, *The Accumulation of Capital or What the Epigones Have Made of Marx's Theory. An Anticritique by Rosa Luxemburg*, Franke, Leipzig 1921; Ead., *The Accumulation of Capital*, translated by B. Maffi, Einaudi, Turin 1972.
33. The best work, in this regard, remains that of G.G. Chang, *The Coming Collapse of China*, Arrow Books, London 2001. See also M. Dassù, T. Saich (eds.), *The Reform Decade in China. From Hope to Dismay*, Routledge, London 2020.
34. Crucial to understanding the problem, H. Meier, *Carl Schmitt, Leo Strauss and "The Concept of the Political". Towards a Dialogue Among Absentees*, J.B. Metzler und C.E. Poeschel Verlag, Stuttgart 1998, and the translation edited by C. Badocco with the expansion of the documentary collection: H. Meier, *Carl Schmitt and Leo Strauss. For a Critique of Political Theology. With the Essay by Leo Strauss on "The Concept of the Political" and His Letters to Carl Schmitt from 1932–1933*, Cantagalli, Siena 2011.
35. See, by Yan Xuetong, *Moral Realism and Strategy for China's Rise*, Social Science Academic Press, Beijing 2018; *Beyond Keeping a Low Profile*, Tianjin People Press, Tianjin 2016; *Shift of World Power: Political Leadership and Strategic Competition*, Beijing University Press, Beijing 2015; *Inertia of History: China and the World in the Next 10 Years*, China CITIC Press, Beijing 2013; *Ancient Chinese Thought, Modern Chinese Power*,

Princeton University Press, Princeton 2011; *Strategic Thinking About China's Rise*, Hunan People Press, Hunan 2010.

36. All his works are fundamental, starting with the one dedicated to German power: D.P. Calleo, *The German Problem Reconsidered*, Cambridge University Press, Cambridge 1978, and *Rethinking Europe's Future*, Princeton University Press, Princeton 2001, leading to the beautiful *Follies of Power: America's Unipolar Fantasy*, Cambridge University Press, Cambridge 2009, and *Rethinking Europe's Future*, Princeton University Press, Princeton 2001, which follows the important *Beyond American Hegemony: The Future of the Western Alliance*, Twentieth Century, Washington 1987.
37. As I already argued in G. Sapelli, *Southern Europe Since 1945. Tradition and Modernity in Portugal, Spain, Italy, Greece and Turkey*, Longman, London-New Delhi-New York-Sidney 1994.
38. Mangia, "The Emergency and the Three Great Breaks", afterword to G. Sapelli, *2020. Pandemic and Resurrection*, Guerini e Associati, Milan 2020.
39. G. Vico, *The "New Science" of 1744*, edited by M. Sanna and F. Tessitore, in M. Sanna and V. Vitiello (eds.), *The New Science*, Giunti-Bompiani, Florence-Milan 2018, p. 1253.
40. See R. Girard, *The Scapegoat*, Adelphi, Milan 1987, pp. 283–284.
41. K. Polanyi, *The Great Transformation*, cit.
42. M. Lévy-Leboyer, *European Banks and International Industrialization in the First Half of the 19th Century*, PUF, Paris 1964.
43. K. Polanyi, *The Great Transformation*, cit.
44. The two fundamental texts are always: S. Eisenstadt, *Traditional Patrimonialism and Modern Neopatrimonialism*, Sage, London 1973, and G. Roth, "Personal Rulership, Patrimonialism, and Empire-Building in the New States", in *World Politics*, n. 20, 1968, pp. 194–206.
45. Fundamental T. Ali, *An Indian Dynasty: The Story of the Nehru-Gandhi Family*, Oxford University Press, Oxford-London 1985.
46. On the original core of the always important conflict A. Lamb, *Kashmir: A Disputed Legacy*, Oxford University Press, Oxford-London 2001.

47. The fundamental text of A. Filippi was prophetic, *Institutions and Ideologies in Hispanic American Independence*, Alianza Editorial, Buenos Aires 1988.
48. All already written in *The Fragments of Power: From the Argentine Oligarchy to Polyarchy*, compiled by T. Di Tella and T. Halperin Donghi, J. Alvarez, Buenos Aires 1969.
49. J.J. Linz, *Totalitarian and Authoritarian Regimes*, Rienner, Bonn 2000; Italian translation *Totalitarian Systems and Authoritarian Regimes: A Historical-Comparative Analysis*, Rubbettino, Soveria Mannelli 2006.
50. P. Temin, *The Vanishing Class. Prejudice and Power in a Dual Economy*, The MIT Press, Cambridge, MA-London 2017.
51. F.L. Neumann, "Fear and Politics", in *Economy, State, Democracy. Essays 1930–1954*, Carsten Knop, Frankfurt am Main 1978; Italian translation "Anxiety and politics", in *il Mulino*, n. 6, 1972.
52. C. Mortati, *The Constitution in a Material Sense*, Giuffrè, Milan 1940.
53. T. Lowi, M. Calise, *Hyperpolitics. An Interactive Dictionary of Political Science*, Chicago University Press, Chicago 2010, and the fundamental essay by T. Lowi, "American Business, Public Policy, Case-Studies, and Political Theory", in *World Politics*, vol. 16, n. 4, 1964, pp. 677–715.
54. J. Ortega y Gasset, *Invertebrate Spain. Sketch of Some Historical Thoughts*, Espasa Calpe, Madrid 1922. And the always indispensable work of A. Elorza, *The Reason and the Shadow. A political Reading of Ortega y Gasset*, Editorial Anagrama, Barcelona 1984.
55. G. Mosca, *Elements of Political Science*, Fratelli Bocca, Turin 1898.
56. See I.S. Cámara, *The Theory of the Select Minority in the Thought of Ortega y Gasset*, Tecnos, Madrid 1988.
57. Fundamental for me is always the reference to the concept of "Dominion" in Weber. Now we can finally have a magnificent Italian translation that erases the errors of the historic "dramatic" translation by Pietro Rossi (who confused *Herrschaft* with *Macht* creating great confusion) thanks to M. Weber, *Economy and Society. The City*, critical text of the Max Weber-Gesamtausgabe edited by W. Nippel, Italian edition edited by M. Palma, Donzelli, Rome 2003–2016. This is a fundamental work

by Massimo Palma, with an exceptional and meritorious effort by the Publisher and the editor.

58. E. Mounier, *Personalism*, Presses Universitaires de France, Paris 1950; Italian translation *Personalism*, Garzanti, Milan 1952.
59. On Morgenthau one cannot fail to refer to C. Frei, *Hans J. Morgenthau: An Intellectual Biography*, Louisiana State University Press, Baton Rouge 2001, and especially to W.E. Scheuerman, *Morgenthau*, Polity, Cambridge 2009, and M.C. Williams (ed.), *Realism Reconsidered: The Legacy of Hans Morgenthau in International Relations*, Oxford University Press, Oxford 2007. Lastly, see L. Zambernardi, *The Limits of Power. Ethics and Politics in Hans J. Morgenthau's International Theory*, Il Mulino, Bologna 2010.
60. K. Waltz, "Realist Thought and Neorealist Theory", in *Journal of International Affair*, n. 1, 1990, pp. 21–37, and "The Emerging Structure of International Politics", in *International Security*, 18 (Fall 1993), pp. 44–79.
61. This is an important series of works, from R. Gilpin, *War and Change in World Politics,* Cambridge University Press, Cambridge 1981 (Italian translation *War and Change in International Politics*, Il Mulino, Bologna 1989), to Id., *Global Political Economy: Understanding the International Economic Order*, Princeton University Press, Princeton 2001 (Italian translation *Global Political Economy: International Economic Relations in the 21st century*, Bocconi University, Milan 2009).
62. R. Kaplan, *The Revenge of Geography. What the Map Tells Us About Coming Conflicts and the Battle Against Fate*, Random House, New York 2011.
63. Let the reference to R. Gilpin, *The Political Economy of International Relations*, with the assistance of J.M. Gilpin, Princeton University Press, Princeton 1987; Italian translation *Politics and Economy of International Relations*, Il Mulino, Bologna 1990.
64. R. Gilpin, *The Political Economy of International Relations*, cit., p. 367.
65. On this concept, see the fascinating book by P. Anderson, *The H-Word: The Peripeteia of Hegemony*, Verso Books, New York 2017.
66. C. Kindleberger, *The World in Depression: 1929–1939*, University of California Press, San Francisco 1973; Italian translation, *The Great Depression in the World, 1929–1939*, Etas, Milan 1982.

67. M. Olson, *The Logic of Collective Action: Public Goods and the Theory of Groups*, Harvard University Press, Cambridge, MA 1965; Italian translation, *The Logic of Collective Action: Public Goods and the Theory of Groups*, Feltrinelli, Milan 1983.
68. On this, see the fascinating work by P. Anderson, *The H-Word*, cit.
69. G. Botero, *On the Reason of State*, edited by L. Firpo, UTET, Turin 1948; L. Firpo, *The Ideal State of the Counter-Reformation. Ludovico Agostini*, Laterza, Bari 1957; Id., *The Reason of State. Notes and texts*, Bottega d'Erasmo, Turin 1976. But fundamental for the discussion undertaken here, by G. Borrelli, "Reason of State, *gouvernamentalité, Governance* Globalization Policies and Transformations of Neoliberalism", in *Science and Politics*, n. 42, 2010.
70. In M. Foucault, *Security, Territory, Population. Course at the Collège de France 1977–1978*, Seuil, Paris 2004, p. 245; Italian translation, *Security, Territory, Population. Course at the Collège de France (1977–1978)*, Feltrinelli, Milan 2005.
71. G. Borrelli, "The Studies of Reason of State in the Last Two Decades of the Twentieth Century: Motivations and Critical Considerations", in *Politics. Journal of Political Studies*, n. 4, 2/2015, pp. 8–9.
72. H. Kissinger, *Diplomacy of the Restoration*, translated by E. Brambilla, Garzanti, Milan 1973.
73. H.J. Mackinder, "The Geographical Pivot of History" (1904), in *The Geographical Journal*, vol. 170, December 2004, pp. 298–321.
74. A.T. Mahan, *The Influence of Sea Power upon History, 1660–1783*, Cambridge University Press, Cambridge 2010 (1889). Of great interest: L.D. Ferreiro, "Mahan and the 'English Club' of Lima, Peru: The Genesis of the Influence of Sea Power upon History", in *The Journal of Military History*, n. 3, 1972, pp. 901–906.
75. N.J. Spykman, *America's Strategy in World Politics: The United States and the Balance of Power*, Yale University Press, New Haven 1942.
76. R. Aron, *Peace and War Among Nations*, Calmann-Lévy, Paris 1962; Italian translation *Peace and War Among Nations*, Edizioni di Comunità, Milan 1970.

77. See the still wonderful texts by E. Jones, *European Miracle: Environment, Economies and Geopolitics in the History of Europe and Asia*, Cambridge University Press, Cambridge 1981 (Italian translation *The European Miracle: Environment, Economy and Geopolitics in European and Asian History*, Il Mulino, Bologna 1984), and especially *Growth Recurring: Economic Change in World History*, Oxford University Press, Oxford 1988.
78. N.J. Spykman, *The Social Theory of Georg Simmel*, University of Chicago Press, Chicago 1925.
79. See on this the beautiful pages of the biography by Olivier Zajec, *Nicholas John Spykman. The Invention of American Geopolitics*, Librairie Pups, Paris 2016.
80. On which D. Calleo has written unsurpassable pages in *Follies of Power*, cit.
81. N.J. Spykman, *The Social Theory of Georg Simmel*, cit., p. 427.
82. On which the book by M. Paléologue, *A Major Turning Point in World Politics (1904–1906)*, Plon, Paris 1934, is always indispensable and irreplaceable.
83. See the beautiful picture given by J. Heffer in *The United States and the Pacific: History of a Frontier*, University of Notre Dame Press, Note Dame 2002.
84. F. Neumann, *Behemoth. Structure and Practice of National Socialism*, Harper & Collins, New York 1942; Eng. trans. *Behemoth: Structure and Practice of National Socialism*, Feltrinelli, Milan 1977.
85. Always indispensable, by A. Nove, *An Economic History of the USSR, 1917–1991*, Penguin Books, London 1992; Eng. trans. *Economic History of the Soviet Union*, UTET, Turin 1969.
86. Important is D. Treisman, "Russian Politics in a Time of Turmoil", in A. Åslund, S. Guriev, A.C. Kuchins (eds.), *Russia after the Global Economic Crisis*, Peterson Institute for International Economics, Centre for Strategic and International Studies, New Economic School, 2010, pp. 39–59.
87. J. Gans-Morse, *Property Rights in Post-Soviet Russia: Violence, Corruption, and the Demand for Law*, Cambridge University Press, Cambridge 1997.

88. The Kautsky of *The Dictatorship of the Proletariat*, Avanti Publishing Company, Milan 1921, and the Lenin of *The Proletarian Revolution and the Renegade Kautsky*, Avanti Publishing Company, Milan 1921.
89. It is a concept well expressed in the first important text of our author: S.P. Huntington, *Soldier and the State: The Theory and Politics of Civil-Military Relations*, Balkan Press, Harvard 1957.
90. The reference goes to the two masterpieces of D. Lieven, *Towards the Flame: Empire, War and the End of Tsarist Russia*, Allen Lane/Penguin, New York-London 2015, and *The End of Tsarist Russia: The March to World War I and Revolution*, Penguin Random House, London 2015. They are indispensable for understanding what is happening today in Russia.
91. On this I refer to my *Southern Europe Since 1945*, cit.
92. S.M. Lipset, *American Exceptionalism: A Double-Edged Sword*, Stanford University Press, Stanford 1996.
93. P. Dibb, *The Soviet Union: The Incomplete Superpower*, Springer, Berlin-New York-London 1986.
94. On this the fundamental pages of T.J. Lowi, *The End of Liberalism: The Second Republic of the United States*, W.W. Norton, New York 1969.
95. The unavoidable reference is to P. Renouvin, *History of International Relations*, 4 vols., Hachette, Paris 1954 and 1994.
96. This is the title of a fundamental text to understand the new era that opens with the Iranian revolution and the Carter presidency: D. Kilcullen, *The Dragons and the Snakes: How the Rest Learned to Fight the West*, Oxford University Press, Oxford 2020.
97. I only refer here to the texts that, in my opinion, were fundamental to inspire, as it were, that change: L. Strauss, *Natural Right and History* (Walgrene Lectures, 1949), University of Chicago Press, Chicago 1953 (Italian trans. *Natural Right and History*, Il Melangolo, Genova 2009); Id., "Existentialism (Public Lecture on Martin Heidegger's Thought)", in *Interpretation*, vol. 22, n. 3, 1955, pp. 303–318; Id., *Thoughts on Machiavelli*, The Free Press, Glencoe 1958 (Italian trans. *Thoughts on Machiavelli*, Giuffrè, Milano 1970); Id., *History of Political Philosophy* (co-editor with J. Cropsey), Chicago University Press, Chicago 1963 (Italian trans. *History of Political Philosophy*, Il Melangolo,

Genova 2000); Id., *The Predicament of Modern Politics*, University of Detroit Press, Detroit 1964; Id., *The City and Man*, Rand McNally, Chicago 1964 (Italian trans. *The City and Man: Essays on Aristotle, Plato, Thucydides*, Marietti, Genova 2010); Id., *Liberalism Ancient and Modern*, Basic Books, New York 1968, reissued with foreword by A. Bloom, 1989, reissued, University of Chicago Press, Chicago 1995 (Italian trans. *Ancient and Modern Liberalism*, Giuffré, Milano 1973).

98. These works are essential: R.N. Gardner, *Mission Italy: On the Front Lines of the Cold War*, foreword by Z. Brzezinski, Rowman & Littlefield, Lanham 2005 (Italian trans. *Mission: Italy. The Years of Lead Told by the American Ambassador to Rome (1977–1981)*, Mondadori, Milano 2005); V. Giscard d'Estaing, *Power and Life*, 3 vols., Éditions Compagnie, Paris 2006 (Italian trans. *Power and Life*, Sperling & Kupfer, Milano 1993); B. Honegger, *October Surprise*, Tudor Communications, New York-Los Angeles 1989; G. Corera, *Shopping for Bombs: Nuclear Proliferation, Global Insecurity, the Rise and Fall of the A.Q. Khan Network*, Oxford University Press, London-New York 2006; V. Ostrovsky, *The Other Side of Deception: A Rogue Agent Exposes The Mossad's Secret Agenda*, Harper Collins, New York 1994; and the fundamental works of P. Cucchiarelli, *Ustica & Bologna. Attack on Italy*, La Nave di Teseo, Milano 2020, and *The Last Night of Aldo Moro. Where, How, When, by Whom and Why the DC President Was Killed*, Ponte alle Grazie, Florence 2018.
99. Fundamental to understanding the "neocon" cultural transformation I refer to is Leo Strauss's text *Thoughts on Machiavelli*, cit.
100. R. Dumas, *New International Stakes. War or Peace* (with C. Crettien), Éditions Le Cherche Midi, Paris 2014.
101. Abdel-Malek, *Egypt. Military Society*, La Decouverte, Paris 1965; Italian translation *Army and Society in Egypt, 1952–1967*, Einaudi, Turin 1967.
102. The work of a great expert on the issue like B. Riedel in *Beirut 1958. How America's Wars in the Middle East Began*, Brookings Institution Press, Washington 2020, is beautiful.
103. Greenspan, *The Age of Turbulence*, Penguin Books, New York 2007; Italian translation *The Era of Turbulence*, Sperling & Kupfer, Milan 2007.

104. N. Kaldor, *Essays on Economic Stability and Growth*, Cambridge University Press, Cambridge 1960 (Italian translation *Essays on Economic Stability and Development*, Einaudi, Turin 1965), and, by the same author, *Capital Accumulation and Economic Growth*, Cambridge University Press, Cambridge 1961.
105. G. Myrdal, "The Equality Issue in World Development", in *The American Economic Review*, vol. 79, n. 6, 1989.
106. P. Sylos Labini, *Oligopoly and Technological Progress*, Einaudi, Turin 1967.
107. See L. Haimson, G. Sapelli (eds.), *Strikes, Social Conflict and the First World War. An International Perspective*, Annali della Fondazione Giangiacomo Feltrinelli 1990–1991, Feltrinelli, Milan 1992; of C. Tilly see the 2nd ed. of *Social Movements, 1768–2008*, Paradigm Publishers, New York 2009.
108. Following the interpretation of the seminal work by H. Batatu, *The Old Social Classes and the Revolutionary Movements of Iraq: A Study of Iraq's Old Landed and Commercial Classes and of Its Communists, Ba'thists and Free Officers*, Cambridge University Press, Cambridge 2004.
109. See D. Atzori, *Islamisation and Globalisation in Jordan*, Routledge, London 2015.
110. S. Huntington, *The Clash of Civilizations and the Remaking of World Order*, Simon & Schuster, New York 1996; Italian translation. *The Clash of Civilizations and the New World Order*, Garzanti, Milan 1997.
111. The reference cannot but be to the work of G. Prunier, *From Genocide to Continental War: The "Congolese" Conflict and the Crisis of Contemporary Africa*, C. Hurst & Co, London 2009.
112. H. Kumarasingham, *Viceregalism: The Crown as Head of State in Political Crises in the Postwar Commonwealth* (Cambridge Imperial and Post-Colonial Studies Series), Palgrave-Macmillan, New York-London 2020.
113. R. Hinnebusch, *The International Politics of the Middle East*, Manchester University Press, Manchester 2004.
114. On this, I cannot fail to mention my *Why Companies Exist and How They Are Made*, Bruno Mondadori, Milan 1999 and then Guerini and Associates, Milan 2019.
115. G. Sapelli, *2020. Pandemic and Resurrection*, cit.

116. L. Murray, "Amanda's Painting", in *Conscious and Verbal*, Duffy & Snellgrove, Sydney 1999, p. 122.
117. G. Sapelli, *Dangerous Games. Comparing Capitalisms. Enron and Parmalat*, Bruno Mondadori, Milan 2005.
118. On this, the reference is to P. Hirst, G. Thompson, *Globalization in Question. The International Economy and the Possibilities of Governance*, Polity Press, Cambridge 1996 (Italian translation. *The Globalization of the Economy*, United Publishers, Rome 1997), and the review by R. Robertson in *American Journal of Sociology*, vol. 102, n. 4, 1997, pp. 204–216.
119. E.L. Jones, in *Growth Recurring: Economic Change in World History*, cit.
120. Fundamental on this are the studies of L. Tomba, *The Government Next Door: Neighborhood Politics in Urban China*, Cornell University Press, Ithaca-London 2014.
121. S.M. Lipset, S. Rokkan, "Cleavage Structures, Party Systems, and Voter Alignments: An Introduction", in S.M. Lipset, S. Rokkan (eds.), *Party Systems and Voter Alignments: Cross-National Perspectives*, The Free Press, New York 1967, pp. 1–64.
122. Fundamental by F. Heisbourg, *After Al Qaeda. The New Generation of Terrorism*, Stock, Paris 2009; Italian trans. *After Al Qaeda: The New Generation of Terrorism*, Armando, Rome 2013.
123. D. Atzori, *Islamisation and Globalisation in Jordan*, cit.
124. A fundamental text (after the masterpiece by E.L. Peters, *The Bedouin of Cyrenaica. Studies in Personal and Corporative Power*, Cambridge University Press, Cambridge 1991, and the very important new edition, edited by J. Goody and E. Marx, always for the same publisher in 2009) is by W. Lacher, *Libya's Fragmentation. Structure and Process in Violent Conflict*, I.B. Tauris, London-New York 2020.
125. H. Strachan, *The First World War in Africa*, Oxford University Press, Oxford 2004.
126. F. Fuglestad, *A History of Niger, 1850–1960*, Cambridge University Press, Cambridge-London 1983.
127. L. Strauss, *Thoughts on Machiavelli*, cit.
128. H. Minsky, "The Financial-Instability Hypothesis: Capitalist Processes and the Behavior of the Economy", in C.P. Kindleberger, J.-P. Laffargue (eds.), *Financial Crises: Theory, History, and Policy*, Cambridge University Press, Cambridge 1982.

129. On this always fundamental E. Jones, *Growth Recurring: Economic Change in World History*, cit., and, lastly, the important work of J. Briceño-Ruiz, *The Political Economy of New Regionalisms in the Pacific Rim*, Routledge, London 2019.
130. R.D. Blackwill, S.A. Karaganov, *Damage Limitation or Crisis? Russia and the Outside World* (CSIA Studies in International Security), Routledge, London 1994.
131. The pages on this matter in O.A. Hathaway, S.J. Shapiro, *The Internationalists*, cit.
132. The best work on these topics is always that of D. Atzori, *Islamisation and Globalisation in Jordan*, cit.
133. G. Bronner, *The Democracy of the Gullible*, PUF, Paris 2013; Italian trans. *The Democracy of the Gullible*, Aracne, Rome 2016.
134. S. Pollard, *Pacific Conquest. Industrialization in Europe*, Oxford University Press, Oxford 1981.
135. G. Sapelli, *Southern Europe Since 1945*, cit.
136. H. Kissinger, *On China*, Penguin, London 2011; Italian trans. *China*, Mondadori, Milan 2011.
137. O. Brunner, *Land and Rule. Basic Questions of the Territorial Constitutional History of Southeast Germany in the Middle Ages*, Baden bei Wien 1939; Italian trans. *Land and Power*, Giuffrè, Milan 1983.
138. "The aim of the ancients was the sharing of social power among all the citizens of the same homeland. This is what they called freedom. The aim of the moderns is security in private enjoyments; and they call freedom the guarantees granted by institutions to these enjoyments". I quote from B. Constant, "On the Liberty of the Ancients Compared to that of the Moderns", in *Political Writings*, Gallimard, Paris 1997, p. 210; Italian trans. *The Liberty of the Ancients Compared to That of the Moderns*, Einaudi, Turin 2001. Today it is this "liberty of the moderns" that is being questioned by the institutions of neoliberalism, transformed into unelected and illegitimate technocracies...
139. On this, see the extraordinary work of J. Bariéty and R. Poidevin, *Franco-German Relations, 1815–1975*, Armand Colin, Paris 1977.
140. D.P. Calleo, *Follies of Power*, cit.
141. "The Obama Doctrine", Story by Jeffrey Goldberg, in *The Atlantic*, April 2014.

142. The guiding thread is all in R. Aron, *Imperial Republic. The United States in the World*, Calmann-Lévy, Paris 1977.
143. G. Allison, *Destined for War: Can America and China Escape Thucydides's Trap?*, Houghton Mifflin Harcourt, Boston 2017.
144. M. Mackinder, "The Geographical Pivot of History", in *The Geographical Journal*, vol. XXIII, n. 4, April 1904.
145. N. Spykman, *American Strategy in World Politics*, cit.
146. D. Calleo, *Follies of Power*, cit.
147. P. Dibb, *The Soviet Union: The Incomplete Superpower*, cit.
148. R. Gilpin, *The Political Economy of International Relations*, cit.
149. R. Aron, *Peace and War Between Nations*, cit.
150. M. Frigessi di Rattalma (ed.), *The Dieselgate: A Legal Perspective*, Springer, Berlin-London 2017.
151. J. Needham, *Science and Civilisation in China*, Cambridge University Press, Cambridge 1954 (Italian translation *Science and civilization in China*, 3 vols., Einaudi, Turin 1981–1985) and, by the same author, "Science and Society in East and West", in J. Needham (ed.), *The Grand Titration: Science and Society in East and West*, Allen & Unwin, London 1969, pp. 190–217.
152. Of M. Granet it is impossible not to read the unforgettable *Chinese civilization*, La renaissance du livre, Paris 1929, in the series "The Evolution of Humanity" of the "Library of Historical Synthesis" founded by Henri Berr; Italian translation *Ancient Chinese civilization*, Einaudi, Turin 1950.
153. K.A. Wittfogel, *Oriental Despotism: A Comparative Study of Total Power*, Yale University Press, New Haven-New York 1957; Italian translation *Oriental despotism*, Vallecchi, Florence 1968, then Pigreco, Milan 2012.
154. A communist since his teenage years and a supporter of Mao Tse-tung, Liu was the second president of the People's Republic of China. His criticisms of Mao's failing economic policy in 1961, and his attempt to marginalize him from the state leadership, however, cost him imprisonment and death.
155. See M. Paléologue, *A Major Turning Point in World Politics 1904–1906*, Fayard, Paris 1914.
156. On this, I allow myself to refer to G. Sapelli, *Southern Europe Since 1945*, cit., pp. 155 sgg.
157. See the beautiful work of L. Vergallo, *Deindustrialization. A New Era?*, GoWare, Florence 2013.

158. Appadurai, *Modernity at Large*, cit.
159. J. Gray, *Seven Types of Atheism*, Allen Lane, London 2017.
160. The reference is to the masterpiece of the unforgettable P. Pera, *The Old Believers and the Antichrist*, Marietti, Genoa 1992.
161. D.P. Calleo, *Follies of Power*, cit.
162. R. Aron, *Peace and War Between Nations*, cit.
163. E.L. Peters, *The Bedouin of Cyrenaica*, cit.
164. On this, see the fascinating work of P. Anderson, *The H-Word*, cit.
165. H.J. Mackinder, "The Geographical Pivot of History", cit.
166. A.T. Mahan, *The Influence of Sea Power upon History*, cit. Of great interest: L.D. Ferreiro, "Mahan and the 'English Club' of Lima, Peru", cit.
167. N.J. Spykman, *America's Strategy in World Politics*, cit.
168. See the still wonderful texts by E. Jones, *European Miracle*, cit., and *Growth Recurring*, cit.
169. On this, the fundamental pages of T.J. Lowi, *The End of Liberalism*, cit.
170. The inescapable reference is to P. Renouvin, *Histoire des relations internationales*, 4 vols., Hachette, Paris 1954 and 1994.
171. M. Nicolazzi, *Elogio del petrolio. Energia e disuguaglianza dal mammut all'auto elettrica*, Feltrinelli, Milan 2019.
172. See on this the prescient and too little valued essay by S. Müller-Kraenner, *China's and India's Emerging Energy Policy*, Discussion Paper, Deutsches Institut fur Entwicklungspolitik, Bonn 2008.
173. Mackenzie, "Miners Have a Part to Play in Fighting Climate Change", in *Financial Times*, July 23, 2019, p. 9.
174. A.-M. Slaughter, *A New World Order*, Princeton University Press, Princeton 2004. But much more important is her never enough read book written with A. Stone Sweet and J.H.H. Weiler, *The European Court and National Courts: Doctrine and Jurisprudence*, Hart Publishing, Oxford 1997.
175. G. Sapelli, *Oltre il capitalismo. Macchine, lavoro e proprietà*, Guerini e Associati, Milan 2018, and the recent expanded edition *Beyond Capitalism: Machines, Work and Property*, Palgrave-Macmillan, London-New York 2019.

176. U. Beck, *Der kosmopolitische Blick oder: Krieg ist Frieden*, Suhrkamp, Frankfurt am Main 2004 (Eng. trans. *The Cosmopolitan Vision*, Carocci, Rome 2005), and especially *Nachrichten aus der Weltinnenpolitik*, Suhrkamp, Berlin 2010.
177. Unsurpassed by D. Hewitt, *China. Getting Rich First: A Modern Social History*, Pegasus, London 2009.
178. See a beautiful edition with German text on the opposite page: W. Benjamin, *Capitalism as Religion*, edited by C. Salzani, Il Melangolo, Genova 2013.
179. E. Scribano, *Guide to the Reading of Spinoza's "Ethics"*, Laterza, Roma-Bari 2008, pp. 27 ff.
180. S. Blackburn, *Oxford Dictionary of Philosophy*, Oxford University Press, Oxford 2008.
181. Fundamental by A. Kojève and M. Filoni, *Identity and Reality in Pierre Bayle's "Dictionary"*, NRF, Gallimard, Paris 2010.
182. E. Scribano, *Guide to the Reading of Spinoza's "Ethics"*, cit., pp. 166–168.
183. R.K. Williamson, *Hegel's Philosophy of Religion*, State University of New York Press, Albany 1984.
184. M. Ravera, *Invitation to the Thought of Spinoza*, Mursia, Milan 1987, p. 205.
185. As H. Gouhier addresses the theme, *Anti-humanism in the 17th Century*, Vrin, Paris 1997, p. 223.
186. B. Pascal, Thoughts, 72, in *Complete Works*, vol. II, ed. M. Le Guern, NRF, Éditions de La Pléiade-Gallimard, Paris 2000, p. 347.
187. L. Goldmann, *The Hidden God. Study on the tragic vision in Pascal's "Thoughts" and in Racine's Theatre*, Gallimard, Paris 1956.
188. As it is in the essay by E. Auerbach "Figure", in Id., *Studies on Dante*, edited by D. Della Terza, Feltrinelli, Milan 2005 (but the first edition is from 1929).
189. The obligatory reference for anyone wishing to understand the event in which we are immersed as humans is M. Onfray, *Decadence. Life and death of Judeo-Christianity*, Flammarion, Paris 2017: a text never enough divulged.
190. We return to the always enlightening M. Horkheimer, T.W. Adorno, *Dialectic of Enlightenment* (with a preface by the authors to the Italian edition), Einaudi, Turin 1966.

191. M. de Montaigne, "Des Cannibales", in *Les Essais*, Éditions de la Pléiade, Paris 1962, Book I, chapter 31.
192. The reference, which could be ironic if it were not dramatic, is naturally to the most emblematic work of pre-pandemic decay (and perhaps unfortunately also post-pandemic): F. Fukuyama, *The End of History and the Last Man*, Free Press, New York 1992 (Italian trans. *The End of History and the Last Man*, Rizzoli, 1992).
193. J. Starobinski, *The Living Eye. Essay*, NRF-Gallimard, Paris 1961 (Eng. trans. *The Living Eye. Essays on Corneille, Racine, Rousseau, Stendhal, Freud*, Einaudi, Turin 1975).
194. Ibid., p. 202.
195. M. de Montaigne, "Of Age", in *The Essays*, cit., chapter LVII, p. 312.
196. M. Mauss, "Essay on the Gift. Form and Reason of Exchange in Archaic Societies", in *Sociological Year 1923–1924*, PUF, Paris 1924 (Italian trans. *Essay on the Gift: The Form and Reason for Exchange in Archaic Societies*, Einaudi, Turin 2002).
197. C. Lévi-Strauss, *Introduction to the Work of Marcel Mauss*, PUF, Paris 1950, p. 21 (Italian translation: "Introduction to the Work of Marcel Mauss", in M. Mauss, *General Theory of Magic and Other Essays*, Einaudi, Turin 1965).
198. Ibid., p. 22.
199. The reference, of course, is to B. Croce, *History of the Kingdom of Naples*, Laterza, Bari 1925.
200. E. De Martino, "Kingdom of Naples and jettatura", now in Id., *South and Magic*, Feltrinelli, Milan 1959, p. 175.
201. "**mana**s.m., invar. – Term of Melanesian origin (which can be translated as 'vital force') indicating an impersonal force believed to be possessed, temporarily or permanently, by people, animals or things, and which manifests itself in unusual and extraordinary effects" (Treccani online dictionary).
202. C. Lévi-Strauss, *Introduction to the work of Marcel Mauss*, cit.
203. Always current, by M. McLuhan: *The Gutenberg Galaxy: The Making of Typographic Man*, Routledge & Kegan Paul, London 1962 (Italian trans. *The Gutenberg Galaxy: Birth of the Typographic Man*, Armando, Rome 1962); *Understanding Media: The Extensions of Man*, Gingko Press, New York 1964 (Eng. trans. *The Tools of Communication*, Il Saggiatore, Milan 1967); and

(with Quentin Fiore), *The Medium Is the Message*, Jerome Agel-Random House, New York 1967 (Eng. trans. *The Medium Is the Message*, Feltrinelli, Milan 1968).

204. We now have the new critical edition edited by B. Clausen and D. Haselbach: F. Tönnies, *Community and Society. 1880–1935*, De Gruyter, Berlin-Boston 2019.
205. M. Godelier, *The Ideal and the Material. Thought, Economies, Societies*, Flammarion, Paris 2010, p. 28 (Italian trans. *The Ideal and the Material. Thought, Economies, Societies*, Editori Riuniti, Rome 1985).
206. Ibid., p. 222.
207. M. Douglas, *Purity and Danger*, Routledge & Kegan Paul, London 1966 (Eng. trans. *Purity and Danger. An Analysis of Concepts of Pollution and Taboo*, Il Mulino, Bologna 1976).
208. M. Douglas, *Leviticus as Literature*, Oxford University Press, New York 1999.
209. J-P. Willaine, "Introduction", to É. Durkheim, *The Elementary Forms of Religious Life. The Totemic System in Australia*, PUF, Paris 2013, p. XVII.
210. M. Douglas, *Purity and Danger*, cit., p. viii.
211. Ibid., p. 124.
212. M.Mauss, *Works. 1. The Functions of the Sacred*, Éditions de Minuit, Paris 1968, Chapter 4, "Prayer and Oral Rites", p. 448.
213. M. Douglas, *Purity and Danger*, cit., p. 126.
214. M. Douglas, "Risk Acceptability According to the Social Sciences", in *Social Research Perspectives. Occasional Reports on Current Topics*, Russell Sage Foundation, New York, n. 11, 1997, p. 39.
215. Prosperi, *A Time Without History. The Destruction of the Past*, Einaudi, Turin 2021.
216. K. Pomian, *The Order of Time*, Gallimard, Paris, 1952.
217. Ibid., p. 27.
218. F. Hartog, *Regimes of Historicity. Presentism and Experiences of Time*, Le Seuil, Paris 2003.
219. M. Agier (ed.), Regional Research and Intervention Group (GRIR), *COVID-19: A Total Social Fact. Historical, Political, Social, and Human Perspectives*, University of Quebec, Chicoutimi 2020.
220. Ibid., p. 21.

221. G. Marramao, *Kairos. Apology of Due Time*, Bollati Boringhieri, Turin 2020, p. 89.
222. E. De Martino, "Cultural Apocalypses and Psychopathological Apocalypses", in *New Arguments*, n. 69–71, 1964, pp. 105–141, then collected in Appendix I of Id., *The End of the World. Contribution to the Analysis of Cultural Apocalypses*, new ed. edited by G. Charuty, D. Fabre and M. Massenzio, Einaudi, Turin 2016, p. 578, from which we quote.
223. F. Keck, "Conflicts of Experts. Zoonoses, Between Animal Health and Public Health", in *French Ethnology*, vol. 1, 2009, pp. 80–81, and, importantly, *Bats. At the Borders Between Species*, CNRS Editions, Paris 2021.
224. Ibid., p. 83.
225. M. Mauss, "A Category of the Human Spirit: The Idea of the Person, the Idea of 'Self': A Plan", in *Journal of the Royal Anthropological Institute*, vol. 68, Jul.–Dec. 1938, pp. 263–281.
226. C. Tarot, *Sociology and Anthropology of Marcel Mauss, The Discovery*, Paris 2003, p. 122. And, of the same, the fundamental *The Symbolic and the Sacred: Theories of Religion, The Discovery*, Paris 2008.
227. G. Sapelli, *Beyond Capitalism*, cit.
228. K. Karpat, *The Gecekondu: Rural Migration and Urbanization*, Cambridge University Press, Cambridge 1964.
229. P. Collier, *The Future of Capitalism*, Harpers Collins, New York 2019; Eng. trans. *The Future of Capitalism*, Rome-Bari, Laterza 2020.
230. Cederna, "The Villa Among the Ruins", in *The World*, February 4, 1964.
231. P. Temin, *The Vanishing Class*, cit.
232. P. Veltz, *Globalization, Cities and Territories*, PUF, Paris 2005.
233. P. Collier, *The Future of Capitalism*, cit.
234. Of A.J. Scott I quote the most significant titles: *A World in Emergence*, Edward Elgar, Cheltenham 2012; *Social Economy of the Metropolis: Cognitive-Cultural Capitalism and the Global Resurgence of Cities*, Oxford University Press, Oxford 2008 (Eng. trans. *Cities and Regions in the New Capitalism: The Social Economy of Metropolises*, Il Mulino, Bologna 2011); with D. Power, "Social Economy of the Metropolis: Cognitive-Cultural Capitalism and the Global Resurgence of Cities", in *Regional Studies*, Taylor &

Francis Journals, vol. 44, n. 1, 2008, pp. 131–132; *Global City-Regions: Trends, Theory, Policy*, Oxford University Press, Oxford 2001; *Regions and the World Economy: The Coming Shape of Global Production, Competition, and Political Order*, Oxford University Press, Oxford 1999 (Eng. trans. *Regions in the World Economy: Production, Competition and Politics in the Era of Globalization*, Il Mulino, Bologna 2001).

235. See N. Smith, *The Production of Nature; The Production of Space*, Open University System, National Autonomous University of Mexico, Mexico City 2006; *The Endgame of Globalization*, Routledge, London 2006; with D. Harvey, *Financial Capital, Real Estate and Culture*, Macba & Publications of the Autonomous University of Barcelona, Barcelona 2003; *American Empire: Roosevelt's Geographer and the Prelude to Globalization*, University of California Press, Berkeley 2003; with C. Katz, *Globalization: Urban Transformations, Social Precarity and Gender Discrimination*, New Graphics, S.A.L. La Cuesta, La Laguna 2001; *The New Urban Frontier: Gentrification and the Revanchist City*, Routledge, London 1996; *Geography and Empire: Critical Studies in the History of Geography* (edited with A. Godlewska), Basil Blackwell, Oxford 1994; *Gentrification of the City* (edited with P. Williams), George Allen and Unwin, London 1988.
236. H. Minsky, *Can "It" Happen Again?*, M.E. Sharpe, Armonk 1982; Italian translation *Could It Happen Again? Instability and Finance After the '29 Crisis*, Einaudi, Turin 1984.
237. F. Farinelli, in "The World Is No Longer Made of Stairs. Conversation with Pasquale Alferj", in *International Dialogues*, n. 7, June 2008, p. 159.
238. C.K. Dyson, I. Mars, *Architects of the Euro. Intellectuals in the Making of European Monetary Union*, Oxford University Press, Oxford 2016.
239. On this fundamental, the essay by A. Mangia, "The interruption of the Great Work. Brief notes on the dialogue between the Courts", soon to be published in *Constitutional Law Review*.
240. Always indispensable, the essay by L. Stone, "Prosopography", in *Daedalus. Historical Studies Today*, vol. 100, n. 1, 1967, pp. 46–79. But undoubtedly the masters of this discipline were all from the great French school of the Seventies and Eighties of the twentieth century, such as the masterpieces of R. Szramkiewicz,

The Regents and Censors of the Bank of France Appointed Under the Consulate and the Empire, Droz, Geneva 1974; A. Plessis, *Regents and Governors of the Bank of France Under the Second Empire*, Droz, Geneva 1985; or again C. Charle, *Biographical Dictionary of Academics in the 19th and 20th Centuries*, 1. *The Faculty of Letters of Paris: 1809–1908*, INRP-CNRS, Paris 1985; Id., *The Elites of the Republic: 1880–1900*, Fayard, Paris 1987. To L. Stone, however, it is always indispensable to refer, starting from his unforgettable *The Crisis of the Aristocracy, 1558–1641*, Clarendon Press, London 1965.

241. E.H. Kantorowicz, *The King's Two Bodies. A Study in Medieval Political Theology*, introduction by C. Leyser and a preface by W.C. Jordan, Princeton University Press, Princeton 2016; Italian translation *The Two Bodies of the King: The Idea of Royalty in Medieval Political Theology*, Einaudi, Turin 1989.
242. C.K. Dyson, I. Mars, *Architects of the Euro*, cit.
243. G. Quagliariello, "Jean Monnet", in M.E. Cavallaro and F.M. Giordano (eds.), *Historical Dictionary of European Integration*, Rubbettino, Soveria Mannelli 2018.
244. Very effective on these topics, G. Bossuat, A. Wilkens (dir.), *Jean Monnet, Europe and the paths of peace*, Publications de la Sorbonne, Paris 1999.
245. "From Mao to Xi Jinping: notes on the XIX congress of the CCP", in N. Bianconi (ed.), *China. The voice of power*, GoWare, Florence 2018, pp. 7–24.
246. It should be remembered that the much—by most—praised Tommaso Padoa Schioppa, high priest of the euro masses, never expressed a thought different from that of marginalism and the prevailing neoclassical school.
247. G. Berti, "Informal rule of law", in *Riv. trim. dir. pubbl.*, 1992, pp. 3 sgg.
248. C. Schmitt, *Doctrine of the Constitution* (1928), Giuffrè, Milan 1981, p. 503.
249. A.L. Hansen, *Business Cycles and National Income*, Allen and Unwin, London 1964.
250. R. Boyer, *Institutions in the Theory of regulation*, CNRS Working Paper, No. 8, 2003, p. 3.
251. R. Triffin, *Europe and the Money Muddle*, Yale University Press, New Haven 1957.

252. Rollat, *Delors*, Flammarion, Paris 1993.
253. J. Delors, "Europe Needs a Soul", in *EU Affairs*, October 10, 2010, pp. 13–48.
254. Predieri, *The Emergence of Independent Administrative Authorities*, Passigli, Florence 1997, p. 122.
255. Published in "his" *Cesifin Notebooks*, n. 1, Giappichelli, Turin 1998.
256. C.E. Lindblom, *Politics and Markets: The World's Political-Economic Systems*, Basic Book, New York 1977, and the *review* made by R. Solo, D.R. Fusfeld, J.M. Buchanan in *Journal of Economic Issues*, vol. 13, n. 1, 1979, pp. 207–217.
257. G. Sapelli, *Democracy Transformed. Representation Between Territory and Function: A Theoretical-Interpretative Analysis*, Bruno Mondadori, Milan 2000. The reference is to the fundamental text by A. Pizzorno, *The Roots of Politics*, Feltrinelli, Milan 1993.
258. G. Sapelli, *Why Companies Exist and How They Are Made*, cit.; Id., *Morality and Corporate Governance: Firm Integrity and Spheres of Justice*, Springer, Heidelberg-London 2013.
259. G. Sapelli, *The Global Economic Crisis. Ten Considerations*, with a Preface by G. De Lucia Lumeno, Bollati Boringhieri, Turin 2008.
260. See the useful work of G. Ferri, "English Constitutionalism and the Idea of the State in Liberal Italy. The Library of Political Sciences by Attilio Brunialti", in *Historia et jus. Journal of Legal History of Medieval and Modern Italy*, n. 8, 2015, pp. 1–12.
261. Predieri, *Carl Schmitt. A Nazi Without Courage*, La Nuova Italia, Florence 1999.
262. Naturally, the reference is to the giants: S. Romano, *The Legal Order*, Sansoni, Florence 1946, and C. Mortati, *The Constitution in a Material Sense*, Giuffrè, Milan 1940; and the indispensable G. Volpe, *The Constitutionalism of the Twentieth Century*, Laterza, Rome-Bari 2000.
263. Y. Mersch, *Central Bank Independence Revisited*, European Central Bank, Directorate General Communication, Frankfurt am Main, March 30, 2017.
264. The reference is explicit to the judgment of the German Constitutional Court of January 14, 2014: BVerfG, 2BvR2728/13, and equally direct the reference to the text of F. Amtenbrink, *The Democratic Accountability of Central Bank*, Hart Publishing, Leiden 1999. In fact, it was an appeal against the OMT (*Outright*

Monetary Transactions), which constituted the foundation of the "unorthodox" monetary policy of the ECB in recent years, and which has always been contested by the German Court and public opinion. To do this, the Court adopted the technique of the preliminary ruling, i.e., the mechanism, provided for by Art. 267 TFEU, through which a national judge asks the Court of Justice of the European Union to rule on the validity or interpretation of a rule of Community law.

265. D. Sardo, "The Unfriendly Confrontation Between the German Constitutional Court and the Court of Justice of the European Union: Dialogue or Negotiation?", in *Pandora*, n. 4, August 2014.
266. O. Hart, J.H. Moore, "Contracts as Reference Points", in *Quarterly Journal of Economics*, February, 2008, pp. 1–48.
267. R.R. Nelson, S.G. Winter, *An Evolutionary Theory of Economic Change*, Harvard University Press, Cambridge, MA 1982.
268. Y. Mersch, *Central Bank Independence Revisited*, cit., p. 9.
269. N.D. Kondratiev, "Die langen Wellen der Konjunktur", in *Archiv für Sozialwissenschaft und Sozialpolitik*, 56, 1926, pp. 573–609, then taken up in *Review of Economic Statistics* (1935), and always by the same "The Long Waves in Economic Life", in *Review of Economic Statistics*, vol. 17, n. 6, 1935, pp. 105–115. After his death, shot during the purges of 1938, his main works were collected in *Dynamics of Economic Development: Long Cycles and Industrial Growth in Historical Context*, Macmillan, London 1998.
270. W. Eucken, *Die Grundlagen der Nationalökonomie*, Fischer, Jena 1940.
271. J. Rueff, *Défense et illustration de l'étalon-or*, Alcan, Paris 1932.
272. D.P. Calleo, *Follies of Power*, cit.
273. G. Sapelli, *Southern Europe Since 1945*, cit.
274. W. Eucken, *Die Grundlagen der Nationalökonomie*, cit.
275. W. Röpke, *International Order and Economic Integration*, Springer, Heidelberg-London 1959.
276. H. Minsky, *The Financial Instability Hypothesis*, Jerome Levy Economics Institute of Bard College, Working Paper No. 74, 1992, available at http://www.levyinstitute.org/pubs/wp74.pdf.

277. See it in B. Croce, *The Philosophical Presupposition of the Liberal Conception*, Laterza, Bari 1927, and of the same, "A Mistaken Historical Concept: The 'Bourgeoisie'", in *The Critique*, 1928, pp. 261–274.
278. É. Farvaque, "Constitutional Foundations of the Independence of Central Banks: From the Founding Fathers of the American Nation to the European Central Bank", in *French Review of Economics*, n. 87, 2007, pp. 2–16.
279. Ibid., p. 1.
280. J.L. Talmon, *The Origins of Totalitarian Democracy*, Secker & Warburg, London 1960. A wrong but useful text...
281. É. Farvaque, "Constitutional Foundations", cit., pp. 4–5.
282. Blinder, "Central Banking in a Democracy", Federal Reserve Bank of Richmond, in *Economic Quarterly*, vol. 82, n. 4, Fall 1996, pp. 1–14, available at https://www.richmondfed.org/~/media/richmondfedorg/publications/research/economic_quarterly/1996/fall/pdf/blinder.pdf.
283. J.-C. Trichet, "Introductory Remarks", in *Independence and Responsibility, Evolution of the Central Banker's Profession, Bicentennial colloquium*, Banque de France, 2000, pp. 49–54.
284. The most beautiful scientific justification of this assumption can be found in B. Ackerman, *We the People*, vol. 1: *Foundations*, Harvard University Press, Cambridge, MA 1991.
285. M. Calise, *After the Party System. Italy Between Models and Reality*, Einaudi, Turin 1994, pp. 28–29.
286. I refer, for example, to J. Wissel, *Staasprojekt Europa. Features of a Materialistic Theory of the European Union*, Westfalisches Dampfboot, Münster 2015.
287. E. Dehay, "The Ordo-Liberal Justification of the Independence of Central Banks", in *French Review of Economics*, April 1995, pp. 10–31.
288. G. Mosca, *Elements of Political Science*, Fratelli Bocca, Turin 1896–1923.
289. C. Bresciani Turoni, *The Events of the German Mark*, Hoepli, Milan 1936.
290. E. Dehay, "The Ordo-Liberal Justification of the Independence of Central Banks", cit., p. 6.

291. See, for example, A. Cukierman, *Central Bank Strategy, Credibility and Independence: Theory and Evidence*, MIT Press, Harvard 1992, chap. 18, and C. Noyer, "About the Status of Independence of Central Banks", in *Financial Economy Review*, n. 22, autumn 1992.
292. See first of all a text always essential for general framing: A. Peacock, H. Willgerodt, *German Neo-liberals and the Social Market Economy*, Macmillan, London 1989. And then the fundamental, always little studied and understood in their theoretical finiteness and their social damage: W. Eucken, "State Structural Changes and the Crisis of Capitalism", in *World Economic Archive*, vol. 36, 1932, pp. 297–321; F. Böhm, "The Research and Teaching Community Between Lawyers and Economists at the University of Freiburg", in *From the History of Law and State Sciences in Freiburg*, Freiburg 1957; and D. Schmidtchen, "German 'Ordnungspolitik' as Institutional Choice", in *Journal for the Entire State Science*, vol. 140, 1984, pp. 54–57.
293. Two essential references to understand what has been happening for years and that the pandemic crisis only accelerates are the works of G. Pietropolli Charmet, *The Engine of the World. How Feelings Have Changed*, Solferino, Milan 2020, and A. Case and A. Deaton, *Deaths of Despair and the Future of Capitalism*, Princeton University Press, Princeton-Oxford 2020.
294. On these topics, the reference to V. Ronchi is unavoidable, *Comprehensive Cooperation. History of "El Hogar Obrero"*, Ediciones Fabro, Buenos Aires 2016.
295. Many ideas from this chapter of the book I find under a different light in P. Collier, *The Future of Capitalism*, cit.
296. I remember the most meaningful works: *Governing the Commons: The Evolution of Institutions for Collective Action*, Cambridge University Press, Cambridge 1990 (Eng. trans. *Governing the Collective Goods*, Marsilio, Venice 2006); with S.E.S. Crawford, "A Grammar of Institutions", in *American Political Science Review*, vol. 89, n. 3, September 1995, pp. 582–600; "A Behavioral Approach to the Rational Choice Theory of Collective Action: Presidential Address, American Political Science Association, 1997", in *American Political Science Review*, vol. 92, n. 1, 1998, pp. 1–22; with J. Walker, *Trust and Reciprocity: Interdisciplinary Lessons for Experimental Research*, vol. VI of the

Russell Sage Foundation Series on Trust, Russell Sage Foundation, New York 2003; *Understanding Institutional Diversity*, Princeton University Press, Princeton 2005. And my "The Common Goods", in *International Dialogues. Cities in the World*, n. 14, 2011, pp. 57–115.

297. E. Ostrom, *Governing the Commons*, cit.
298. G. Sapelli, "Introduction", in K.J. Hopt and G. Teubner (eds.), *Corporate Governance and Responsibility of Senior Management. Legal, Economic and Sociological Analysis of Corporate Social Responsibility*, ISVET-Franco Angeli, Milan 1986, pp. 11–38.
299. G. Sapelli, *Goods and People. Moral Action in the Economy. With an Essay on the Sanctity of Adriano Olivetti*, Rubbettino, Soveria Mannelli 2002.
300. The reference to E.F. Fama is mandatory: E.F. Fama, "Agency Problems and the Theory of the Firm", in *Journal of Political Economy*, April 1980. But it was Roberta Garruccio who pointed out to me the relevance of the historical and theoretical sense of the transformation, which she well illustrated in her "Preface" to F. Novara, R. Rozzi, R. Garruccio, *Men and Work at Olivetti*, Bruno Mondadori, Milan 2005, pp. 13–14.
301. H. Hansmann, *The Ownership of Enterprise*, The Belknap Press of Harvard University Press, Cambridge, MA-London 1996, p. 3.
302. J. Rawls, "Justice as Fairness", in *Philosophical Review*, April 1958, pp. 164–194. I thank Domenico Siniscalco who reminded me of the importance of this contribution by an author who is always indispensable and too rarely invoked these days (but always see J. Rawls, *A Theory of Justice*, Feltrinelli, Milan 1999).
303. On this my *Morality and Corporate Governance: Firm Integrity and Spheres of Justice*, Springer, London-Berlin 2012.
304. J. Attali, M. Guillaume, *The Anti-economic*, PUF, Paris 1974, p. 235; Italian translation *The Anti-economic: A Counter-Manual*, Marsilio, Venice 1977.
305. G. Simondon, *On the Technique*, Orthotes, Nocera Inferiore 2018, and also, by the same author, *On the Technique*, PUF, Paris 1984.
306. Leroi-Gourhan, *Gesture and Speech*, Albin Michel, Paris 1964–1965; Italian translation *Gesture and Speech*, Einaudi, Turin 1977. It is worth remembering that ten years after this edition Jacques Attali published *Speech and the Tool*, PUF, Paris 1975, largely

inspired, in the analytical part and not in the utopian one, by this foundational work.

307. The reference to J.-J. Rousseau is absolutely necessary, as S. Corbin masterfully wrote in "Between Gift and Necessity. Jean-Jacques Rousseau, Anthropologist of Language", in *Revue du Mauss*, vol. 50, n. 2, 2017, pp. 241–256.
308. Leroi-Gourhan, *Living Mechanics*, Albin Michel, Paris 1983 (Italian translation *Living Mechanics*, Jaca Book, Milan 1986), and my *Anthropology of Globalization*, Bruno Mondadori, Milan 2002.
309. The work of É. Durkheim is immense and all of extreme relevance. I only recall, for the purposes of this essay: *The Division of Labor in Society*, Alcan, Paris 1893 (Italian translation *The Division of Social Labor*, Il Mulino, Bologna 1972); *The Rules of Sociological Method*, Alcan, Paris 1895 (Italian translation *The Rules of Sociological Thought*, Community Editions, Milan 1969); *Suicide*, Alcan, Paris 1897 (Italian translation *Suicide*, UTET, Turin 1970); *The Elementary Forms of Religious Life: The Totemic System in Australia*, Alcan, Paris 1912 (Italian translation *The Elementary Forms of Religious Life*, Community Editions, Milan 1963).
310. G. Sapelli, *Community and Market*, Rubbettino, Soveria Mannelli 1991, and developing the issue, Id., *Goods and People*, cit.
311. B. Stiegler, *Technique and Time*, Volume 1: *The Fault of Epimetheus* (1994); Volume 2: *Disorientation* (1996); Volume 3: *The Time of Cinema and the Question of Malaise* (2001), now all published by Fayard, Paris 2018.
312. Especially in *The Fault of Epimetheus*, cit.
313. Beautiful by R. Arena, M. Quéré, *The Economics of Alfred Marshall: Revisiting Marshall's Legacy*, Palgrave-Macmillan, New York 2016.
314. B. Milanovic, *Global Inequality. The Fate of the Middle Classes, the Ultra-Rich and Equal Opportunities*, La Decouverte, Paris 2019.
315. G. Sapelli, *Community and Market*, cit.
316. P.N. Howard, *Pax Technica: How the Internet of Things May Set Us Free or Lock Us Up*, Yale University Press, New Haven 2015; Id. (ed.), *State Power 2.0: Authoritarian Entrenchment and Civic Engagement Worldwide*, Ashgate Press, Farnham 2013.

317. M. Lind, *Land of Promise: An Economic History of the United States*, Harper, New York 2018, p. 245.
318. G. Sapelli, *Beyond Capitalism*, cit., pp. 86–88, and the expanded edition *Beyond Capitalism*, cit.
319. Sen, *Commodities and Capabilities*, Oxford University Press, Oxford 1999.
320. F. Braudel, *Material Civilization and Capitalism*, A. Colin, Paris 1967; Italian translation *Capitalism and Material Civilization*, Einaudi, Turin 1977.
321. G. Sapelli, "Trust, Legitimation and Faith", in *Equilibri*, n. 1, 2013, pp. 9–15.
322. N. Georgescu-Roegen, *Analytical Economics: Issues and Problems*, Harvard University Press, Cambridge, MA 1966, and the fundamental *The Entropy Law and the Economic Process*, Harvard University Press, Cambridge, MA 1971.
323. J. Navarro Valls, G. Sapelli, "Can Benevolence Change the World?", in G. Sapelli, *Economy, Business, Society. Essays and Articles from 1998 to 2016*, GoWare-Fondazione Eni Enrico Mattei, Florence-Milan 2016, pp. 5–18.
324. B. Stiegler, *Taking Care, of Youth and Generations*, Flammarion, Paris 2008 (Italian trans. *Taking Care: Of Youth and Generations*, Orthotes, Salerno 2014), and his fundamental *Technique and Time*, cit., vols. 1–2.
325. J. Derrida, *Plato's Pharmacy*, Tel Quel, Paris 2004; Italian trans. *Plato's Pharmacy*, Jaca Book, Milan 1968.
326. G. Simondon, *Individuation in the Light of the Notions of Form and Information*, Jérôme Millon, Grenoble 2005; Italian trans. *Individuation in the Light of the Notions of Form and Information*, Mimesis, Milan-Udine 2011.
327. The most ambitious text is undoubtedly J. Porcher, *Living with Animals. A Utopia for the 21st Century*, preface by A. Caillè, La Decouverte, Paris 2014; Italian trans. *Living with Animals: A Utopia for the 21st Century*, Slow Food, Bra 2017.
328. On this impressive article appeared on the occasion of the Paris Agriculture Fair 2019 in *Le Monde* on February 23, 2019 on p. 1 of the "Ecoentreprise" insert: P. Escande, "The Farm in the Urban Era", in which "genetic" and urban agriculture is magnified by citing a farming company "in the suburbs of Amiens: it will raise mealworms (*Tenebrio molitor*) in order to produce

20,000 tons of protein per year initially intended for fish and pet food".

329. J. Porcher, *Breeders and Animals, Reinventing the Link*, PUF, Paris 2002, and the same, with V. Despret, *Being Beast*, Actes Sud, Arles 2007.
330. N. Irti, *The Legal Order of the Market*, Laterza, Rome-Bari 2003.
331. H. Pirenne, *Mohammed and Charlemagne*, Alcan, Paris-Brussels 1937; Italian translation *Mohammed and Charlemagne*, Laterza, Bari 1939.
332. F. Debenedetti, "More Competition, More EU Integration", in *Il Sole 24 Ore*, February 27, 2019.
333. Predieri, *The Emergence of Independent Authorities*, cit.
334. K.G. Elzinga, M. Webber, "Louis Brandeis and Contemporary Antitrust Enforcement", in *Touro Law Review*, vol. 33, n. 1, 2017.
335. H.A. Simon, *Administrative Behavior. A Study of Decision-Making Processes in Administrative Organizations*, Cambridge University Press, New York-London 1947 (Italian translation *Administrative Behavior*, Il Mulino, Bologna 1958); Id., with J.G. March, *Organizations*, Blackwell, Malden, MA 1958 (Italian translation *Theory of the Organization*, Community Editions, Milan 1979); Id., *The Shape of Automation: For Men and Management*, Evanston, New York 1965 (Italian translation *Business Management and Automation*, Etas Kompass, Milan 1968); Id., *Reason in Human Affairs*, Stanford University Press, Palo Alto 1983 (Italian translation *Reason in Human Affairs*, Il Mulino, Bologna 1984); Id., *Models of My Life*, Basic Books, New York 1991 (Italian translation *Models for My Life*, Rizzoli, Milan 1992).
336. G. Sapelli, *The Company as a Historical Subject*, Il Saggiatore, Milan 1986, then republished by GoWare in 2008.
337. J.A. Schumpeter, *Business Cycles: A Theoretical, Historical, and Statistical Analysis of the Capitalist Process*, Macmillan, London 1939; Italian translation *The Capitalist Process: Economic Cycles*, Boringhieri, Turin 1964.
338. P. Sylos Labini, *Oligopoly and Technological Progress*, cit.
339. F. Balbo, *Works*, Boringhieri, Turin 1963.

340. C.F. Casula (ed.), *Believing in Social Development. The Intellectual Lesson of Giorgio Ceriani Sebregondi*, introduction by G. De Rita, Edizioni Lavoro, Rome 2010.
341. By A. Sen, see *Choice of Techniques: An Aspect of the Theory of Planned Economic Development*, Basil Blackwell, Oxford 1960; *On Economic Inequality* (expanded edition), Clarendon Press-Oxford University Press, Oxford-New York 1973; *Poverty and Famines: An Essay on Entitlement and Deprivation*, Oxford University Press, Oxford-New York 1979; *Commodities and Capabilities*, Elsevier Science Publishing Co, New York 1983.
342. G. Sapelli, *Morality and Corporate Governance. Firm Integrity and Spheres of Justice*, Springer Verlag, New York-Berlin 2012.
343. See the magnificent text edited by M. Augier and J.G. March, *Models of a Man: Essays in Memory of Herbert A. Simon*, The MIT Press, Cambridge, MA 2004.
344. G. Sapelli, "Pervasive and Post-modern Modernization", in *Journal of Southern Europe and the Balkans*, n. 1, 1999, pp. 77–80.
345. G. Sapelli, *2020. Pandemic and Resurrection*, cit.
346. On this, see the unsurpassed studies of the much lamented P. Monzini, among which I remember *Criminal Groups in Naples and Marseille: Organized Crime in the History of Two Cities: 1820–1990*, Donzelli, Rome 1999; with M. Massari, *The Market of Women: Prostitution, Trafficking and Exploitation*, Donzelli, Rome 2000; *Sex Traffic: Prostitution, Crime and Exploitation*, Sage, Berlin-London 2005; "Trafficking in Women and Girls and the Involvement of Organised Crime in Western and Central Europe", in *International Review of Victimology*, n. 4, 2004; with F. David and M. Peruffo, "Human Smuggling and Trafficking: A Desk Review on the Trafficking in Women from the Philippines", n. 3, 2000, NCJR; "Schengen's Soft Underbelly? Irregular Migration and Human Smuggling Across Land and Sea Borders to Italy", in *Working Paper. UNCTAD*, n. 8, 2001; with F. Pastore and G. Sciortino, *Human Smuggling to/Through Italy, Project Research of the UNCTAD Centre*, 234, 2001.
347. G. Sapelli, *Southern Europe Since 1945*, cit., p. 48, and Id., "Northern and Southern Mediterranean Cities", in *Equilibri*, n. 1, 1998, pp. 63–82, and, always mine, "European Cities

and the Rise of Non-European Metropolises: The Challenges of Freedom", in *International Dialogues*, n. 1, 2006, pp. 78–87.
348. G. Sapelli, *Southern Europe Since 1945*, cit.
349. P. Collier, *Exodus. How Migration Is Changing Our World*, Oxford University Press, Oxford-New York 2013.
350. As understood by A. Masullo, *The Archisense. Dialectic of Solitude*, Quodlibet, Macerata 2018.
351. L. Spitzer, "Linguistics and Literary History", in A. Schiaffini (ed.), *Stylistic Criticism and History of Language*, Laterza, Bari 1966, pp. 137–138.
352. See C. Corduas, G. Sapelli, "Reification and Managerialism in the Company of the New Century", in *Business Itineraries*, n. 10, 2006, pp. 37–55.
353. G. Leopardi, *Zibaldone of Thoughts*, edited by G. Pacella, Garzanti, Milan 1991, vol. I, pp. 347–348.
354. The reference to P. Barcellona, *The Nostalgia for God in the Contemporary Age*, Macondo Libri, Pove del Grappa 2011, is fundamental.
355. Predieri, *The Emergence of Independent Administrative Authorities*, cit.
356. E.W. Böckenförde, *State, Society, Freedom Studies on State Theory and Constitutional Law*, Suhrkamp, Berlin 1976, p. 122.
357. Mangia, "The Emergency and the Three Great Breaks", Afterword to G. Sapelli, *2020. Pandemic and Resurrection*, cit., pp. 91–118.
358. Maalouf, *The Shipwrecks of Civilizations*, Grasset, Paris 2019; Italian translation *The Shipwreck of Civilizations*, La nave di Teseo, Milan 2019.
359. J. Sainte-Marie, *Bloc Against Bloc. The Dynamics of Macronism*, Éditions du Cerf, Paris 2019.
360. C. Guilly, *Peripheral France: How We Sacrificed the Working Classes*, Champs Actuel Éditions, Paris 2015, and from the same *The Twilight of the France from Above*, Champs Actuel, Paris 2017.
361. P. Vermeren, *The France That Downgrades: The Yellow Vests, a Jacquerie in the 21st Century*, Éditions Tallandier, Paris 2019.
362. G. Casati (pseudonym of four managers who wished to remain anonymous), *Luigini Against Peasants. The Dark Side of the Northern Question*, Guerini e Associati, Milan 2015.

363. R. Davies, *Extreme Economies: Survival, Failure, Future. Lessons from the World's Limits*, Transworld, London 2020.
364. Exemplary to illustrate the catastrophe that was preparing well before Covid is the beautiful work of D. Graeber, *Bullshit Jobs, A Theory*, Simon & Schuster, New York 2018; Italian translation *Bullshit Jobs*, Garzanti, Milan 2018.
365. Fundamental to understand the contrasts within the PCC is the text by F. Godement and A. Vasselier, *China at Our Doors: A Strategy for Europe*, Odile Jacob, Paris 2018, pp. 22–27.
366. F.-X. Fauvelle-Aymar, *The Golden Rhinoceros: Stories of the African Middle Ages*, Alma Éditeur, Paris 2013.
367. R. Lewontin, R. Levins, *Biology Under the Influence: Dialectical Essays on the Coevolution of Nature and Society*, NYU Press-Monthly Review Press, New York 2007.
368. H. Hansmann, *The Ownership of Enterprise*, Belknap Press, Boston 2000; Italian trans. *The Ownership of the Company*, Il Mulino, Bologna 2005.
369. M. Godelier, *The Ideal and the Material*, Fayard, Paris 1984; Italian trans. *The Ideal and the Material: Thought, Economies, Society*, Editori Riuniti, Rome 1985.
370. O. Hathaway, S. Shapiro, *The Internationalists*, cit.
371. G. Sapelli, "The Management of the Company Between Economy and Politics", in *History and Market*, August 1984, pp. 161–188.
372. Exemplary D. Lieven, *Empire: The Russian Empire and Its Rivals*, Yale University Press, New Haven 2000.
373. On Hintze and this theme, I refer to my *Community and Market*, cit.
374. A clear example of absolute shortsightedness is the diligent work of W. Lacher, *Libya's Fragmentation. Structure and Process in Violent Conflict*, I.B. Tauris, London-New York-Oxford-New Delhi-Sydney 2020.
375. P. Tucker, *Unelected Power: The Quest for Legitimacy in Central Banking and the Regulatory State*, cit.
376. J.A. Hobson, *Imperialism: A Study*, J. Potton and Company, New York 1902.
377. I can never forget the gratitude I owe to Luigi Firpo for having made me discover, through the reading of the famous essay by Federico Chabod, the thought of Meinecke in the fervent

Turin of the late sixties of the twentieth century, forcing me to read the article of the great historian and partisan from Aosta Valley: F. Chabod, "A Contemporary German Historian: Federico Meinecke", in *New Historical Review*, vol. XI, 1927, pp. 592–603.

378. On this G. Sapelli, *Beyond Capitalism*, cit.
379. M. Castells, "Class, State and Urban Marginality", in *Class Structure and Urban Policy in Latin America*, Ediciones Siap, Buenos Aires 1974; F. Fernandes, *Class Society and Underdevelopment*, Zahar, Rio de Janeiro 1968. And more modestly my *South American Diary*, Guerini and Associates, Milan 2014.
380. L. Wacquant, "Three Pernicious Premises in the Study of the American Ghetto", in *International Journal of Urban and Regional Research*, vol. 21, n. 2 (June 1997), pp. 341–354; Id., "The Rise of Advanced Marginality: Notes on Its Nature and Implications", in *Acta Sociologica*, vol. 39, 1996; Id., "Urban Marginality in the Coming Millennium", in *Urban Studies*, vol. 36, September 1999.
381. J. Perlman, *The Myth of Marginality: Urban Poverty and Politics in Rio de Janeiro*, Oxford University Press, Oxford 1976.
382. I had glimpsed this process in *Democracy Transformed. Representation Between Territory and Function: A Theoretical-Interpretative Analysis*, Bruno Mondadori, Milan 2007, then taken up again in G. Sapelli, *Kleptocracy. The Unique Mechanism of Corruption*, Feltrinelli, Milan 1994, then reissued by Guerini and Associates in 2018 with essays by L. Festa and A. Pilati.
383. On this G. Sapelli, *Italian Capitalism. Transformation or Decline*, Feltrinelli, Milan 1994.
384. See the beautiful pioneering work of C.A. Figueroa and O.H. Moreno, *Coupism and Neocoupism in Latin America. Violence and Political Conflict in the Twenty-First Century*, University of Puebla, 2020.
385. Cf. on this my *Ukraine. A War Between Worlds*, preface by L. Caracciolo, Guerini and Associates, Milan 2022.
386. C. Brinton, *The Anatomy of Revolution*, the first edition is from 1953 by Vintage Books-Random House, New York, and the latest from 1965 by Prentice Hall, New York, from which I quote at pp. 265–266.

387. G.G. Merlo (ed.), *Arsenio Frugoni. Arnaldo da Brescia. Giovanni Miccoli. Fra Dolcino*, Editions of the Normal Superior School of Pisa, 2017.
388. Ibid., p. 106.
389. G. Miccoli, "The Heresiological Tradition of Pauperism", in *History of the City. International Journal of Urban and Territorial History*, nn. 26–27, 1983, pp. 33–43.

Index

Note: The page numbers followed by 'n' represents notes.

G. Sapelli, *States, Markets and Wars in Global History*,
https://doi.org/10.1007/978-3-031-26716-1

D

E

F

G

The manufacturer's authorised representative in the EU is Springer Nature Customer Service Centre GmbH, Europaplatz 3, 69115 Heidelberg, Germany. If you have any concerns regarding our products, please contact ProductSafety@springernature.com

Printed and bound by CPI Group (UK) Ltd, Croydon, CR0 4YY

01/10/2026

02225894-0008